W9-BRF-076

DISCARD

DISCARD

THE MISSING AMERICAN JURY

Criminal, civil, and grand juries have disappeared from the American legal system. Over time, despite their significant presence in the Constitution, juries have been robbed of their power by the federal government and the states. For example, leveraging harsher criminal penalties, executive officials have forced criminal defendants into plea bargains, eliminating juries. Capping money awards, legislatures have stripped juries of their power to fix damages. Ordering summary judgment, judges dispose of civil cases without sending them to a jury. This is not what the Founders intended. Examining the Constitution's text and historical sources, the book explores how the jury's authority has been taken and how it can be restored to its rightful, co-equal position as a "branch" of government. Discussing the value of juries beyond the Constitution's requirements, the book also discusses the significance of juries worldwide and argues jury decision-making should be preferred over determinations by other governmental bodies.

SUJA A. THOMAS is a professor of law at the University of Illinois College of Law. Her research on the jury has received extensive national attention in news outlets such as *The New York Times*, in testimony to the U.S. Senate and House of Representatives, and in federal and state court opinions. She practiced law for many years in New York City, including at Cravath, Swaine & Moore and Vladeck, Waldman, Elias & Engelhard, participating in jury trials and arbitration. Her past experience also includes participating in several criminal trials on behalf of the federal public defender.

THE MISSING AMERICAN JURY

Restoring the Fundamental Constitutional Role
of the Criminal, Civil, and Grand Juries

SUJA A. THOMAS

University of Illinois College of Law

CAMBRIDGE
UNIVERSITY PRESS

CAMBRIDGE
UNIVERSITY PRESS

32 Avenue of the Americas, New York NY 10013

Cambridge University Press is part of the University of Cambridge.

It furthers the University's mission by disseminating knowledge in the pursuit of education, learning, and research at the highest international levels of excellence.

www.cambridge.org
Information on this title: www.cambridge.org/9781107055650

© Suja A. Thomas 2016

This publication is in copyright. Subject to statutory exception and to the provisions of relevant collective licensing agreements, no reproduction of any part may take place without the written permission of Cambridge University Press.

First published 2016

A catalogue record for this publication is available from the British Library.

Library of Congress Cataloging in Publication Data
Names: Thomas, Suja A., author.
Title: The missing American jury : restoring the fundamental constitutional role of the criminal, civil, and grand juries / Suja A. Thomas, University of Illinois, Champaign
Description: New York, NY : Cambridge University Press, 2016. | Includes bibliographical references and index.
Identifiers: LCCN 2015050998 | ISBN 9781107055650 (Hardback) | ISBN 9781316618035 (Paperback)
Subjects: LCSH: Jury–United States.
Classification: LCC KF8972 .T477 2016 | DDC 347.73/752–dc23 LC record available at http://lccn.loc.gov/2015050998

ISBN 978-1-107-05565-0 Hardback
ISBN 978-1-316-61803-5 Paperback

Cambridge University Press has no responsibility for the persistence or accuracy of URLs for external or third-party Internet Web sites referred to in this publication and does not guarantee that any content on such Web sites is, or will remain, accurate or appropriate.

CONTENTS

ACKNOWLEDGMENTS

My interest in the jury stems from a trial over two decades ago. In that trial the plaintiff accused his employer of discriminating against him and then retaliating against him by firing him. Prior to the trial, we spent significant time picking a jury, with each side exercising the ability to challenge jurors for cause and without cause. After evidence was presented in the case, the jury rendered a verdict against the plaintiff on the discrimination claim and in favor of the plaintiff on the retaliation claim, awarding backpay and over $200,000 for emotional distress. When the employer protested the jury's verdict for emotional distress, arguing that the jury conferred an excessive amount, the judge ordered the award reduced to $20,000 or required the plaintiff to retry the case. As a young lawyer, I was surprised. I thought a right to a jury trial existed. How could a judge make this decision after a jury deliberated and assessed the value of the distress that the plaintiff suffered. I began to research this procedure of remittitur or the reduction of a jury verdict, and I learned that the Supreme Court had called remittitur "doubtful precedent." After reading the late eighteenth-century English case law on which the Founders had relied to frame our constitutional jury trial provisions, I discovered that no such practice as remittitur where a judge reduced a jury verdict existed at that time. The American judiciary invented it. Later, I saw judges take away other decisions from juries. For example, they would dismiss employment discrimination cases before jury trials when they thought there was insufficient evidence showing discrimination. Again, I looked at the past English case law and found judges could not dismiss cases, ordering such "summary judgment" for one side. My interest in these procedures in civil cases has led me to see parallels between the civil, criminal, and grand juries and their fates, resulting in this book.

A few words about the cover. The cover was the idea of my friend Jeffrey Miller, an accomplished author, who helped me with many questions related to the book. The milk carton is an American symbol of something that has gone missing that is terribly important and must be found. As described in this book, the jury has disappeared and must be restored.

It is always difficult to put together a list of people to thank, particularly after a project like this that has lasted for several years. I begin by thanking my spouse Scott Bahr, who has given me spectacular comments that have been incorporated into this book. Most importantly, Scott supported me by believing in the significance of this topic. My friend Benjamin Glassman read the draft chapter by chapter and provided invaluable comments. Over the years, I have also worked with students who researched issues related to the jury. Many years ago, my first research assistant Tod Thompson did outstanding work from which I still draw today. I also thank Jessica Bartlett for her excellent research, as well as Kaitlyn Luther, Prachi Mehta, and Joseph Bozdech for their work that has supported this project. Recently, I had the good fortune to work with Allison Slocum who performed a role as a talented editor and as a trusted research assistant.

Several academics and friends helped me with this project in a variety of ways including: Akhil Amar, Vikram Amar, Laura Appleman, Caitlin Borgmann, Paul Caron, Robert Chang, Jack Chin, Jacob Cogan, Ruth Colker, Brooke Coleman, Sally Cook, Elizabeth Daniel, Scott Dodson, Melissa Englund, Margareth Etienne, Roger Fairfax, Marc Galanter, Jim Gardner, Dan Hamilton, Valerie Hans, David Hyman, Eric Johnson, Robin Kar, Karen Kohut, Charlotte Ku, Niki Kuckes, James Kuklinski, John Langbein, Bob Lawless, Andrew Leipold, Jason Mazzone, Darrell Miller, William Nelson, James Oldham, Frank Partnoy, Martin Redish, Jamelle Sharpe, Bruce Smith, Lawrence Solum, Jeffrey Stempel, Steve Subrin, Stephen Vladeck, Melissa Wasserman, Lesley Wexler, and Ingrid Wuerth.

Recently, I had a very useful conversation with my colleague Jacqueline Ross that helped me frame Chapter 6 in which I discuss several juries in other countries. In addition to her guidance and comments on drafts, many people very generously provided their expertise on lay participation in other countries including: Shawn Boyne (Germany), Matilde Cohen (France), Jasbir Dhillon (England), Gennady Esakov (Russia), Hiroshi Fukurai (China), Moosi Ghazi (Iran), Elisabetta Grande (Spain), Cheryl Lloyd-Bostock (England), Renee Morhe (Ghana), Andrew Novak (Ghana), Izabel Nunez (Brazil), Walter Perron (Germany), and Dimitri Vanoverbeke (Japan).

Thanks is also due to my colleague Kurt Lash who read the book proposal and has spoken with me about my work on many occasions.

I am particularly appreciative of his introduction of me to Cambridge University Press Senior Editor John Berger.

Finally, I want to acknowledge the *Virginia Law Review, Notre Dame Law Review, Washington University Law Review, Ohio State Law Journal, Illinois Law Review Slip Opinions*, and *Boston College Law Review*, which have published articles that are relied upon in this book.

The Missing American Jury

An Introduction

Jorge has worked for a shipping company for thirty years, receiving great reviews throughout his tenure. He is sixty-years-old when the company terminates him, replacing him with Martin, a twenty-nine-year-old. A few months before Jorge was fired, his boss commented that the company needed an infusion of young blood. Believing that the company discriminated against him on the basis of his age, Jorge brings a lawsuit. In its defense, the company files for "summary judgment." It requests that the judge throw out Jorge's claim, asserting that it hired Martin to replace Jorge only to reduce labor costs, not because of Jorge's age. The judge dismisses the case, depriving Jorge of the chance to present his case to a jury.

Mary is accused of selling an ounce of crack cocaine. She wants a jury to hear her case. But her lawyer has advised her that if a jury convicts her, the statutory sentencing guidelines dictate a severe mandatory minimum sentence. Mary's sole chance of serving less time lies with the prosecutor. He can modify the charge to an offense that has a lower mandatory minimum, but will do so, only if Mary agrees to forgo a jury trial by taking a plea. Mary pleads guilty.

David is charged with insider trading after a grand jury indicts him. The judge gives the prosecutor and David, through his lawyer, the opportunity to select a fair jury, eliminating jurors who may be biased and excluding a certain number of jurors without giving any reasons. During the trial, the prosecutor presents evidence of insider trading, and David's lawyer sets forth proof that he did not commit the crime. The jury unanimously convicts David of insider trading, subjecting him to a prison sentence of ten years. Deciding there is insufficient evidence of insider trading, the judge acquits David, resulting in David going free.

The American jury captivates us. In high-profile cases, juries are portrayed as fundamental and pivotal to the government of the United States. They are not, however. Despite frequent highlights in media and pop-cultural displays in movies and television, juries have come to play almost no role in the American legal system. The examples involving Jorge, Mary, and David paint a more accurate picture of the jury's role. The jury has essentially vanished.

Although statistics from America's founding are sparse, we know that juries decided the final fates of nearly every defendant accused of a crime at that time. In most cases, the government could not even prosecute a criminal defendant without a grand jury's stamp of approval. With rare exception, juries also determined civil cases in which people sought money for wrongs allegedly committed against them.

But by 1962 – when much of trial statistics becomes available – juries tried only 8.2% of criminal cases in federal court.[1] And by 2013, juries tried just 3.6% of these cases.[2] In 1976, in the courts of the most populous twenty-two states, juries decided only 3.4% of criminal cases. By 2002, juries decided even fewer cases, with jury verdicts in just 1.3% of criminal cases in these state courts.[3] While federal courts still employ grand juries for serious crimes, most state courts do not.[4]

The jury's role in civil cases has followed the same downward trend of the criminal jury. In 1962, civil juries decided just 5.5% of federal court cases,[5] further dwindling to 0.8% by 2013.[6] In 1976, in the courts of the most populous twenty-two states, juries decided only 1.8% of civil cases. And by 2002, juries tried just 0.6% of these cases.[7]

This decline of the American jury remains hidden to all but a few. Many of those who are aware of the jury's fate have failed to admonish

---

[1] Marc Galanter, *The Vanishing Trial: An Examination of Trials and Related Matters in Federal and State Courts*, J. EMP. LEG. STUD. 459, 554 tbl.A-17 (2004).

[2] Administrative Office of the United States Courts, Table D Cases – U.S. District Courts – Criminal Judicial Business (Sept. 30, 2013), www.uscourts.gov/uscourts/Statistics/Judicial Business/2013/appendices/D00CSep13.pdf; Administrative Office of the United States Courts, Table T-1 – U.S. District Courts – Trials Judicial Business (Sept. 30, 2013), www.uscourts.gov/uscourts/Statistics/JudicialBusiness/2013/appendices/T01Sep13.pdf.

[3] Galanter, *supra* note 1, at 510.

[4] SARA SUN BEALE ET AL., GRAND JURY LAW AND PRACTICE 1–3 (2d ed. 2013); Suja A. Thomas, *Nonincorporation: The Bill of Rights After* McDonald v. Chicago, 88 NOTRE DAME L. REV. 159, 201 (2012).

[5] Galanter, *supra* note 1, at 462 tbl.1.

[6] Administrative Office of the United States Courts, Table C – U.S. District Courts – Civil Judicial Business (Sept. 30, 2013), www.uscourts.gov/uscourts/Statistics/JudicialBusiness/2013/appendices/C00Sep13.pdf; Administrative Office, tbl.T-1, *supra* note 2.

[7] Galanter, *supra* note 1, at 507 tbl.4; *see also* Carol J. DeFrances et al., Bureau of Justice Statistics Special Report, *Civil Justice Survey of State Courts, 1992: Civil Jury Cases and Verdicts in Large Counties*, www.bjs.gov/content/pub/pdf/cjcavilc.pdf.

this occurrence, instead, declaring juries at best obsolete and at worst dangerous, arguing that other methods to resolve cases, like plea bargaining, summary judgment, settlement, and arbitration, are more efficient, rational, and accurate.

This book sounds the overdue alarm, demonstrating the jury's plight while exploring the role that people through juries should play in government in relationship to other parts of the state. Exposing the silent diminution of the American jury from its constitutional role, it reveals that the executive, the legislature, the judiciary, and the states ("traditional constitutional actors") have caused the decline of the jury by usurping its authority. The traditional constitutional actors now decide matters that juries decided in the past. For example, the executive charges, convicts, and sentences, despite juries indicting, convicting, and sentencing in the past. The legislature can set damages, although only the jury historically had that power. The judiciary circumvents juries by dismissing cases via mechanisms such as the motion to dismiss, summary judgment, acquittal, and judgment as a matter of law, procedures nonexistent at our Constitution's founding. Many states have also appropriated jury authority, including by empowering prosecutors and judges to decide the propriety of criminal charges instead of grand juries. The American jury has been marginalized.

Juries do not try some cases because cases are settled or are decided in arbitration instead of court. Because this book concerns only procedures imposed by the government to which parties do not consent or procedures such as plea bargaining to which a party may unwillingly consent, it does not discuss settlement and arbitration.

The denigration of the jury by the government has taken place despite the jury's similarity to the traditional constitutional actors. With respect to the traditional actors, the Constitution gives significant authority to them, and the Supreme Court has recognized this authority. The Founders established divisions between the traditional actors to protect as well as limit their authority. For example, they provided that both houses of Congress must pass on legislation along with the President before a bill becomes law. The Supreme Court, through which we see the most transparent display of the authority of the traditional actors, has recognized that separation of powers between the executive, the legislature, and the judiciary, and federalism, the division of authority between the federal government and the states, co-actively empower and limit each of the traditional constitutional actors.

The Constitution similarly empowers and limits the jury in relationship to the traditional actors. For example, the prosecutor as an officer of the executive branch charges a defendant, and the jury decides whether the defendant is guilty. Likewise, the legislature makes laws and the jury decides facts and applies the facts to the law. The judiciary and the jury also share power. If a jury decides a case, the judiciary can alter that determination only in certain circumstances. Lastly, the states and the jury share power. States enact laws and juries apply those laws in particular cases.

Similar to the display in Supreme Court decisions of the rivalry between the traditional constitutional actors, the Court is the best place to view how the competing authority of the traditional constitutional actors and the jury has been handled. Different from its robust recognition of the authority of each of the traditional actors, the Court has reduced the jury's authority by failing to analyze the authority of the jury in terms like separation of powers and federalism.

While the Founders established the jury as a check on the executive, the legislature, the judiciary, and the states, the Supreme Court presently does not recognize this function. Often the Court has admitted a division of authority between the jury and the traditional constitutional actors, only later to disinherit the jury of its independence and power. For example, the Court initially permitted only a jury to try serious crimes but later changed its decision to allow judges to try such crimes. Similarly, at first, the Court prohibited a judge from second-guessing a civil jury's verdict but subsequently, judges were permitted to act in this manner. Many other similar shifts of authority away from the jury have occurred.

In fracturing the jury from the greater structure of American government, the Court has disempowered the jury. The jury is often viewed as having a relationship with only the judiciary. Even this recognized relationship with the judiciary is looked upon as one by which only the judge oversees the jury, not one where the jury checks the judiciary. At the same time, the jury is also not thought of as having any sort of power-sharing relationship with the legislature, the executive, and the states. Compounding this problem, the jury has no ability to act against the traditional actors' power by, for example, constituting itself to hear a case after a court dismisses a case. For all of these reasons – related to the failure of the traditional actors to recognize an equal, fundamental place in the constitutional structure for the jury – the jury serves an inferior role in the American government, with the traditional actors essentially exercising one-way power against the jury.

Despite this enfeebled jury, removed from the greater constitutional structure, some might argue that the jury has as much or even more power than it should. For example, the jury hears some causes of action such as employment discrimination claims that did not exist in the past. Also, the jury may not actually possess any power. People instead may simply have the "right" to a jury trial. Arguably then people can freely forgo a jury, pleading guilty or choosing a judge to decide instead of a jury. These types of arguments will be explored. Briefly regarding the examples here, while the jury hears some new types of cases, those claims are within its constitutional authority. Moreover, many other pre-existing claims have been improperly removed from the jury's purview. Also, despite contentions to the contrary, there is significant evidence that the jury held affirmative power at the time of the founding and thus jury authority should not be limited to the exercise of a right to a jury. Additionally, people generally do not freely decide whether to have juries decide their cases. Judges may dismiss their cases or people may avoid a jury trial knowing that a case can be affected by the traditional actors using various modern procedures as a sword against them, including charge bargaining, summary judgment, and caps on damages.

This book investigates a new theory for the decline of the American jury. Disposing of the usual suspects of the inefficiency, cost, incompetence, and inaccuracy of the jury, it demonstrates that the traditional actors led by the Supreme Court have seized the domain of the jury. Depriving the jury of the same doctrines essential to the preservation of the authority of the traditional constitutional actors, the Court has pushed the jury to the periphery. Offering a novel argument about the role of juries in the very fabric of our political system, the book argues that the jury should be recognized as a co-equal of the traditional actors and specifically as a significant check to balance their powers – essentially as a "branch."

The book also hypothesizes about why the traditional actors currently do not treat the jury as an equal including recognizing its authority under the Constitution. At times, the traditional actors and particularly the Supreme Court have recognized that the jury holds significant authority under the Constitution. Since the 1930s, a recognizable shift has occurred, however, with the Court acting less favorably towards the jury. Although a difficult question to answer, the book begins to examine this issue of why this change against jury authority has occurred.

Taking the unique view of the jury as a branch, the book proposes that the traditional actors should exercise restraint when their power com-petes with the power of the jury. Because of the jury's unique inability to protect its own authority and the ability and desire of the traditional actors to take the jury's power, restraint by the traditional actors is necessary. The book explores the extent of restraint that is appropriate, including the use of originalism, the original public meaning of the constitutional text. Concluding that originalism should be employed to interpret the criminal, civil, and grand jury provisions to limit the traditional actors' actions, the book argues that the jury of today should look more like the predecessor jury that existed in late eighteenth-century England at the time the jury provisions were adopted in America.

Restoring the jury's past role means preventing the executive, the legislature, the judiciary, and the states from usurping the jury's authority. For example, judges should not be able to dismiss criminal and civil cases by assessing the evidence and deciding juries could find only one way. Accordingly, factually intensive cases like employment discrimination cases should be left to juries to decide. Also, the legislature should not be able to shift cases that juries were to decide to judges. Moreover, if the government alleges individuals or companies violated the law, juries, not the government, should decide whether those sued by the government should pay monetary fines to the government. And grand juries should decide whether charges proceed against criminal defendants in state courts prior to any plea discussions by the government.

Whether the American jury can be restored depends on how we view the government that is set forth in the Constitution. If the jury is recognized as a constitutional actor that has competing relationships with the traditional actors, the jury can be legitimized as an essential, indispensible part of government in the same way that the executive, legislature, judiciary, and the states are already recognized.

The book also addresses the question of the role the jury should play if the past does not govern the jury's place in the government. This potential role can be informed by the role of lay people in other countries. Despite a prevailing view that the jury is part of American exceptionalism, lay people actually participate in various forms in judicial systems of many other nations including through traditional juries and mixed panels of lay people and judges. The role of lay people in several other major countries shows significant value has been placed on the use of lay people in judicial decision-making. At the same time, many of these same nations have established controls on juries similar to the procedures in effect in the United States, seemingly showing a common distrust for lay judicial decision-making. Moreover, some countries have lesser controls on the jury than employed in the United States.

The presence of the jury in various forms throughout the world gives us the opportunity to examine the role that the jury should play in our government. Putting aside any requirements to adhere to the past, a fresh look at the appropriate role of the jury involves assessing its abilities and flaws, along with those of other governmental actors. The jury can perform important functions, including involving people in the operation of government on a more regular basis, thus engaging them in appreciating and policing the government. While, like any other governmental entity, juries do not perform every function well, the incentives of juries and competing decision-makers, including judges, differ in important ways. Most apparently, juries lack monetary and status incentives to decide in a certain manner. Examining these biases, as well as possible differences in judicial and jury decision-making, the book argues that juries, not judges or other traditional constitutional actors, should decide criminal and civil cases.

The book ends with additional thoughts about the importance of the jury and ways to improve it. It recognizes the essential role that juries can play to preserve civil liberties and civil rights. Also, brief recommendations regarding the current system are offered, including necessitating that prosecutors give juries the same options on which to convict as offered to the defendant in plea bargaining and requiring consensus for summary judgment on appeal.

Chapter 2 begins the discussion by describing the vibrant role of the criminal, civil, and grand juries in the late eighteenth century in England and in America. Next, several examples of how the traditional constitutional actors have taken the authority of juries are used to illustrate the fall of the jury. Finally, after the arguable rise of the jury is recognized, the overall decline of the jury is demonstrated through the virtual absence of the jury authority that existed in the past and the consequent inability of the jury to check any governmental actors.

Chapter 3 proceeds to explore why the jury has fallen. It first sets forth the traditional reasons offered for the declines of each of the criminal, civil, and grand juries. It then offers a new theory for the fall that acknowledges the common fate of the three juries. Despite their powerful presence in the constitutional text and their similarity to the traditional actors in separation of powers or federalism-type relationships with the traditional actors, the traditional actors have failed to recognize the jury's fundamental role as a co-equal in the government. To attempt to assess why the traditional actors, led by the Supreme Court, have changed their views on jury authority over time, this chapter concludes with a review of news articles in the time period when much jury power shifted to the traditional actors.

Chapter 4 addresses the future interpretation of the jury provisions. It explores how they should be interpreted. Discussing the original public meaning of the Seventh Amendment, it concludes that originalism and specifically the late eighteenth-century English common law civil jury trial should govern the scope of the civil jury trial today. Further, describing a concept called relational originalism, the chapter argues that originalism is also the best methodology to protect the authority granted to the criminal and grand juries.

Chapter 5 then initiates a discussion on how the jury can be restored. It applies originalism to four commonly accepted present-day procedures and practices, concluding that they improperly take away jury authority.

Not all agree that history should govern some or all of the Constitution. Chapter 6 recognizes the arguments against using the past to govern the present. It explores the role the jury should have under an evolving Constitution. Examining the value that other nations grant lay people, this chapter shows the important role that lay people can play in government. This chapter proceeds to discuss who should decide criminal and civil cases. It assesses the incentives of lay people versus traditional constitutional actors and concludes that the jury is the most attractive decision-maker.

Chapter 7, the concluding chapter, first discusses how the jury can play a significant role to protect civil liberties and civil rights. It then briefly introduces five ideas to restore the jury in the event the jury-infringing modern procedures discussed in Chapter 5 continue to remain in place.

This book's examination of the fall of the jury gives us the opportunity to review what lay people have offered in the past and determine the place that they should hold in the future in the United States and in other nations.

PART I

The Jury Now

2

The Fall of the Criminal, Civil, and Grand Juries and the Rise of the Executive, the Legislature, the Judiciary, and the States

When America was founded, criminal, civil, and grand juries were integral to government in both England and the colonies. Between the founding and today, power shifted from juries to other governmental institutions – the executive, the legislature, the judiciary, and the states – the very entities that juries were to check.

The Vibrant Jury of the Late Eighteenth Century

The jury has a long history in England. Informed by this past, the American colonists and the Founders understood that the jury restrained the government and preserved liberty. From their experiences in England and in the colonies, they also learned what could happen without juries. For example, they knew of the Star Chamber, a court of law – composed of judges, Parliament members, and other leaders – through which the monarchy abused authority by prosecuting people for political reasons. The colonists and Founders also suffered from aggressive actions by Parliament and royal judges: Parliament rescinded their legislation; royal judges removed from colonial juries cases regarding whether taxes should be paid on goods; and English courts heard some of the crimes that English officers committed in the colonies.[1]

When the Founders established their government, they wanted juries. Their desire was expressed in several discussions about the jury before the enactment of the Constitution. Delegates of several state assemblies gathered and proclaimed the necessity of the jury to preserve liberty. The First and Second Continental Congresses asserted Americans' entitlement to criminal and civil juries.[2] The colonists adopted the Declaration of

---

[1] *See* Akhil Reed Amar, The Bill of Rights: Creation and Reconstruction 109 (1998); Akhil Reed Amar, America's Constitution: A Biography 233, 237, 329–30 (2005).

[2] *See* Amar, America's Constitution, *supra* note 1, at 329–30.

Independence in part because the King repeatedly had deprived them of trial by jury.[3] Before the Constitutional Convention, all of the states with written constitutions provided some right to a jury trial.[4] As William Nelson has observed "[f]or Americans after the Revolution, as well as before, the right to trial by jury was probably the most valued of all civil rights."[5]

The original Constitution provided the right to a jury trial for all crimes, except those of impeachment, but included no other jury rights.[6] Concern about this omission and the constitutional power over law and fact that was granted to the Supreme Court on appeal delayed the Constitution's ratification. Adoption of the Constitution in 1787 was ultimately conditioned upon a Bill of Rights providing jury protections. The first Congress fulfilled this promise when the Bill of Rights was ratified in 1791, creating more robust criminal jury protections, in addition to civil and grand jury protections.[7]

As for the particular jury rights in the Bill of Rights, the Sixth Amendment contained further protections for the criminal jury trial such as rights to a speedy and public trial.[8] The Seventh Amendment preserved jury trials in suits at common law where the value in controversy exceeded twenty dollars.[9] And the Fifth Amendment required a presentment or an indictment of a grand jury before a person could be formally accused of a capital or infamous crime.[10]

How were these jury provisions in the federal Constitution to be interpreted? At this point, suffice it to say that although jury rights were prevalent among the states at the founding, and even in some circumstances greater than those in England, these jury rights varied.[11] The colonists and Founders were acquainted with the English jury as chronicled in English legal commentaries like Blackstone's *Commentaries on the Laws of England*, which was a best-seller in the colonies.[12] Daniel

---

[3] THE DECLARATION OF INDEPENDENCE para. 20 (U.S. 1776) ("For depriving us in many cases, of the benefits of Trial by Jury.").

[4] See AMAR, AMERICA'S CONSTITUTION, *supra* note 1, at 330.

[5] WILLIAM E. NELSON, AMERICANIZATION OF THE COMMON LAW 96 (1975).

[6] U.S. CONST. art. III, § 2, cl. 3.

[7] See AMAR, AMERICA'S CONSTITUTION, *supra* note 1, at 233–36.

[8] U.S. CONST. amend. VI.

[9] U.S. CONST. amend. VII.

[10] U.S. CONST. amend. V.

[11] See THE FEDERALIST PAPERS No. 83, at 501–03 (Alexander Hamilton) (Clinton Rossiter ed., 1961).

[12] See M.H. HOEFLICH, LEGAL PUBLISHING IN ANTEBELLUM AMERICA 131–34 (2010); William B. Stoebuck, *Reception of English Common Law in the American Colonies*, 10 WM. & MARY L. REV. 393 (1968).

Boorstin has called *The Commentaries* the "bible of American legal institutions," and Forrest McDonald has referred to the influence of Blackstone on the Constitution as "pervasive."[13]

To interpret the jury provisions in the Constitution, the U.S. Supreme Court has supposedly relied on English judicial interpretation ("English common law") of the English jury's authority found in prominent sources such as *The Commentaries*. It has also made comparisons to relevant practices in America at the time of the founding. Primarily using the past English common law, this chapter contrasts the jury of the past with the jury of today. Secondarily, this chapter distinguishes the past American jury from the present jury. Whether the jury provisions should be interpreted using any such historical test will be revisited in Chapter 4.

The Criminal Jury

Article III, Section 2 of the Constitution establishes the criminal jury trial as follows:

> The Trial of all Crimes, except in Cases of Impeachment, shall be by Jury; and such Trial shall be held in the State where the said Crimes shall have been committed; but when not committed within any State, the Trial shall be at such Place or Places as the Congress may by Law have directed.[14]

The Sixth Amendment further states:

> In all criminal prosecutions, the accused shall enjoy the right to a speedy and public trial, by an impartial jury of the State and district wherein the crime shall have been committed, which district shall have been previously ascertained by law.[15]

What do these provisions mean? When the criminal jury was established in the U.S. Constitution in the late eighteenth century, the English jury held significant power. Some viewed the criminal jury as an essential institution of the English government, alongside the Crown, Parliament, and the judiciary. Many eighteenth-century commentators believed the jury was necessary to check the executive, the legislature, and the

---

[13] DANIEL J. BOORSTIN, *Preface* to THE MYSTERIOUS SCIENCE OF THE LAW (1941); FORREST McDONALD, NOVUS ORDO SECLORUM: THE INTELLECTUAL ORIGINS OF THE CONSTITUTION 7 (1985). McDonald remarked that in his discussion of the origins of the Constitution, he "usually followed Blackstone" but described the occasions when modern scholars have shown he was wrong. *See* McDONALD, *supra*, at xii.

[14] U.S. CONST. art. III, § 2, cl. 3.

[15] U.S. CONST. amend. VI.

judiciary. For example, some stated that the jury was "an element in the constitution . . . especially as a necessary surrogate for what [was] viewed as a corrupt and unrepresentative parliament." Others explained that the jury countered the judiciary, which depended upon the executive for money and dominion.[16] As Blackstone declared, the jury was "the grand bulwark of [every Englishman's] liberties." It checked the King's power to appoint a partial judge who could preside in a suit between the King and the subject.[17]

In England, criminal juries tried serious crimes – felonies (crimes that were subject to the death penalty) including murder, rape, and property crimes of one shilling or more in value. Juries also heard misdemeanors – crimes not punishable by death – but judges tried summary offenses – crimes that generally did not involve imprisonment.[18]

An informal, lay set of people, including the victim, conducted pretrial investigations of almost all alleged crimes. For a trial in a felony or misdemeanor case to move forward, a grand jury had to approve the indictment drafted from this investigation.[19]

If a case was tried, the victim would prosecute the crime to a jury of property owners.[20] Jurors – typically farmers, tradesmen, and artisans – were "neither 'aristocratic nor democratic,'" and generally did not interact in society with the alleged criminals whom they judged.[21] Defendants had various rights, including challenging jurors for cause and without cause. And even foreign defendants were entitled to a jury of half Englishmen and half foreigners.[22]

---

[16] THOMAS ANDREW GREEN, VERDICT ACCORDING TO CONSCIENCE: PERSPECTIVES ON THE ENGLISH CRIMINAL TRIAL JURY 1200–1800, at 290–91, 305, 332–34 (1985); Thomas A. Green, *The English Criminal Trial Jury and the Law-Finding Traditions on the Eve of the French Revolution, in* THE TRIAL JURY IN ENGLAND, FRANCE, GERMANY 1700–1900, at 61, 66–67 (Antonio Padoa Schioppa ed., 1987).

[17] 4 WILLIAM BLACKSTONE, COMMENTARIES ON THE LAWS OF ENGLAND 342–43 (University of Chicago Press 1979) (1769).

[18] *See* John H. Langbein, *The English Criminal Trial Jury on the Eve of the French Revolution, in* THE TRIAL JURY IN ENGLAND, FRANCE, GERMANY 1700–1900, *supra* note 16, at 16–17.

[19] *See* Langbein, *supra* note 18, at 19–23.

[20] *See* GREEN, *supra* note 16, at 270–71; 3 WILLIAM BLACKSTONE, COMMENTARIES ON THE LAWS OF ENGLAND 362 (University of Chicago Press 1979) (1768); JAMES OLDHAM, TRIAL BY JURY: THE SEVENTH AMENDMENT AND ANGLO-AMERICAN SPECIAL JURIES 130–32 (2006).

[21] Langbein, *supra* note 18, at 25; *see* JOHN HOSTETTLER, THE CRIMINAL JURY OLD AND NEW: JURY POWER FROM EARLY TIMES TO THE PRESENT DAY 99 (2004).

[22] *See* 4 BLACKSTONE, *supra* note 17, at 346.

Jury trials, governed by undeveloped rules of evidence, were frequent and quick.[23] Juries participated actively in trials asking questions of witnesses.[24] A conviction required the unanimous agreement of the twelve jurors who sat in the case.[25] Juries were instructed to convict only upon such standards as being "'perfectly satisfied'" that the act was committed, "'absolutely coerced to believe'" the witness, or having "'no doubt that the prisoner [was] guilty.'"[26] At times voluntarily or under questioning by the judge, juries provided rationales for their verdicts.[27]

The public nature of the English criminal jury trial contributed to the role of the jury as a check on government. People could observe the government in action in court.[28]

When cases were tried, the jury's duty, particularly its power to decide law, was somewhat complicated. Commentators debated the jury's general authority to make legal determinations as well as the jury's authority to reduce a defendant's punishment by selecting the crime that the defendant committed. Some insisted that the jury was empowered to decide law and fact and that seditious libel cases demonstrated these powers. The English government used those laws to silence people who allegedly published material to incite action against the state.[29] While the jury could decide certain legal issues, a jury could ignore the judge's instruction on the law by finding the defendant not guilty under a general verdict, which did not require the jury to state facts or otherwise give reasons for its decision. Beyond this authority to issue such a verdict, the jury had no express power to decide law.[30]

Outside England, the criminal jury also had a significant presence in the American colonies. Every colony provided for jury trials though in some colonies statutes provided that the defendant could waive the jury

---

[23] See GREEN, *supra* note 16, at 271–72; John H. Langbein, *On the Myth of Written Constitutions: The Disappearance of Criminal Jury Trial*, 15 HARV. J.L. & PUB. POL'Y 119, 122–23 (1992).

[24] See John H. Langbein, *The Criminal Trial before the Lawyers*, 45 U. CHI. L. REV. 263, 288–89 (1978).

[25] See 4 BLACKSTONE, *supra* note 17, at 343.

[26] BARBARA J. SHAPIRO, "BEYOND REASONABLE DOUBT" AND "PROBABLE CAUSE" 22–23 (1991); JAMES Q. WHITMAN, THE ORIGINS OF REASONABLE DOUBT: THEOLOGICAL ROOTS OF THE CRIMINAL TRIAL 192–200 (1987).

[27] See Langbein, *supra* note 24, at 289–91.

[28] See AMAR, BILL OF RIGHTS, *supra* note 1, at 112–13.

[29] See Green, *supra* note 16, at 48–71; Mark DeWolfe Howe, *Juries as Judges of Criminal Law*, 52 HARV. L. REV. 582, 583 (1939).

[30] See OLDHAM, *supra* note 20, at 28–29; Howe, *supra* note 29, at 583.

trial if the prosecution agreed.[31] The colonial jury possessed power to decide law akin to the English jury's authority in the late eighteenth century. Akhil Amar has noted "it was widely believed in late-eighteenth-century America that the jury, when rendering a general verdict, could take upon itself the right to decide both law and fact," and that sedition cases may have influenced this view.[32] The law-finding authority was actually greater in some parts of America than in England, and the jury may have possessed some of its authority because of distrust of American judges.[33]

Bill Nelson has carefully studied law-finding powers of colonies in the eighteenth century. He concluded that some colonies' juries had significant law-finding power while others' did not. Nelson stated that New England juries held this power in civil and criminal cases. Other published sources have indicated that Virginia juries also held this power. However, New York, Pennsylvania, North Carolina, and South Carolina juries did not wield significant law-finding power.[34]

Returning to the English criminal jury, outside of political cases, it held authority to decide law in one other significant context – sentencing. Offenses at the time were associated with specific sanctions, particularly death.[35] Engaging in what Blackstone called "pious perjury,"[36] juries could essentially sentence by choosing the offense on which the defendant was convicted.[37] John Langbein has remarked that "[t]his mitigation practice was widespread and immensely important.... [T]he English criminal jury trial of the later eighteenth century ... was primarily a sentencing proceeding."[38] A jury could find the defendant not guilty or

---

[31] See Matthew P. Harrington, *The Economic Origins of the Seventh Amendment*, 87 Iowa L. Rev. 145 (2001); *see, e.g.*, Massachusetts Body of Liberties 29 (1641).

[32] Amar, Bill of Rights, *supra* note 1, at 100–01.

[33] See John H. Langbein, Renee Lettow Lerner & Bruce P. Smith, History of the Common Law: The Development of Anglo-American Legal Institutions 463, 484–85 (2009); William E. Nelson, *The Lawfinding Power of Colonial American Juries*, 71 Ohio St. L.J. 1003, 1004–05 (2010).

[34] See Nelson, *supra* note 33, at 1003–28. John Adams also discussed the juror's role to find law. "It is not only [the juror's] right, but his duty, in that case, to find the verdict according to his own best understanding, judgment, and conscience, though in direct opposition to the direction of the court." John Adams, Diary, *in* 2 The Works of John Adams 255 (1865) (Diary, Feb. 12, 1771).

[35] See Langbein, *supra* note 18, at 36–37.

[36] 4 Blackstone, *supra* note 17, at 239.

[37] See Akhil Reed Amar, America's Unwritten Constitution: The Precedents and Principles We Live By 424 (2012); Langbein, *supra* note 18, at 36–37.

[38] Langbein, *supra* note 18, at 37.

guilty. Alternatively, the jury could pronounce a partial verdict under which the jury could acquit the defendant of the indicted offense but convict him of a lesser charge within the indicted offense.[39] Partial verdicts could take into account the seriousness of the offense, the conduct and character of the accused, and punishment.[40] In one significant sample of English jury verdicts examined by Peter King, juries acquitted a third of the accused in property cases and returned partial verdicts in 10% of the cases.[41] In another sample studied by John Beattie, juries acquitted approximately a third of defendants accused in capital cases and issued partial verdicts in another 30%.[42]

During English trials, usually only one judge presided. More than one judge was perceived as unnecessary to guard against judicial overbearance because of the protective role served by the jury.[43] English judges influenced juries in different ways. They could state the issues and the supporting evidence. They could direct the jury to find a verdict for or against the defendant based on the evidence presented at trial.[44] A judge could also recommend that the jury decide the case using a special verdict. Under a special verdict, the jury decided only the facts, and the judge decided the case based on those facts. If the jury decided by a general verdict instead and convicted the defendant, the court could conclude that the evidence presented in the case did not support the jury's decision. The court could order a new trial but could not do so in felony cases.[45]

Statutes increasingly imposed the death penalty and judges sought pardons of defendants in some cases. If a judge did not want the defendant to be executed because of the harshness of the sentence or an incorrect jury verdict, the judge could recommend a reprieve, staying execution of the sentence, and the King could decide to pardon the

---

[39] *See* JOHN M. BEATTIE, CRIME AND THE COURTS IN ENGLAND, 1660–1800, at 336–37, 406 (1986).

[40] *See* HOSTETTLER, *supra* note 21, at 99.

[41] P.J.R. King, *"Illiterate Plebeians Easily Misled": Jury Composition, Experience, and Behavior in Essex, 1735–1815 in* TWELVE GOOD MEN AND TRUE: THE CRIMINAL TRIAL JURY IN ENGLAND 1200–1800, at 255 (J.S. Cockburn & Thomas Green eds., 2014).

[42] J.M. Beattie, *Crime and Courts in Surrey, 1736–1753 in* CRIME IN ENGLAND 1550–1800, at 176 (J.S. Cockburn ed., 1977).

[43] John H. Langbein, *Shaping the Eighteenth-Century Criminal Trial: A View from the Ryder Sources*, 50 U. CHI. L. REV. 1, 35 (1983).

[44] *See* 3 BLACKSTONE, *supra* note 20, at 375; 4 BLACKSTONE, *supra* note 17, at 350 (explaining that most evidence rules are the same for criminal and civil trials), 354.

[45] *See* 4 BLACKSTONE, *supra* note 17, at 354–55.

defendant. The defendant could win his freedom or a lesser sentence – often transportation to America for a period of years.[46]

After a jury conviction, judges also possessed power in noncapital property cases. Two people convicted of the same crime could receive different sentences. Factors such as the impact that a sentence might have on a defendant's employment and the nature of the offense could influence a judge's sentence.[47]

Despite judges' control, juries retained significant independence. The jury was not required to follow a judge's instruction to find for or against the defendant.[48] As previously discussed, juries could also issue general verdicts pronouncing the accused guilty or not guilty.[49] While a judge could recommend that a jury decide by special verdict stating the facts, judges could not require juries to decide in this manner, and juries rarely used this verdict. Further, after a jury convicted, a judge could order a new trial only in limited circumstances, and after an acquittal, a judge could not order a new trial. Moreover, because juries gave no reasons for their decisions, there was generally little room for review of convictions.[50]

Although juries and judges each possessed particular powers and independence, where they disagreed were "exceptional cases in the everyday work of the courts in the eighteenth century."[51] For the most part, they worked in tandem and the recommendations of the judge carried significant weight with jurors.[52]

Plea bargaining did not occur at this time: "Virtually every prisoner charged with a felony insisted on taking his trial, with the obvious support and encouragement of the court." The certainty of the sentence motivated defendants to go to trial.[53]

---

[46] See BEATTIE, *supra* note 39, at 406, 409, 421, 430–36.

[47] See BEATTIE, *supra* note 39, at 610–13.

[48] See Suja A. Thomas, *The Seventh Amendment, Modern Procedure, and the English Common Law*, 82 WASH. U. L.Q. 687, 728–30 (2004).

[49] See 4 BLACKSTONE, *supra* note 17, at 354.

[50] See 4 BLACKSTONE, *supra* note 17, at 354–55; Langbein, *supra* note 18, at 37–38. Blackstone stated the jury decided whether to order a special verdict. See 4 BLACKSTONE, *supra* note 17, at 354. However, Langbein believes that a judge could force a special verdict. See Langbein, *supra* note 24, at 296.

[51] BEATTIE, *supra* note 39, at 410.

[52] See GREEN, *supra* note 16, at 285; Langbein, *supra* note 18, at 36.

[53] BEATTIE, *supra* note 39, at 336–37, 446–47 (1986). For example, in grand larceny and petty larceny cases in the Surrey courts between 1722 and 1802, less than 1% and less than 4% respectively of those indicted pled guilty. See *id.* at 336.

In limited circumstances in England – times of martial law – juries did not hear certain criminal cases. Martial law could be instituted only for "order and discipline in [the] army" during times of war.[54]

The Civil Jury

The Seventh Amendment states:

> In Suits at common law, where the value in controversy shall exceed twenty dollars, the right of trial by jury shall be preserved, and no fact tried by a jury, shall be otherwise re-examined in any Court of the United States, than according to the rules of the common law.[55]

What does this mean? Drawing on the English common law, the English civil jury was in many ways similar to the English criminal jury in the late eighteenth century. Citing Blackstone's treatment of juries in addition to other authorities, John Langbein has written that "[f]or many purposes until the nineteenth century the criminal and civil jury were inseparable." Under these sources, the employment of criminal and civil juries was generally viewed as equally significant.[56] In his chapter on the civil jury, Blackstone designated it "the glory of the English law ... it [had] so great an advantage over others in regulating civil property."[57]

Blackstone considered the jury essential to prevent partiality because, as members of a privileged class, judges "will have frequently an involuntary bias towards those of their own rank and dignity." Although judges were necessary to present the law to juries, judges should not decide facts due to these possible prejudices.

> [I]n settling and adjusting a question of fact, when intrusted [sic] to any single magistrate, partiality and injustice have an ample field to range in; either by boldly asserting that to be proved which is not so, or more artfully by suppressing some circumstances, stretching and warping others, and distinguishing away the remainder.

Blackstone also cautioned against establishing tribunals of judges and other persons to decide facts without juries. Other countries had

---

[54] 1 WILLIAM BLACKSTONE, COMMENTARIES ON THE LAWS OF ENGLAND 400 (University of Chicago Press 1979) (1765); see MATTHEW HALE, THE HISTORY OF THE COMMON LAW OF ENGLAND 42 (Charles Runnington ed., 6th ed. 1820).

[55] U.S. CONST. amend. VII.

[56] Langbein, *supra* note 18, at 15 (citing 3 BLACKSTONE, *supra* note 20, at 379–81; 4 BLACKSTONE, *supra* note 17, at 343).

[57] 3 BLACKSTONE, *supra* note 20, at 379.

done so, eliminating juries, and eventually devolved into aristocracies.[58]

Blackstone also described how a public jury trial, more than private oral or written examinations, promoted the truth to be revealed. Moreover, he discussed the importance of witnesses being cross-examined. The "manner" of the evidence was as important as the "matter" of the evidence. Live testimony before a jury contrasted with a written record.

> In short by this method of examination [the jury], and this only, the persons who are to decide upon the evidence have an opportunity of observing the quality, age, education, understanding, behaviour, and inclinations of the witness. . . . [A]ll persons must appear alike, when their depositions are reduced to writing, and read to the judge, in the absence of those who made them.[59]

James Oldham has written that in some cases, a special jury – composed of people with certain characteristics such as property owners of a greater social status and wealth or experts in a particular area – could be convened. A special jury could resolve issues that were too difficult for a common jury though Oldham stated that "few reports of such cases exist." Such a jury also could hear a case when the sheriff who assembled the common jury could be biased. Additionally, a party could ask for a special jury and could pay the extra expense even where the court deemed it unnecessary.[60]

In the English system, jury trials were frequently held in civil cases.[61] Juries heard cases in which parties alleged they suffered monetary damages.[62] Their authority included protecting against government overreaching by awarding damages to people who were falsely

---

[58] 3 BLACKSTONE, *supra* note 20, at 379–81.

[59] 3 BLACKSTONE, *supra* note 20, at 373–74.

[60] *See* OLDHAM, *supra* note 20, at 127–73; *see also* 3 BLACKSTONE, *supra* note 20, at 357–58. Less frequently, special juries were convened in criminal cases. *See* OLDHAM, *supra* note 20, at 154. Several definitions for special juries have emerged, including a jury of higher social class, a jury of experts, and a jury established through a procedure where the parties strike jurors. *See id.* at 127–28.

[61] *See* James Oldham, *Law-making at Nisi Prius in the Early 1800s*, 25 J. LEG. HIST. 221, 226–29 (2006).

[62] *See* Suja A. Thomas, *A Limitation on Congress: "In Suits at common law,"* 71 OHIO ST. L.J. 1073, 1083–1101 (2010); *see also* OLDHAM, *supra* note 20, at 21, 49–56 (among other things, describing that when defendants defaulted, upon a writ of inquiry, a jury would decide the damages).

arrested.[63] Judges in other courts made non-monetary decisions such as whether a party should be prevented from taking an action against another party.[64]

Civil juries like criminal juries decided cases without significant interference from other parts of government. For example judges rarely decided damages, and when they did, the circumstances were controversial.[65] Courts could dismiss cases before, during, or after jury trials but this power was limited. Prior to trial, a party in the case could demur to the pleadings of the other party, admitting their facts, and arguing that no cause of action or defense existed upon those facts. During a trial a similar procedure existed – demurrer to the evidence. Using this procedure, a party could admit the evidence of the other party, arguing that the evidence did not constitute a claim or defense.[66] In the late eighteenth-century case *Gibson v. Hunter*, the House of Lords explained the demurrer to the evidence. It proclaimed that even if it was unclear whether the facts were true, if the facts were to be "proved by presumptions or probabilities" the defendant must admit these facts to demur to the evidence. After the explanation that the defendant must admit "every fact, and every conclusion, which the evidence given for the Plaintiff conduced to prove," the House of Lords stated a similar demurrer would not be presented again.[67]

Another English procedure was the nonsuit. In circumstances in which the plaintiff thought he did not have sufficient evidence to win a case, the plaintiff could refuse to appear in court when the jury was called to render the verdict. In this situation, the court would nonsuit the plaintiff.[68] This practice occurred frequently.[69] The plaintiff would be required to pay the defendant's costs, but the plaintiff could bring the same suit again.[70]

---

[63] See Stephan Landsman, *Appellate Courts and Civil Juries*, 70 U. Cin. L. Rev. 873, 908 n.176 (2002).

[64] See Thomas, *supra* note 62, at 1084–85.

[65] See Thomas, *supra* note 62, at 1086–96.

[66] See 3 Blackstone, *supra* note 20, at 314–15, 373, 395; Thomas, *supra* note 48, at 704–48 (discussing the procedures at common law in detail).

[67] Gibson v. Hunter, 126 Eng. Rep. 499, 510 (1793).

[68] See Thomas, *supra* note 48, at 722–25.

[69] See Oldham, *supra* note 20, at 10; *see, e.g.*, James Oldham, Case Notes of Sir Soulden Lawrence 1787–1800, at 10 n.15, 56, 68 (2013).

[70] See Thomas, *supra* note 48, at 722. What has been referred to as "compulsory nonsuits" were rare. *See* James Oldham, *The Seventh Amendment Right to Jury Trial: Late-Eighteenth-Century Practice Reconsidered*, in Human Rights and Legal History: Essays in Honour of Brian Simpson 231 n.35 (2000); *see also* Thomas, *supra* note 48, at 723–25 (discussing compulsory nonsuits).

Similar to the procedure for a criminal jury, if the case was tried, the jury in a civil case could render a general verdict or a special verdict. Additionally, a unanimous jury of twelve was required for the plaintiff to win.[71]

After a jury verdict, if the court believed the evidence presented at trial did not support the verdict, a new trial could be ordered. Both the demurrer to the evidence and the bill of exceptions had fallen into disuse in favor of this procedure. If the case was sent to a second jury, Blackstone emphasized that a third jury was rarely constituted if the second agreed with the first jury. He stated that "for the law will not readily suppose, that the verdict of any one subsequent jury can countervail the oaths of two preceding ones."[72] A court could also order a new trial if it believed that the damages rendered by the jury were excessive.[73] Again, a third trial would rarely be ordered if the second jury agreed with the first. On appeal, the only method to attack the judgment was an error of law.[74]

As briefly described previously, the civil jury also had a significant presence in colonial America, including in some circumstances, possessing the power to find law and fact.

The Grand Jury

The Fifth Amendment provides:

> No person shall be held to answer for a capital, or otherwise infamous crime, unless on a presentment or indictment of a Grand Jury, except in cases arising in the land or naval forces, or in the Militia, when in actual service in time of War or public danger.[75]

What does this mean? Blackstone discussed the English grand jury as one of a "strong and two-fold barrier, of a presentment and a trial by jury, between the liberties of the people, and the prerogative of the crown."[76] An oft-cited example of its power is a seventeenth-century grand jury's refusal to indict Lord Shaftesbury for treason for speaking out against the Crown.[77]

---

[71] See 3 BLACKSTONE, supra note 20, at 365, 375, 377–79. For a discussion of another procedure called the special case, see id. at 378.

[72] 3 BLACKSTONE, supra note 20, at 372–73, 387.

[73] See Suja A. Thomas, Re-Examining the Constitutionality of Remittitur Under the Seventh Amendment, 64 OHIO ST. L.J. 731, 775–84 (2003).

[74] See 3 BLACKSTONE, supra note 20, at 372, 387, 405–06.

[75] U.S. CONST. amend. V.

[76] 4 BLACKSTONE, supra note 17, at 343.

[77] See RICHARD D. YOUNGER, THE PEOPLE'S PANEL: THE GRAND JURY IN THE UNITED STATES, 1634–1941, at 2 (1963). But see Andrew D. Leipold, Why Grand Juries Do Not

Blackstone referred to presentments as the notice by a grand jury of a crime from their own information. A court official would frame an indictment thereafter.[78] Outside of presentment, private people generally brought criminal accusations to the grand jury, so the grand jury largely functioned without a governmental prosecutor.[79]

In the grand jury proceeding, which was closed to the public, only the prosecutor, whether private or governmental, presented evidence. At least twelve of the jurors – freeholders, "usually gentlemen of the best figure in the county" – were to be "thoroughly persuaded of the truth of an indictment" and "not to rest satisfied merely with remote probabilities."[80] The grand jury may have been required to find more than probable cause to indict the defendant. If the grand jury did not indict, another grand jury could be convened to decide the same charges.[81]

Although grand juries were intended to protect people who were falsely accused from the "stigma, risk, and expense of a criminal trial," some commentators were critical of them. Such criticisms included that they could be tampered with to prevent proper indictments.[82] Also grand juries indicted in most cases.[83] Thus, perhaps they were an unnecessary additional proceeding to check the government. Finally, although grand juries prevented some weak cases from proceeding, (indictments did not occur in approximately 10–20% of the cases),[84] the grand jury arguably was not necessary because even when they indicted, criminal juries would not convict where evidence was lacking.[85]

In addition to a role in criminal matters, grand juries served as "the voice of the community about matters of broad interest or matters that

---

[78] *See* 4 BLACKSTONE, *supra* note 17, at 298.

[79] *See* JOHN H. LANGBEIN, THE ORIGINS OF ADVERSARY CRIMINAL TRIAL 40–48 (2003).

[80] 4 BLACKSTONE, *supra* note 17, at 299–301.

[81] *See* 4 BLACKSTONE, *supra* note 17, at 300–01; SHAPIRO, *supra* note 26, at 81–83; Niki Kuckes, *Retelling Grand Jury History, in* GRAND JURY 2.0: MODERN PERSPECTIVES ON THE GRAND JURY 142–47 (Roger Anthony Fairfax, Jr. ed., 2011).

[82] HOSTETTLER, *supra* note 21, at 115–17.

[83] *See* Beattie, *supra* note 42; King, *supra* note 41, at 254–55 (discussing property cases).

[84] BEATTIE, *supra* note 39, at 402 tbl.8.1; BEATTIE, *supra* note 39, at 319 (the grand jury took "its duties seriously" and "continued in the 1790s to refuse to indict a significant number of accused offenders"); GREEN, *supra* note 16, at 274–75; HOSTETTLER, *supra* note 21, at 97–98; Langbein, *supra* note 18, at 23.

[85] *See* Langbein, *supra* note 18, at 22 ("English grand jury was largely an anachronism, more a ceremonial than an instrumental component of the criminal procedure").

The text preceding note 78 begins: *(and Cannot) Protect the Accused,* 80 CORNELL L. REV. 260, 282–83 (1995) (discussing the subsequent pressure to indict in the case).

required administrative attention." Their involvement might include weighing in on issues such as whether to repair a road.[86]

The American grand jury was similar to its English counterpart but possibly more significant. Some American grand juries declined to indict people who criticized the Crown. In the frequently cited case of John Peter Zenger, two grand juries refused to indict him for publishing an editorial critical of the Crown.[87] Some American grand juries also challenged the Crown including with presentments and indictments against British soldiers, and by promoting boycotts.[88] Characterized as "indispensable" in the colonies, grand juries also acted to denounce actions by Parliament and even called for support for the war after independence was declared. They also protested local problems.[89]

*****

In summary, the late eighteenth-century English and colonial criminal, civil, and grand juries played significant roles in the English and colonial government to check the executive, the legislature, and the judiciary.

The Fall of the Jury

As previously discussed, this chapter assumes the American jury was largely modeled after the late eighteenth-century English jury. There were significant differences between the actual systems that enshrined the jury in the United States and England, however. The English had no written constitution. Jury power was simply historical, subject to change according to the will of Parliament. In the mid-nineteenth century, Parliament modified the English jury's authority by transferring power for some civil and criminal matters from juries to courts, and jury use

---

[86] BEATTIE, *supra* note 39, at 319–20.

[87] *See* Kevin K. Washburn, *Restoring the Grand Jury*, 76 FORDHAM L. REV. 2333, 2343 (2008). The criminal jury also served as a check on the executive in this case. *See* RANDOLPH N. JONAKAIT, THE AMERICAN JURY SYSTEM 23–24 (2003).

[88] *See* MARVIN E. FRANKEL & GARY P. NAFTALIS, THE GRAND JURY: AN INSTITUTION ON TRIAL 10–12 (1977); Roger A. Fairfax, Jr., *The Jurisdictional Heritage of the Grand Jury Clause*, 91 MINN. L. REV. 398, 409–10 (2006); Renee Lettow Lerner, *Reviving Federal Grand Jury Presentments*, 103 YALE L.J. 1333, 1337 (1994).

[89] YOUNGER, *supra* note 77, at 26, 36. On the other hand, the "information" by a prosecutor that replaced a grand jury indictment was "effectively labeled . . . as an odious instrument of British tyranny." *Id.* at 37.

began to wane. Increased caseloads, the costs of jury trials, and the democratization of the jury contributed to this decline in England.[90]

Although the jury in the United States had an auspicious beginning, with inclusion in the original Constitution and a central role in the Bill of Rights, by the nineteenth century, use of the jury in the United States also began to decline.[91] Some disagree with this proposition, arguing the jury's power has been sustained or has even increased since the late eighteenth century. The section below shows how jury authority has declined since the Constitution and Bill of Rights were enacted, and the section that follows concludes that any arguable gains in jury authority do not compensate for more substantial losses, which now place the jury in a position where it fails to check any governmental actors.

The Criminal Jury

Blackstone warned of "secret machinations" that could undermine the jury, including the "introduc[tion of] new and arbitrary methods of trial, by justices of the peace." He declared that although these may seem "*convenient*," they were "fundamentally opposite to the spirit of our constitution" and would lead to the elimination of the jury.[92] For the most part, the criminal jury has disappeared, displaced by modes similar to what Blackstone noted that we should fear. Moreover, when the jury actually hears a case, although some powers of the jury remain, much authority has been reduced.

Plea Bargaining

Juries presided over almost every serious criminal case in the late eighteenth century. In contrast, today, juries rarely decide whether a defendant is guilty. In many cases in state court, often where no grand jury is required, prosecutors can charge defendants by "information" or a complaint and obtain guilty pleas without a trial.[93] In some cases in federal court, prosecutors also may proceed without grand juries and secure

---

[90] *See* HOSTETTLER, *supra* note 21, at 109–22, 131, 140; Thomas, *supra* note 62, at 1098–1104; *see also* Chapter 6.

[91] *See* Comment, *The Changing Role of the Jury in the Nineteenth Century*, 74 YALE L.J. 170, 170–71 (1964).

[92] 4 BLACKSTONE, *supra* note 17, at 343–44.

[93] *See* Roger A. Fairfax, Jr., *Remaking the Grand Jury*, *in* GRAND JURY 2.0: MODERN PERSPECTIVES ON THE GRAND JURY, *supra* note 81, at 333–34.

guilty pleas without a trial.[94] Criminal defendants almost always plead to crimes because prosecutors offer leniency unavailable to defendants convicted by a jury.[95] For example, the prosecutor can motivate pleas using mechanisms such as charge or sentence bargains. In the former, the prosecutor can threaten additional or more serious charges. In the latter, she may offer to recommend to a sentence below the maximum. In these circumstances, she agrees not to prove predicate offenses or not to charge the defendant as a recidivist, or agrees that mitigating factors exist or aggravating factors do not.

Blackstone documented that defendants in England could plead guilty without a jury trial. However, he advised that promises before conviction should not occur because they could be unjustly used. For instance, decision-makers could employ them for monetary gain. Under one practice, after the defendant was convicted of a misdemeanor, the court could permit the defendant to speak to the prosecutor (again, often a private citizen). The court could give the defendant a trivial punishment – possibly ordering the defendant to pay the prosecutor monetary compensation – if the prosecutor agreed to it. Blackstone warned this was a "dangerous practice" because the prosecutor could commence an action solely for monetary gain. The right to punish belonged not to an individual but rather to society or the government that represented society.[96] In the eighteenth century, this right in certain nation-states for juries to decide defendants' fates was contrasted with the power that existed in other countries to compel an innocent to plead guilty because of the conditions that the state imposed.[97]

At the time of the founding in England and America, guilty pleas had little effect on jury trials; they were "highly atypical," and plea bargaining was not viewed positively.[98] Pleas did not occur in the manner in which they happen today with pressure from the prosecutor.[99] Plea bargaining developed in the 1800s – after the enactment of the Constitution and the Bill of Rights.[100]

---

[94] Fed. R. Crim. P. 7(b); Fairfax, *supra* note 93, at 333–34.

[95] *See* Langbein, *supra* note 23, at 121; Ronald F. Wright, *Trial Distortion and the End of Innocence in Federal Criminal Justice*, 154 U. Pa. L. Rev. 79, 91–100 (2005) (describing possible theories of plea bargaining).

[96] 4 Blackstone, *supra* note 17, at 355–57, 372.

[97] *See* Sir John Hawles, Knight, The Englishman's Right: A Dialogue Between a Barrister at Law and a Juryman 11 (1763).

[98] Amar, Bill of Rights, *supra* note 1, at 108 (citing Albert W. Alschuler, *Plea Bargaining and Its History*, 79 Colum. L. Rev. 1, 1–24 (1979)).

[99] *See* Langbein, *supra* note 23, at 121–22.

[100] *See* Beattie, *supra* note 39, at 337.

Trial by Judge

Article III, Section 2 of the Constitution provides that "[t]he Trial of all Crimes, except in Cases of Impeachment, shall be by Jury."[101] In other words, under the Constitution's text, if a trial in a criminal case occurs, other than in an impeachment case, a jury should decide the case. When cases are tried, however, some matters have shifted from juries to judges.

In the late eighteenth century, judges did not try criminal cases other than minor offenses.[102] Citing this history, in the late nineteenth century, the Supreme Court recognized that a criminal defendant could not agree to waive the jury trial and consent to a trial by a judge. It stated that "[t]he public has an interest in [the defendant's] life and liberty. Neither can be lawfully taken except in the mode prescribed by law."[103] Some years later, in the twentieth century, the Court changed its jurisprudence, deciding a defendant could choose to forgo a jury in favor of a judge. Citing Blackstone and Justice Story, who characterized the jury trial as a "privilege" to be used, the Court concluded that the jury trial was not "part of the structure of government." Instead, it "only [guaranteed] the accused the right to such a trial."[104] So, judges now determine guilt or innocence in some cases that juries decided in the past.[105]

Military Tribunals

Despite their limited use in late eighteenth-century England, in the United States, military tribunals have been used to try military service members, civilians who are citizens, and foreigners who are civilians and combatants. Although the merits and deficiencies of military tribunals have been debated,[106] the question remains whether the Constitution authorizes such trials without grand and criminal juries. Several constitutional provisions have been used to justify congressional or presidential

---

[101] U.S. CONST. art. III, § 2, cl. 3.

[102] See Susan C. Towne, *The Historical Origins of Bench Trial For Serious Crime*, 26 AM. J. L. HIST. 123 (1982).

[103] Thompson v. Utah, 170 U.S. 343, 353–54 (1898) (holding defendant could not waive requirement of jury of twelve).

[104] Patton v. United States, 281 U.S. 276, 293, 296 (1930) (holding defendant could waive jury trial of twelve); AMAR, BILL OF RIGHTS, *supra* note 1, at 108.

[105] FED. R. CRIM. P. 23(c); Andrew D. Leipold, *Why Are Federal Judges So Acquittal Prone?*, 83 WASH. U. L.Q. 151, 159 (2005) (describing from 1983 to 2002, 77% of defendants who were tried were tried by juries).

[106] See Laura K. Donohue, *Terrorism and Trial by Jury: The Vices and Virtues of British and American Criminal Law*, 59 STAN. L. REV. 1321, 1341–43 (2007).

authority to establish tribunals, including the jury provisions and Congress's Article I, Section 8 powers.[107] Most relevant to this discussion are the Fifth Amendment, which states that a grand jury must be constituted "except in cases arising in the land or naval forces, or in the Militia, when in actual service in time of War or public danger"[108] and Congress's power under Article I, Section 8 "[t]o make Rules for the Government and Regulation of the land and naval Forces"[109] and "[t]o define and punish . . . Offences against the Law of Nations."[110]

Military Service Members   In most circumstances, the Supreme Court has deemed juries unnecessary in cases involving military service members. In some cases, the Court has changed its jurisprudence from favoring jury authority to disfavoring it. In a case alleging that a military member sexually assaulted a civilian off-base, the Court concluded that a grand jury was required in such a case that was unconnected to service.[111] The Fifth Amendment required a grand jury there because the case did not "aris[e] in the land or naval forces." Less than twenty years later, the Court heard a case involving the same circumstances – an alleged off-base sexual assault – and applied Congress's "make Rules for the Government and Regulation of the land and naval Forces" clause in Article I. There, the Court decided differently that the Constitution did not require a grand jury (or a criminal jury) to try a defendant in a case unconnected to service. Ignoring the jury provisions and emphasizing what it characterized as ambiguous history, the Court decided that military tribunals alone could properly try these cases.[112]

The Fifth Amendment phrase not requiring grand juries and thus permitting decisions by other tribunals "in the Militia, when in actual

---

[107] *See, e.g.*, United States v. Al Bahlul, 820 F. Supp. 2d 1141, 1167–68 (U.S.C.M.C.R. 2011) (discussing several constitutional provisions). Ingrid Wuerth has undertaken an extensive study of the Captures Clause, which gives Congress the power to "make Rules concerning Captures on Land and Water." U.S. CONST. art. I, § 8, cl. 11. She concludes that this clause relates only to property, not to people. *See* Ingrid Wuerth, *The Captures Clause*, 76 U. CHI. L. REV. 1683 (2009).

[108] U.S. CONST. amend. V.

[109] *Id.* art. I, § 8, cl. 14.

[110] *Id.* art. I, § 8, cl. 10.

[111] *See* O'Callahan v. Parker, 395 U.S. 258 (1969).

[112] *See* Solorio v. United States, 483 U.S. 435 (1987); Stephen I. Vladeck, *The Laws of Wars as a Constitutional Limit on Military Jurisdiction*, 4 J. NAT'L SEC. L. & POL'Y 295, 308–09 (2010). The Court may recognize juries for trial of a capital offense that is not connected to service. *See* Vladeck, *supra*, at 311 n.95.

service in time of War or public danger" also has been somewhat broadly interpreted against jury authority. English commentary occurring around the time of the adoption of the Bill of Rights argued against greater jurisdiction for military courts. It also emphasized that they should be used only at times of war for order and discipline in the army. Consistent with this history, the Supreme Court decided that state militia are subject to military tribunals only in times of war or public danger. But in cases involving the federal military, the Court expansively interpreted the text against jury authority deciding that the federal military is subject to such tribunals at all times, not only during war or public danger.[113]

Nonmilitary Citizens and Noncitizens   In some circumstances, non-military citizens and noncitizens have been tried by military tribunals without juries.[114] Assuming Congress can enact certain laws pursuant to the Offenses against the Law of Nations clause in Article I,[115] the question is whether Congress has power to place matters involving nonmilitary citizens and noncitizens before military tribunals.[116] While an early decision by the Supreme Court provided support for juries for noncitizens and nonmilitary citizens,[117] the Court subsequently attempted to distinguish that case. Using the jury provisions and Congress's authority to regulate Offenses against the Law of Nations as

---

[113] See Johnson v. Sayre, 158 U.S. 109, 114 (1895).

[114] 10 U.S.C. §§ 821, 948a–950w (2006); Ex parte Quirin, 317 U.S. 1, 20, 48 (1942); United States v. Al Bahlul, 820 F. Supp. 2d 1141, 1155–57 (U.S.C.M.C.R. 2001).

[115] Despite this assumption, according to the discussion around the adoption of the clause, unless all nations agreed to the prohibition of additional crimes, these crimes could not be proscribed as offenses against the law of nations. See Vladeck, supra note 112, at 329–31; see also 4 BLACKSTONE, supra note 17, at 66–73 (discussing offenses against the law of nations). The clause has been accepted as an evolving law of nations, which should be based on international law. See Vladeck, supra note 112, at 332–36.

[116] See Thomas McDonald, Comment, A Few Good Angry Men: Application of the Jury Trial Clause of the Sixth Amendment to Non-Citizens Detained at Guantanamo Bay, 62 AM. U. L. REV. 701 (2013); Vladeck, supra note 112, at 336–39. The Court has stated that "[t]he military commission, a tribunal neither mentioned in the Constitution nor created by statute, was born of military necessity." Hamdan v. Rumsfeld, 548 U.S. 557, 590 (2006). Congress's "make Rules for the Government and Regulation of the land and naval Forces" has been interpreted to apply only to Congress's court-martial regulation of service members. Stephen Vladeck has argued that this interpretation makes the same clause inapplicable to other people, voiding any congressional authority to subject others to military tribunals absent another constitutional provision. See Vladeck, supra note 112, at 311–12. Of course, the Fifth and Sixth Amendments can provide independent constraints on this authority. See id.

[117] See Ex parte Milligan, 71 U.S. (4 Wall.) 2, 122–23 (1866).

support, the Court subjected noncitizens and an apparent nonmilitary citizen to military tribunals.[118]

Despite the present state of the law, one could imagine that the Founders were concerned that the President or Congress might persecute in the same manner as the King and Parliament. To prevent a repeat of history, they limited military tribunals to certain prescribed situations. In the earlier decision, the Court warned that in times of unrest, liberty needs the protection of juries.

> This Nation, as experience has proved, cannot always remain at peace, and has no right to expect that it will always have wise and humane rulers, sincerely attached to the principles of the Constitution.... [T]he lessons of history informed [the Framers] that a trial by an established court, assisted by an impartial jury, was the only sure way of protecting the citizen against oppression and wrong.[119]

Other English and American authorities also support a reading of the Constitution to require juries for citizen and noncitizen, nonmilitary personnel. For example, at English common law, noncitizens were indicted and received jury trials. Noncitizens even had the right to have noncitizens on their juries, except in cases of treason, where they were not trusted to determine whether the King's allegiance had been violated.

Historically, there is support for treating opposing military members like our own military members, subjecting them to military tribunals instead of jury trials.[120] Also, it may be illogical to provide greater protections to noncitizens than to our own military members.[121] However, it belies reason, for example, that noncitizens who are nonmilitary could be tried by military tribunals simply by manipulating incidental circumstances, such as the location the government choses to hold a noncitizen.[122]

---

[118] *See Quirin*, 317 U.S. at 41.

[119] *Milligan*, 71 U.S. at 125–26.

[120] Matthew Hale stated that military tribunals were for only the members of the military and the opposing military. *See* HALE, *supra* note 54, at 42.

[121] *See Quirin*, 317 U.S. at 44.

[122] In a recent decision, apparently based on Congress's war powers and the inapplicability of the jury provisions, the Court of Appeals for the Armed Services decided that a noncitizen who was tried in a jurisdiction where the United States was not the sovereign had no jury rights. *See* United States v. Ali, 71 M.J. 256, 269–70 (C.A.A.F. 2012), *reconsideration denied*, 71 M.J. 389 (C.A.A.F. 2012), *cert. denied*, 133 S. Ct. 2338 (2013); Stephen I. Vladeck, *The Civilization of Military Jurisdiction, in* THE CONSTITUTION AND THE FUTURE OF CRIMINAL JUSTICE IN AMERICA 287, 292–95 (2013).

As for citizens, the fact that state courts prohibited military trial of them during the War of 1812 also lends support for jury trials for them.[123]

A Liability-Only Jury

When juries actually hear cases, power has also been taken from them. The jury has lost authority to make determinations of law, such as using the available sentences to decide on which crime to convict a defendant. Unlike the eighteenth-century English jury, most American juries are not informed of the possible sentences,[124] and thus contemporary juries are limited to making only criminal liability determinations.

Lessening the Role of the Jury and the Right of the Defendant

Another law-finding power of the late eighteenth-century English jury has been taken from the criminal jury. While American juries retain the power to acquit criminally culpable defendants, and judges are restrained from overturning such acquittals, the Supreme Court has refused to recognize this "nullification" power. Juries cannot be told that they govern in this respect,[125] and instead they are instructed to follow the law. This misinformation significantly curtails the American jury's power to restrain the executive, which has brought the charge, and the legislature, which has established the law.

The power of American criminal juries has been further reduced where judges acquit defendants who have been convicted by juries. A judge can do so if he finds that the jury's verdict is not supported by the evidence.[126] While at English common law a judge might have directed a jury to find a certain way, and the jury might have followed the judge's order, the jury

---

[123] *See Ex parte* Milligan, 71 U.S. (4 Wall.) 2, 128–29 (1866) (citing Smith v. Shaw, 12 Johns. 257 (N.Y. Sup. Ct. 1815); M'Connell v. Hampton, 12 Johns. 234 (N.Y. Sup. Ct. 1815)); Ingrid Wuerth, *The President's Power to Detain "Enemy Combatants": Modern Lessons from Mr. Madison's Forgotten War*, 98 Nw. U. L. Rev. 1567, 1580–83 (2004) (discussing *Smith*, 12 Johns. at 265 (refusing to permit citizens to be detained); *In re* Stacy, 10 Johns. 328 (N.Y. Sup. Ct. 1813); Case of Clark the Spy, *in* 1 THE MILITARY MONITOR AND AMERICAN REGISTER 121–22 (Feb. 1, 1813)).

[124] However, juries are involved in capital sentencing and in sub-capital sentencing in some states such as Texas. *See* Nancy J. King & Rosevelt L. Noble, *Felony Jury Sentencing in Practice: A Three-State Study*, 57 VAND. L. REV. 885 (2004).

[125] Sparf v. United States, 156 U.S. 51 (1895) (holding that there is no constitutional right for the jury to decide law).

[126] *See* Jackson v. Virginia, 443 U.S. 307, 318–19 (1979). Chapter 5 discusses the constitutional problems with judicial acquittal.

was not required to do so. The jury was the final arbiter of guilt or innocence. At most, a judge could order a new trial, and this could occur only in non-felony cases. A judge could reprieve or stay execution of a sentence in order for the Crown to consider a pardon. While the Crown almost invariably followed the judge's recommendation, the Crown made the final decision, not the judge. Moreover, pardons might involve a sentence reduction instead of freedom.

The power of the American criminal jury has been further limited by its diminution to fewer than the twelve jurors required to convict at English common law. Again, while the Supreme Court initially recognized this requirement,[127] it subsequently changed its mind, and now as few as six jurors are permitted in state cases.[128] Having fewer than twelve jurors reduces the role of the community in the decision-making process by having fewer people involved. It also interferes with the defendant's rights by decreasing possible discussion among jurors and significantly lowering the hurdle for the government to convict.

A related problem is unanimity. In state courts, a jury need not be unanimous to convict a defendant, though unanimity was a requirement at English common law.[129] Once again, the Supreme Court initially recognized unanimity as a constitutional hurdle to conviction.[130] But the Court subsequently limited the unanimity requirement only to federal courts.[131] This lower threshold for state governments can significantly curtail the rights of defendants. Despite this possibility, all states but two, Louisiana and Oregon, require the jury to convict unanimously.

The Civil Jury

Similar to Blackstone's warning about supplanting the criminal jury trial with alternative methods, in describing the civil jury trial, he stated that "the introduction of new and arbitrary methods of trial ... under a

---

[127] See Thompson v. Utah, 170 U.S. 343, 349 (1898) (referring to a jury as "twelve persons, neither more nor less").

[128] See Williams v. Florida, 399 U.S. 78, 103 (1970); see also Ballew v. Georgia, 435 U.S. 223, 245 (1978) (finding that five-member jury was unconstitutional).

[129] See Suja A. Thomas, *Nonincorporation: The Bill of Rights After McDonald v. Chicago*, 88 NOTRE DAME L. REV. 159, 171–72, 189–91, 203–04 (2012). In an odd decision, the Court decided that although the Fourteenth Amendment incorporated the criminal jury requirement against the states, unanimity was not required in the states. *See id.*

[130] See Am. Pub. Co. v. Fisher, 166 U.S. 464, 468 (1897).

[131] See Apodaca v. Oregon, 406 U.S. 404, 406 (1972).

variety of plausible pretences [sic], may in time imperceptibly undermine this best preservative of English liberty."[132] The American civil jury has been displaced by such methods in many circumstances. Also, where the civil jury still exists, it has been significantly disempowered.

Delegation of Damages to Other Tribunals

In late eighteenth-century England, the jury almost invariably decided cases involving monetary remedies or damages. Now, in many circumstances, the jury's jurisdiction over cases with these types of remedies has shifted to other tribunals. For example, a jury trial will not be required for a new cause of action for which money remedies are available unless the action is analogous to one that existed at common law. Moreover, Congress can direct certain causes of action with monetary remedies to other bodies that do not provide juries, including federal administrative agencies and bankruptcy courts.[133]

The jury also does not hold the authority that it should possess in the states. By not applying the Seventh Amendment to the states, the Supreme Court has not required states to hold jury trials in civil cases. Although almost all states require civil juries anyway, most states do not require juries for matters that involve smaller amounts, including in some circumstances, amounts near $100,000.[134]

Procedures Before, During, and After Trial

Jury decision-making authority has shifted to other bodies through the use of procedures that did not exist in late eighteenth-century England.

Judges as Fact-finders   Using three new procedures, judges now dismiss civil cases before, during, and after a jury trial. First, at the beginning of a case, the defendant can move to dismiss a claim brought by the plaintiff, arguing that the facts the plaintiff alleges do not state a claim for which the law provides relief.[135] Early on, this rule was interpreted in a manner that was complementary to the jury. In *Conley v. Gibson*, the Supreme Court decided a case should not be dismissed "unless it appears beyond

---

[132] 3 BLACKSTONE, *supra* note 20, at 381.

[133] *See* Thomas, *supra* note 62, at 1078–1108; *see also* Russell G. Ryan, Opinion, *The SEC as Prosecutor and Judge*, WALL ST. J., Aug. 5, 2014 (discussing movement of cases charging activity such as alleged insider trading from juries to SEC administrative law judges under 2010 Dodd–Frank law).

[134] *See* Thomas, *supra* note 129, at 172–75, 191–96, 198–203.

[135] FED. R. CIV. P. 12(b)(6).

doubt that the plaintiff can prove no set of facts in support of his claim which would entitle him to relief."[136] For the most part, cases appear to have survived this pleading stage, and few defendants moved to dismiss under this standard.[137] In 2007, and again in 2009, the Court changed its interpretation of the rule in a manner that took power away from the jury.[138] Under this standard, a judge can decide whether a claim is plausible. To decide this question, the judge takes into account not only the inferences from the facts that favor the plaintiff but also those that favor the defendant, and uses his "judicial experience and common sense" to decide whether the claim is plausible.[139] Although it is too early to tell how many and what types of cases will be dismissed at this early stage, a case is now easier to dismiss than it was in the past,[140] which results in fewer cases being tried by juries.

Second, after discovery – an exchange of information by the parties – a claim may be dismissed through a procedure called summary judgment. In many ways the motion to dismiss mirrors this procedure.[141] Originally, the standard to dismiss a case upon summary judgment was more difficult to meet.[142] In three cases during 1986, the Supreme Court made it easier for judges to dismiss cases using this procedure. A judge can decide whether a reasonable jury could find for the plaintiff and can consider inferences that favor the plaintiff in addition to inferences that favor the defendant.[143] Although a judge is not supposed to use his

---

[136] 355 U.S. 41, 45–46 (1957).

[137] *See* Suja A. Thomas, *The New Summary Judgment Motion: The Motion to Dismiss Under Iqbal and* Twombly, 14 Lewis & Clark L. Rev. 15, 24 (2010).

[138] *See* Ashcroft v. Iqbal, 556 U.S. 662 (2009); Bell Atlantic Corp. v. Twombly, 550 U.S. 544 (2007). *Compare* Suja A. Thomas, *Why Summary Judgment Is Unconstitutional*, 93 Va. L. Rev. 139, 150 n.39 (2007) (arguing that the motion to dismiss under *Conley* is constitutional under the Seventh Amendment), *with* Suja A. Thomas, *Why the Motion to Dismiss Is Now Unconstitutional*, 92 Minn. L. Rev. 1851 (2008) (arguing that the motion to dismiss is unconstitutional under *Twombly*).

[139] *See Twombly*, 550 U.S. at 567–69 & n.13; *Iqbal*, 556 U.S. at 677–84 (majority opinion), 687–99 (Souter, J., dissenting).

[140] *See, e.g.*, Joe S. Cecil et al., Fed. Judicial Ctr., Motion to Dismiss for Failure to State a Claim After *Iqbal*: Report to the Judicial Committee on Civil Rules (2011), *available at* www.fjc.gov/public/pdf.nsf/lookup/motioniqbal2.pdf/$file/motioniqbal2.pdf.

[141] *See* Thomas, *supra* note 137, at 31–34.

[142] *See* Patricia M. Wald, *Summary Judgment at Sixty*, 76 Tex. L. Rev. 1897, 1904–07 (1998).

[143] Fed. R. Civ. P. 56; Anderson v. Liberty Lobby, Inc., 477 U.S. 242 (1986); Celotex Corp. v. Catrett, 477 U.S. 317 (1986); *see also* Matsushita Elec. Indus. v. Zenith Radio Corp.,

opinion of the evidence in the decision whether to dismiss, he appears to do so. Then, the result is what a judge determines, not what a reasonable jury might have found.[144] Although there is mixed evidence on whether courts have increased their grant of summary judgment after the 1986 cases, it is clear that courts use summary judgment to dismiss many cases, including factually intensive cases, like employment discrimination cases,[145] reducing the number of cases decided by juries.

A procedure similar to summary judgment that judges use to dismiss cases during and after trial is judgment as a matter of law.[146] Under judgment as a matter of law, during the jury trial or after the trial, if a judge decides a reasonable jury could not find for the plaintiff, the case is dismissed. Early on, judgment as a matter of law was found unconstitutional by the Supreme Court. If a judge decided the evidence was insufficient after a jury found for the plaintiff, only a new trial could be ordered.[147] However, similar to the motion to dismiss and summary judgment, judgment as a matter of law has been interpreted in a manner that has reduced the jury's authority over time. The Court later decided a judge could dismiss the case entirely during a jury trial or after a jury verdict if he decided that a reasonable jury could not find for the plaintiff.[148]

Summary judgment, the motion to dismiss, and judgment as a matter of law contrast with the substance or essentials of the procedures in existence in late eighteenth-century England. Courts were not empowered to make such decisions at that time. At most, a case was sent for a new trial.[149]

Courts as Determiners of Damages   Another new procedure is the remittitur or reduction by a court of the damages that a jury found. After a jury finds for the plaintiff and awards monetary damages to her, the

---

475 U.S. 574 (1986). Although a judge can decide summary judgment for the plaintiff, this rarely occurs.

[144] *See* Suja A. Thomas, *The Fallacy of Dispositive Procedure*, 50 B.C. L. Rev. 759 (2009); Dan M. Kahan et al., *Whose Eyes Are You Going to Believe? Scott v. Harris and the Perils of Cognitive Illiberalism*, 122 Harv. L. Rev. 837, 881–94 (2009).

[145] *See* Memorandum from Joe Cecil and George Cort to Hon. Michael Baylson 2, 6 tbl.3 (June 15, 2007), www.fjc.gov/public/pdf.nsf/lookup/sujufy06.pdf/$file/sujufy06.pdf.

[146] Fed. R. Civ. P. 50.

[147] *See* Slocum v. N.Y. Life Ins. Co., 228 U.S. 364 (1913). A judge could decide judgment as a matter of law for the plaintiff, but this rarely occurs.

[148] *See* Balt. & Carolina Line, Inc. v. Redman, 295 U.S. 654 (1935).

[149] *See* Thomas, *Motion to Dismiss, supra* note 138; Thomas, *Summary Judgment, supra* note 138; *see also* Ellen E. Sward, The Decline of the Civil Jury 288–94 (2001).

defendant can move for a new trial arguing that the jury awarded excessive damages. The defendant can also move for a remittitur of the damages as an alternative result. If the court agrees that the damages are excessive, the court can order a new trial and can determine the maximum amount that a reasonable jury could find. The plaintiff can accept this reduction of the jury verdict instead of embarking on a new trial. This type of remittitur did not exist in the late eighteenth century.[150] In fact, the Supreme Court has called the constitutionality of modern remittitur "doubtful precedent."[151]

The remittitur of the damages effectively forces the plaintiff to take the reduced amount instead of the new trial. The judge has determined the maximum amount that a reasonable jury could find. If the second jury found more than that amount, the second jury would be unreasonable per se, and the court would find that verdict excessive. In other words, there is no reason for the plaintiff to take the new trial. Through this procedure of remittitur, the judge replaces the jury as the decider of damages.[152]

Judges now also order new trials in tort cases when they decide the jury awarded excessive damages – circumstances under which they generally would not order new trials in the past. In England, such new trials for excessive damages were granted only when damages were calculable, as in contract or debt cases as opposed to cases in which damages were uncertain, such as tort cases.[153]

The Legislature as Determiner of Damages   Legislatures have also displaced juries. They have taken on the jury's role by declaring the maximum damages permitted for certain claims. Caps on damages have become commonplace, particularly in state malpractice claims.[154]

---

[150] *See* Suja A. Thomas, *Re-examining the Constitutionality of Remittitur Under the Seventh Amendment*, 64 OHIO ST. L.J. 731 (2003).

[151] Dimick v. Schiedt, 293 U.S. 474, 485–88 (1935).

[152] *See* Thomas, *supra* note 150, at 739–46. Appellate courts also should not be able to review the denial of a new trial motion. *See* Thomas, *supra* note 62, at 1078 & n.29. The Supreme Court has also decided that additur, a judge's increase of a jury verdict, is unconstitutional, despite some evidence of the practice in certain cases. *See* OLDHAM, *supra* note 20, at 60–62; Thomas, *supra* note 150, at 750 n.91.

[153] *See* Thomas, *supra* note 150, at 775–82.

[154] *See* Caitlin Haney, *Trend Continues for Personal Injury Damage Caps*, 38 A.B.A. SEC. LITIG. 5, 4–5 (2013).

They also play a limiting function in some federal statutes, including employment discrimination cases under Title VII.[155] Various reasons have been asserted to justify the constitutionality of caps on damages:

> Caps are constitutional because legislatures, not courts, are reviewing the facts found by a jury; caps are constitutional because the legislature can eliminate causes of action and thus also can limit damages; caps are simply the law that is being applied to a jury's finding of the facts; caps are constitutional because there actually may not be a right to a jury trial in the remedy phase of a jury trial; ... [and] caps are simply a legislative remittitur, analogous to remittiturs [of damages] by courts.[156]

Yet at common law only one method existed to reassess the damages rendered by a jury: a court could order a new trial where it deemed a damage award excessive. The legislature itself had no power to reassess or limit damages.

The Grand Jury

More on Plea Bargaining

In circumstances where a grand jury is required, prosecutors sometimes condition plea agreements on the defendant's waiver of the grand jury indictment. In late eighteenth-century England, a defendant could not be prosecuted for a serious crime without such an indictment. In the first 150 years of our constitutional jurisprudence, grand jury indictment or presentment was required in order for the federal courts to have jurisdiction over any infamous crime.[157] The adoption of Rule 7 of the Federal Rules of Criminal Procedure in 1938, under which a criminal defendant could waive a grand jury indictment for noncapital cases, began to effect significant change.[158] In the late nineteenth century, the Supreme Court previously had decided that a court did not have power over a criminal defendant who was prosecuted under a grand jury's indictment that was amended without the grand jury's approval.[159] Later, the Court changed

---

[155] 42 U.S.C. § 2000e (2006).
[156] Suja A. Thomas, Federal Tort Reform and the Seventh Amendment, Address at the American Association of Law Schools Section on Civil Procedure Program: The Civil Jury in the Shadow of Tort Reform (Jan. 5, 2006).
[157] See Ex parte Wilson, 114 U.S. 417, 426 (1885); see also Fairfax, supra note 88, at 408, 413.
[158] See FED. R. CRIM. P. 7; Fairfax, supra note 88, at 423–25.
[159] See Ex parte Bain, Jr., 121 U.S. 1 (1887).

its mind about the grand jury requirements. It decided a defect in the indictment – in that case, prosecuting the defendant under an indictment that did not support the sentence imposed on the defendant – did not deprive a court of power over the defendant.[160] So, despite history and prior precedent to the contrary, the government can obtain a guilty plea without grand jury indictment and, in some circumstances, proceed to trial on a defective indictment or on an amended indictment not approved by a grand jury.

Taking Away the Power of the Grand Jury Not to Indict

In late eighteenth-century England, the grand jury had complete discretion to indict or not, and there were significant examples of grand juries declining to indict. Although indictment by a grand jury is widely characterized as a mere formality now, the grand jury is empowered to stop the government's prosecution. A grand jury may decline to indict for a variety of reasons including: an unjust or unconstitutional law, an unwise law or application of law, biased or unwise allocation of prosecutorial resources, or improper governmental motivation.[161]

Moreover, one of the grand jury's historical roles – balancing power between the colonists and England – is comparable to the modern role grand juries could play to mediate power between the federal government and the states. Through the grand jury, the local community can restrain federal power exerted through federal laws.[162]

Grand juries are not required in many states. Similar to its decision not to command states to require unanimous convictions by juries and to constitute civil juries, the Supreme Court has not required states to assemble grand juries. As a result, state practices vary widely in how grand juries are used.[163]

---

[160] *See* United States v. Cotton, 535 U.S. 625 (2002).
[161] *See* Roger A. Fairfax, Jr., *Grand Jury Discretion and Constitutional Design*, 93 CORNELL L. REV. 703 (2008); Joe Palazzolo, *Teen Jailed for Facebook Posting About School Shooting*, WALL ST. J., July 5, 2013, at A3 (illustration of grand jury not indicting teenager over Facebook posting). Josh Bowers makes the interesting point that prosecutors use grand juries to indict the most serious crimes for which there will be the least disagreement, and thus it should not be surprising that they indict. *See* Josh Bowers, *The Normative Case for Normative Grand Juries*, 47 WAKE FOREST L. REV. 319, 328 (2012).
[162] *See* Fairfax, *supra* note 161, at 729–31.
[163] *See* Thomas, *supra* note 129, at 181–82, 201.

Lessening the Power of the Grand Jury

When grand juries hear cases, their authority may have been curtailed by three changes. First, today's grand juries must find only probable cause to indict, even though more may have been required in late eighteenth-century England. Lowering what the government must prove to obtain an indictment from the grand jury lessens the authority of the grand jury. Second, although no such authority existed in the past, and such action is not permitted in the federal courts, after a grand jury indictment, most state judges can decide that there is insufficient evidence to support the indictment and dismiss the case.[164] Finally, grand juries do not serve the independent investigative function through presentments that they performed in the past. So, for example, grand juries cannot bring an action against a police officer for shooting a civilian without the acquiescence of the prosecution.

Modern Changes and the Jury

Although civil litigation and criminal cases have changed in many ways since the late eighteenth century resulting in decreased jury authority, modern transformations have also affected change that arguably has enhanced the jury.

Arguments that the Jury Has Risen Over Time

Civil cases subject to jury trial in America today are more complex than those in late eighteenth-century England.[165] To avoid confusing juries

---

[164] See Kaley v. United States, 134 S. Ct. 1090, 1100 (2014) ("we have repeatedly affirmed . . . : A defendant has no right to judicial review of a grand jury's determination of probable cause to think a defendant committed a crime"); see, e.g., State v. Green, 810 P.2d 1023 (Alaska Ct. App. 1991) (upholding trial court's dismissal of murder indictment); People v. Bello, 705 N.E.2d 1209, 1211 (N.Y. 1998) (the trial judge asks "'whether the facts, if proven, and the inferences that logically flow from those facts supply proof of every element of the charged crimes,' and whether 'the Grand Jury could rationally have drawn the guilty inference'"). Niki Kuckes found case law permitting a judge to decide whether sufficient admissible evidence existed for the grand jury to indict. See Kuckes, *supra* note 81, at 139–42 (discussing an example involving United States v. Coolidge, 25 F. Cas, 622, 623 (C.C.D. Mass. 1815)). Blackstone, who sets forth the different ways by which judges can interfere with criminal and civil jury verdicts, does not describe such ways for a judge to interfere with an indictment by a grand jury. See 4 BLACKSTONE, *supra* note 17, at 298–303.

[165] See Douglas King, *Complex Civil Litigation and the Seventh Amendment Right to a Jury Trial*, 51 U. CHI. L. REV. 581, 592 (1984).

and courts, and to control litigation expenses, English juries tried only one matter, unless the court granted permission for more.[166] Most cases that juries heard involved relatively simple tort, property, or contract claims.[167] Juries also heard far less evidence than today, because discovery was not available in the common law courts.[168] In all types of cases, juries were precluded from hearing certain evidence such as any testimony from a witness with an interest in the outcome of the case – testimony permitted in many modern trials.[169] On the other hand, juries heard much more hearsay evidence and other evidence that modern courts exclude.[170] The smaller and less complex jury trials of the past seldom took longer than a day.[171] The common law courts contrasted with equity courts where judges decided longer lasting cases with more complicated issues, additional parties, and greater amounts in controversy.[172]

The volume of cases, frequency of service, and qualifications for eighteenth-century juries also differed from their modern American counterparts. A single jury then would hear many cases, and jurors often served on multiple juries over time.[173] Litigants could request special juries comprised of individuals possessing expert knowledge, such as merchants. Such juries tried most business cases or those cases were referred to arbitration with the consent of the parties.[174] Property ownership requirements and the exclusion of certain groups, including women, also precluded many from participating in jury deliberations.[175] Because such requirements are now prohibited, juries of greater diversity presently sit on cases.[176]

---

[166] See 3 BLACKSTONE, supra note 20, at 308, 311.

[167] See King, supra note 165, at 593, 598–99.

[168] See Thomas, supra note 62, at 1088–89 (discovery could be obtained from the equity courts and the case may proceed back in the common law courts).

[169] See King, supra note 165, at 589.

[170] See Langbein, supra note 24, at 300–06.

[171] See King, supra note 165, at 589; Langbein, supra note 24, at 277–84.

[172] See King, supra note 165, at 603–06.

[173] See Langbein, supra note 24, at 274–76.

[174] See OLDHAM, supra note 20, at 22. Oldham stated that while consent was required, consent may have been pushed upon a party. See James Oldham, On the Question of a Complexity Exception to the Seventh Amendment Guaranty of Trial by Jury, 71 OHIO ST. L.J. 1031, 1036 (2010).

[175] See HOSTETTLER, supra note 21, at 125–27.

[176] See Strauder v. West Virginia, 100 U.S. 303 (1880) (unconstitutional to prevent black jurors from serving on grand or criminal juries).

Juries formerly participated more actively in trials including asking questions of witnesses and after a verdict, at times providing rationales for them.

In the past, the judges' authority to opine on the evidence and recommend verdicts allowed some influence over verdicts that does not exist now. And even if a jury convicted, a judge could recommend that the King pardon a criminal defendant.[177]

Additional changes complicate comparisons to the past. Formerly, in both English civil and criminal cases, fewer lawyers were involved. Under the modern adversarial system, parties use more resources, including lawyers, to prove their cases, resulting in collateral differences such as increased costs. Also, under the English system the losing party recovered costs. Today while the loser pays certain costs,[178] attorneys' fees (generally unrecoverable from the loser) as well as significant discovery costs (that generally are not recovered until the end of the case) have altered the economics of litigation. Earlier settlement to avoid costs has become more attractive and may incentivize settling a case that may have gone to the jury in the past.

Such changes suggest that in some ways modern American juries have greater power. More people participate. Juries hear more causes of action. Juries hear some cases that would have gone to specialized juries or arbitration. And juries hear certain types of evidence that they could not hear in the past. Some changes are attributable to evolutions in American constitutional law, including the adoption of the Fourteenth Amendment, providing all citizens the opportunity to serve on juries and requiring that juries be drawn from a cross section of the community. Many of the other changes, including the merger of courts of law and courts of equity and changes regarding the influence of judges, have occurred over time independent of action required by the Constitution.

Perhaps the most contentious issue is the role that the jury should play in complex cases. In the eighteenth century, English equity courts heard larger claims with more parties and additional complexity.[179] Because juries did not hear such cases,[180] the American jury arguably should not

---

[177] *See* Langbein, *supra* note 24, at 285–87, 291–97.

[178] FED. R. CIV. P. 54(d)(1).

[179] *See* King, *supra* note 165, at 603–06.

[180] *See* Patrick Devlin, *Jury Trial of Complex Cases: English Practice at the Time of the Seventh Amendment*, 80 COLUM. L. REV. 43 (1980); King, *supra* note 165; Oldham, *supra* note 174. *But see* Morris S. Arnold, *A Historical Inquiry into the Right to Trial by Jury in Complex Civil Litigation*, 128 U. PA. L. REV. 829 (1980).

hear them. Even a supporter of this view, James Oldham, has found no case in late eighteenth-century England where a judge decided a case because the facts were too difficult for the jury.[181] Because juries decided damages, juries arguably must hear all cases, including complex ones, in which damages are available.

Finally, two additional changes should be noted. A significant set of civil cases are now settled by the parties or decided in arbitration – accounting for the shift of some of cases from juries. Parties may sign "contracts" to have disputes heard by arbitrators instead of juries. While a troubling development in some circumstances,[182] arbitration does not involve the same power shift that has been otherwise described here. The book's focus is not on circumstances in which people choose to bring their cases elsewhere or decide to settle them. Instead the focus is on the many cases juries were to decide that are now decided by the executive, the legislature, the judiciary, and the states.

The Jury Has Fallen

The significant authority that criminal, civil, and grand juries enjoyed in England in the late eighteenth century has disappeared. In certain ways, though, the jury has even more authority now than it did then.

In order to compare the English jury of the past to the jury of today, the substance or essentials of the English jury should be evaluated to determine whether the most important elements of the past exist today. This may be accomplished by examining whether the purpose of the jury of the past set forth in the Constitution is accomplished through the functions of the jury today. The past jury restrained the judiciary, the executive, the legislature, and the states. Akhil Amar documents that the Constitution's jury was to serve several roles – a populist role by "protecting ordinary individuals against government overreaching," a local role with members from the community, a student role by learning about the law and government, and a political role by participating in government.[183] Included in these roles was the power, and perhaps the duty, of the jury to question whether a law

---

[181] See OLDHAM, *supra* note 20, at 21; Oldham, *supra* note 174, at 1052.

[182] See Suja A. Thomas, *Before and After the Summary Judgment Trilogy*, 43 Loy. U. Chi. L.J. 499, 508 (2012).

[183] AMAR, BILL OF RIGHTS, *supra* note 1, 89–96; *see also* Vikram David Amar, *Jury Service as Political Participation Akin to Voting*, 80 CORNELL L. REV. 203 (1995).

was constitutional. The jury's role was as important as the functions of the judiciary, the legislature, and the executive.[184]

The jury does not play that role any longer, however. For instance, in the past, if the executive accused a person of a crime, the grand and criminal juries in turn had the opportunity to dismiss the case against the defendant, which checked the executive's authority. Now, in the vast majority of circumstances, the jury serves no role in checking the government and a defendant is dependent on the state to decide his fate. Formerly, a litigant would bring a case against the executive and the jury would decide whether the rights of that individual had been violated. Now, a judge can dismiss a litigant's case against the executive, depriving the jury of its power to check this institution.

The historical record compels an inescapable conclusion that the most important elements of the jury of the past have vanished. Juries hear few cases – almost all criminal cases are pled out, grand juries generally are circumvented, judges dismiss many civil cases before trial, and the legislature may give the executive the power to hear cases instead of juries. When a criminal case goes to trial, a judge may try it instead. When a jury hears a criminal or civil case, although the judge cannot comment on the evidence during the jury trial or recommend a verdict, the judge can dismiss the case before it reaches the jury, during the trial, or after the jury verdict. In modern American criminal litigation, prosecutors and judges alone almost invariably determine the outcome. In modern American civil litigation, the judiciary, the legislature, or the executive often have significant authority over the outcome.

*****

In summary, juries now look very different from their English predecessors. Most evident is that these juries hear far fewer cases and have far less power than in the past despite some changes that give authority to the jury.

A Transfer of Authority

The English viewed the jury as a restraint on the judiciary, the executive, and the legislature. Assuming the relevance of the late eighteenth-century

---

[184] See AMAR, BILL OF RIGHTS, supra note 1, at 98–102.

English common law, a transfer of power has occurred, giving authority to the very parts of government that the jury was intended to check. Moreover, when the Fourteenth Amendment was adopted, the jury was viewed as protection against the states. Thus, the failure to apply some of the jury provisions to the states has transferred power intended for juries to the states.

The Executive

Today the jury does not serve as a check on the executive. However, in the past, criminal and grand juries played this role, including stopping the executive's prosecution of people who spoke critically of the government. Also, civil juries protected against government overreaching by awarding damages to people who were falsely arrested.

Now, power has transferred from the jury to the executive in several ways. Most significantly, the executive can enforce any law that it chooses to enforce with little or no jury involvement. Plea bargaining is the most prominent example of this shift in power from the jury to the executive, although it is often recharacterized as a shift in power from the judiciary to the executive.[185] With most cases being resolved by leveraging punishment against the accused, the decision to prosecute is a decision both to indict and to convict with the executive supplanting the grand jury's and the criminal jury's roles.

Despite the perceived need for a more efficient mode of procedure, John Langbein discussed the strange result of modern plea bargaining: "Plea bargaining achieves just what the Framers expected the jury to prevent, the aggrandizement of state power." Government prosecutors are able to convict defendants without any community involvement and without a public trial, preventing the public from viewing the evidence or participating in discussion about the laws and government.[186]

The executive also gains power because of its control over the sentence in plea bargaining. In the past, a criminal jury could determine a sentence by convicting on a charge less punitive than the charge pursued by the government. Now that decision belongs to the executive, in its power to determine the charge it offers to the defendant for a plea. New laws that

---

[185] See Michelle Alexander, *Go to Trial: Crash the Justice System*, N.Y. TIMES, Mar. 11, 2012.
[186] See Langbein, *supra* note 23, at 124.

impose mandatory minimum sentences provide the prosecutor with even greater leverage. With the certainty of a harsher penalty if the defendant is convicted by a jury on the original charge, the defendant essentially cannot turn down the plea to the charge imposing a lesser sentence.[187]

If the government's case is tried by a jury, changes in how jury trials are conducted have also shifted power to the executive. In state cases, the executive must convince only six to twelve jurors, not necessarily twelve. Also, the executive must establish only probable cause to obtain an indictment, though the requirement may have been greater in the past.

Additionally, in cases unconnected to military service, the legislature has shifted grand and criminal jury power over U.S. military members to military tribunals that are established and controlled by the executive. In some circumstances, jury power over nonmilitary citizens and noncitizens has shifted to the executive through military tribunals.

The executive has also taken power from the civil jury. The Supreme Court has decided that the National Labor Relations Board can decide questions of public significance and can decide backpay damages – questions that, arguably, juries should decide.[188] The Securities and Exchange Commission has shifted matters, including insider-trading cases, from federal juries to administrative law judges. Moreover, as a prerequisite to suing for employment discrimination under federal law, the legislature requires individuals to request federal administrative investigation and disposition of their claims. These plaintiffs must jump through a relatively complex charge-filing process, imposed by the executive's Equal Employment Opportunity Commission.[189] If the plaintiff does not satisfy those charge-filing requirements, a jury never hears the plaintiff's case.

---

[187] See Nancy Gertner, From "Rites" to "Rights": The Decline of the Criminal Jury Trial, 24 YALE J.L. & HUMAN. 433, 436 (2012); LAURA I. APPLEMAN, DEFENDING THE JURY: CRIME, COMMUNITY AND THE CONSTITUTION 128–29 (2015); cf. Human Rights Watch, An Offer You Can't Refuse: How US Federal Prosecutors Force Drug Defendants to Plead Guilty 2 (2013) ("In 2012, the average sentence of federal drug offenders convicted after trial was three times higher (16 years) than that received after a guilty plea (5 years and 4 months)").

[188] See Great-West Life & Annuity Ins. Co. v. Knudson, 534 U.S. 204, 212, 218 n.4 (2002); Nat'l Labor Relations Bd. v. Jones & Laughlin Steel Corp., 301 U.S. 1 (1937); Allan Dinkoff, Back Pay Is Not An Equitable Remedy, 7 MEALEY'S LITIGATION REPORT: EMPLOYMENT LAW #8 (Mar. 2011).

[189] See 42 U.S.C. § 2000e-4, 2000e-5(b) (2006).

The Legislature

Once the Seventh Amendment was ratified, the legislature lacked power over the civil jury, because the Amendment gave only juries and judges certain powers. The legislature also lost power over the grand jury when the Fifth Amendment was enacted, because the Amendment gave the grand jury the power not to indict on laws that the legislature enacted. Over time, this power reserved for the jury has shifted to the legislature.

As with the executive, one of the most important shifts of power from the jury to the legislature has occurred in the context of plea bargaining. The legislature establishes significant punishments for crimes, which gives the prosecutor the ability to threaten a defendant with these punishments if he does not take a plea. In the past, the grand jury and the criminal jury could respectively decide not to indict or convict, including by not following the law. Now, in many cases where plea bargaining occurs, the jury cannot decline to follow the law and thus cannot serve as a check on the legislature.

The jury has also lost power to the legislature in the civil context. In the late eighteenth century, juries decided monetary damages. The Seventh Amendment preserved this power, and the legislature was not granted any competing constitutional power to decide damages.[190] Now, Congress has a significant role in the monetary damages determination when it enacts caps on the damages that a jury can award. Such caps ultimately shift the jury's power to decide damages to the legislature, especially when a jury awards damages greater than what the legislature has approved and the jury's award is reduced. Further, with damages caps in place, plaintiffs have less incentive to take a jury trial because they know in advance the most that they can receive – which will influence settlement.

The Judiciary

Power has shifted significantly from the jury to the judiciary as well. The Sixth Amendment gives juries the explicit power to decide criminal cases. However, courts have permitted defendants to waive their jury trial rights, allowing judges to determine their fates.[191] Also, in plea

---

[190] See Colleen P. Murphy, *Determining Compensation: The Tension Between Legislative Power and Jury Authority*, 74 TEX. L. REV. 345, 354 (1995).
[191] See APPLEMAN, *supra* note 187, at 159–64.

bargaining, where the defendants have waived grand jury indictments, judges can sentence without any jury involvement. Where juries hear cases, juries are not permitted to consider mandatory minimums and mandatory enhancements in their conviction decisions, despite the historical analogy. Judges can also acquit defendants whom juries have convicted.

Power has also shifted from the civil jury to the judiciary through modern procedures such as motions to dismiss, summary judgment, and judgment as a matter of law. Using these mechanisms, judges can dismiss cases before or after juries hear them. Thus, judges can decide what happens in cases – for example, whether a defendant employer wins an employment discrimination case – by simply removing cases from juries based on the judges' own beliefs about what the evidence proves. Lastly, judges can also curtail the power of juries to decide damages by remitting damage awards, supplanting jury determinations with their own.

The States

Power has also shifted from juries to states. Nonincorporation has been the primary contributor to this redistribution of power. The Court has never required the states to require unanimity under the Sixth Amendment, to hold civil jury trials under the Seventh Amendment, or to assemble grand juries under the Fifth Amendment grand jury.

State and local authority has increased in direct relation to decreases in the jury's power. For example, because the Fourteenth Amendment has not been interpreted to incorporate the grand jury, they are not required in most states. Likewise, because the unanimity requirement has not been incorporated against the states in criminal cases, power shifts from juries to states that do not require a unanimous jury to convict. States have also benefited from the failure to incorporate the civil jury trial right. In a few states, there is no jury trial right at all, and in the many states where there is such a right, several do not require jury trials in cases that involve significant amounts of money. Incentives to plead in state cases also buttress state authority. Similar to federal cases, states and localities imprison people – bypassing juries entirely.[192]

---

[192] Juveniles accused of crimes and subject to the loss of their liberty do not have a right to a jury trial so judges try those cases in the states. McKeiver v. Pennsylvania, 403 U.S. 528 (1971).

Conclusion

Despite the fact that juries have gained some limited powers since the founding, the jury has fallen far from its late eighteenth-century origins. At the same time, power has transferred to other parts of the government – the executive, the legislature, the judiciary, and the states – the very bodies that the jury was meant to check.

3

The Missing Branch

As described in Chapter 2, the criminal, civil, and grand juries have declined in authority from their late eighteenth-century English roots. Yet, the executive, the legislature, the judiciary, and the states have gained power. Though attempts have been made to explain the jury's diminution, the corresponding rise of these other bodies has never been acknowledged. This chapter introduces a theory accounting for the fall of the three juries and the related increase in authority of these three branches of government and the states.

Reasons Proffered for the Falls of the Criminal, Civil, and Grand Juries

Commentators generally do not recognize the similarity of the reasons proffered for the criminal, civil, and grand juries' declines. However, cost, incompetence, inaccuracy, and inefficiency are commonly touted as explanations for why all three juries hear few cases, and why, even when they do hear cases, their authority may be disregarded.

The Criminal Jury

Much of the decline of the criminal jury in the United States is attributed to plea bargaining. Its systematic use first occurs in the early nineteenth century. While defendants pled to different crimes at various rates, it appears that they generally pled guilty only about 20% of the time. By the early twentieth century, the proportion of defendants who took pleas grew to more than 90% – a figure that continues to climb.[1]

---

[1] *See* GEORGE FISHER, PLEA BARGAINING'S TRIUMPH: A HISTORY OF PLEA BARGAINING IN AMERICA 12, 137, 140, 161, 167 (2003).

Different reasons have been offered for the increase in plea bargaining and subsequent decrease in jury trials.[2] The rise in the number of plea-bargained cases has been associated with changing caseloads. As the absolute number of criminal defendants has increased over time – for example, doubling in the federal courts from 1946 to 2002 – some argue that pleas have become necessary to dispose of cases quickly without trial.[3] Faced with heavy loads, prosecutors and judges alike have similar incentives for plea bargaining. In the 1970s, the Supreme Court's Chief Justice Warren Burger stated that "plea bargaining is to be encouraged because '[i]f every criminal charge were subjected to a full-scale trial, the States and the Federal Government would need to multiply by many times the number of judges and court facilities.'"[4] Or, as John Langbein translates Burger's sentiment, "[w]e cannot afford the Constitution and the Bill of Rights. Sheer expediency is rationale enough for disregarding the constitutional texts."[5]

Scholars have also suggested that plea bargaining substituted for jury trials after legislators introduced mandatory minimum sentencing and mandatory sentencing guidelines in the 1980s.[6] Under the mandatory minimum regime, charges carry particular minimum sentences. The prosecutor can choose a charge with a lesser mandatory sentence for a defendant who forgoes a jury trial and accepts a plea. In such a system, defendants – even innocent ones – have significant incentives to plead guilty and waive their jury trial right. When a jury decides a case, unlike in the past, the jury will acquit or convict on the charges without knowing the punishment associated with the charges. In these circumstances, the jury may acquit on the charges, it may give a verdict on the charge that comes with the greatest punishment, or it may convict on the charge that presents the least time in prison. For a variety of reasons including that the jury does not know the possible sentences and the prosecutor may not prosecute the charge with the

---

[2] *See* MIKE McCONVILLE & CHESTER L. MIRSKY, JURY TRIALS AND PLEA BARGAINING 1–13 (2005).

[3] *See* Andrew D. Leipold, *Why Are Federal Judges So Acquittal Prone?*, 83 WASH. U. L.Q. 151, 156 & n.16 (2005).

[4] John H. Langbein, *On the Myth of Written Constitutions: The Disappearance of Criminal Jury Trial*, 15 HARV. J.L. & PUB. POL'Y 119, 125 (1992); *see* Bruce P. Smith, *Plea Bargaining and the Eclipse of the Jury*, 1 ANN. REV. L. & SOC. SCI. 131, 132 (2005).

[5] Langbein, *supra* note 4, at 125.

[6] *See, e.g.,* Nancy Gertner, *From "Rites" to "Rights": The Decline of the Criminal Jury Trial*, 24 YALE J.L. & HUMAN. 433, 436–37 (2012).

lesser punishment that was offered in plea bargaining, the defendant is unlikely to take a chance with a jury.

In addition to the impact of mandatory minimums on plea bargaining, sentencing guidelines (although now advisory) also encourage guilty pleas. Judges use these protocols to determine the baseline sentence and whether it should be increased or decreased. The guidelines incentivize defendants to take pleas by providing certain discounts to sentences – for example, acceptance of responsibility – that will not be available upon being convicted at trial. Prosecutors also can influence the effect of the guidelines in certain ways including by recommending a particular sentence within the sentencing range or recommending a departure from that range.

Under another view, elected district attorneys who sought to advance particular political agendas in the nineteenth century caused plea bargains to supplant jury trials. The state was said to have adopted "its own social and political agenda," including "aggregate justice" and certainty, which encouraged pleas over jury trials.[7]

Other explanations are offered for the fall of the criminal jury – among them emotional reactions of jury members and the expansion of jury membership across economic lines, sexes, and races – possibly leading to perceptions that juries may render verdicts in favor of criminal defendants, influenced by reasons unrelated to the law.[8] At the same time, democratization of the jury simply may have led certain segments of the population not to desire juries any longer because of the possible results.[9]

The Civil Jury

Commentators criticize the civil jury in some of the same ways as they do the criminal jury. Civil juries have been widely characterized as biased,

---

[7] McConville & Mirsky, *supra* note 2, at 197–98 & 327–37.

[8] *See* Jeffrey Abramson, We, the Jury: The Jury System and the Ideal of Democracy 3–4 (1994); Jon Elster, Securities Against Misrule: Juries, Assemblies, Elections 102–09 (2013). In addition to discussing this possible explanation, Robert Burns sets forth several potential reasons for the decline of the criminal and civil trials, including the jury trial. *See* Robert P. Burns, The Death of the American Trial 88–108 (2009).

[9] *See* Stephen C. Thaman, *A Typology of Consensual Criminal Procedures: An Historical and Comparative Perspective on the Theory and Practice of Avoiding the Full Criminal Trial in* World Plea Bargaining: Consensual Procedures and the Avoidance of the Full Criminal Trial 327–28 (Stephen C. Thaman ed., 2010).

and some say these inclinations are due to increasing diversity. Moreover, members of the general public who comprise the jury are chastised as unable to understand cases involving complicated issues. One of the most common explanations for why the civil jury has fallen derives in part from such assessments. It asserts that parties, such as corporations, have sought alternative methods of dispute resolution, particularly arbitration or settlement, because juries harbor bias for under-dog plaintiffs and are unable to decide complicated cases accurately.[10]

Corporations have also actively sought to limit juries' authority when juries try cases. While the nature of any jury decision is unpredictable, proponents of jury reform argue that because juries are not held accountable for their decisions and can choose not to follow the law, corporations are subject to unacceptable uncertainty.[11] Successfully advocating for tort reform, corporations have secured greater predictability in certain cases through limits on the monetary damages that juries can award.[12]

In addition to the possibility of large jury verdicts being rendered against them, corporations and other defendants must pay attorneys' fees, which increase dramatically when a matter goes to trial. Pursuant to the so-called American Rule, in the vast majority of cases, defendants pay their own attorneys' fees even if they win at trial. So defendants, and often plaintiffs, are incentivized to avoid trial.

Along with corporations and other parties seeking to avoid litigation costs, courts have incentives to avoid civil juries. Like their criminal caseloads, courts' civil dockets have grown exponentially. Although some resources have been devoted to this growth, a perception exists that courts' dockets remain overcrowded.[13] There is also congressional pressure for processing cases in a timely manner. Congress requires federal judges to report cases pending for more than three years and motions

---

[10] *See* Nancy S. Marder, The Jury Process 232 (2005); Neil Vidmar, Medical Malpractice and the American Jury: Confronting the Myths about Jury Incompetence, Deep Pockets, and Outrageous Damage Awards (1995); Marc Galanter, *The Hundred-Year Decline of Trials and the Thirty Years War*, 57 Stan. L. Rev. 1255, 1263, 1266–68 (2005); Valerie P. Hans & Theodore Eisenberg, *The Predictability of Juries*, 60 DePaul L. Rev. 375, 376–78 (2011).

[11] *See* Lars Noah, *Civil Jury Nullification*, 86 Iowa L. Rev. 1601 (2001).

[12] See Sheldon Whitehouse, *Restoring the Civil Jury's Role in the Structure of Our Government*, 55 Wm. & Mary L. Rev. 1241, 1254–55 (2014).

[13] *See* Ellen E. Sward, The Decline of the Civil Jury 136–38 (2001); Renee Lettow Lerner, *The Failure of Originalism in Preserving Constitutional Rights to Civil Jury Trial*, 22 Wm. & Mary Bill Rts. J. 811, 831, 848 (2014).

pending more than six months.[14] Under such pressure, juries, which take time and money to compose, may be disfavored. Judges have also actively reduced their civil caseloads through the use of procedures such as summary judgment that preclude jury trials.[15]

Additionally, increased access to courts "for outsiders," including civil rights plaintiffs, may have led to reform efforts resulting in more limitations on claims such as caps on monetary damages.[16] Legislatures have also shifted matters to administrative agencies for more efficiency, uniformity, and control than they think juries offer.[17] The decline in the civil jury has been associated with "a mutually supportive complex of beliefs and practices – beliefs that we are suffering from a litigation explosion; that juries are biased against corporate defendants; that courts should not be expanding the edges of rights; that litigation is hurting the economy; and that the solution is to curtail remedies, privatize, and deregulate."[18]

In his article on the disappearance of the civil trial, John Langbein asserted another reason for the decline, claiming that "[l]itigants no longer go to trial because they no longer need to." Cases are tried through discovery. Formerly at common law, the trial was the only method available to discover the facts of a case. After the separate courts of law and equity merged under the federal rules (and analogous state rules), fact-finding began to occur earlier when parties exchanged information before trial. Using this evidence and new procedures, judges bypassed juries by dismissing cases they deemed factually insufficient and they encouraged settlement in other cases. Langbein argues that this system makes the trial unnecessary because the parties and courts know the facts earlier in litigation, permitting the disposition of cases before trial, through dismissal or settlement.[19]

---

[14] The Civil Justice Reform Act of 1990, 28 U.S.C. § 476 (1990).

[15] *See* Randy J. Kozel & David Rosenberg, *Solving the Nuisance-Value Settlement Problem: Mandatory Summary Judgment*, 90 Va. L. Rev. 1849 (2004); Arthur Miller, *The Pre-Trial Rush to Judgment: Are the "Litigation Explosion," "Liability Crisis," and "Efficiency Clichés" Eroding Our Day in Court and Our Jury Trial Commitments?*, 78 N.Y.U. L. Rev. 982 (2003); Judith Resnik, *Managerial Judges*, 96 Harv. L. Rev. 374 (1982).

[16] Stephan Landsman, *The Civil Jury in America: Scenes from an Unappreciated History*, 44 Hastings L.J. 579, 606–09 (1993).

[17] *See* Sward, *supra* note 13, at 130–38.

[18] Galanter, *supra* note 10, at 1272.

[19] John H. Langbein, *The Disappearance of Civil Trial in the United States*, 122 Yale L.J. 522, 569–72 (2012).

The Grand Jury

Some early criticisms of the grand jury echo commentary on the criminal and civil jury regarding it as useless and inefficient. In the early twentieth century, studies concluded that grand juries simply rubberstamped prosecutors' decisions to charge defendants.[20] In the 1940s, and culminating in the 1970s, allegations emerged that prosecutors abused the powers of the grand jury, leading to a call for the grand jury's abolition.[21]

Today, people continue to denounce grand juries for being unready to deviate from the direction of prosecutors. Since 1985, following the lead of the then-New York State Chief Judge, the grand jury has often been characterized as willing to indict a "ham sandwich."[22] Available statistics show indictments in many cases – greater than 99% of federal cases and 84–94% of New York state cases, for example.[23] Although these statistics can be interpreted in different ways, one interpretation is that the use of grand juries misallocates resources. Many prosecutors believe, however, that grand juries deliberately approach their task of judging evidence in cases and provide a "'sounding board'" regarding whether sufficient evidence to convict exists.[24]

A related attack is that the grand jury is duplicative, rendering the work of grand juries unnecessarily costly and inefficient. Under this argument, prosecutors, police, and lawyers, all of whom played almost no role at the founding, are now an integral part of the system. Police and prosecutors do in concert what the grand jury did at common law – help to ensure that charges are accurate. Defense lawyers, provided by the state in some circumstances, might offer protections similar to those provided by the grand jury at common law. Judges also obviate the need

---

[20] See RICHARD D. YOUNGER, THE PEOPLE'S PANEL: THE GRAND JURY IN THE UNITED STATES, 1634–1941, at 60, 229 (1963).

[21] See MARVIN E. FRANKEL & GARY P. NAFTALIS, THE GRAND JURY: AN INSTITUTION ON TRIAL 52–59, 117, 119 (1977); Michael E. Deutsch, The Improper Use of the Federal Grand Jury: An Instrument for the Internment of Political Activists, 75 J. CRIM. L. & CRIMINOLOGY 1159, 1176–83 (1984).

[22] Matter of Grand Jury Subpoena of Stewart, 545 N.Y.S.2d 974 (N.Y. Sup. 1989) (quoting Chief Judge).

[23] Andrew Leipold, Prosecutorial Charging Practices and Grand Jury Screening: Some Empirical Observations, in GRAND JURY 2.0: MODERN PERSPECTIVES ON THE GRAND JURY 196 (Roger Anthony Fairfax, Jr. ed., 2011); Ric Simmons, Re-Examining the Grand Jury: Is There Room for Democracy in the Criminal Justice System?, 82 B.U. L. REV. 1, 31–39 (2002).

[24] James C. McKinley & Al Baker, Grand Jury System, With Exceptions, Favors the Police in Fatalities, N.Y. TIMES, Dec. 7, 2014.

for grand juries, by reviewing charges at preliminary hearings where grand juries have not been employed.[25]

Similar to criminal and civil jurors, grand jurors are often disparaged for their lack of qualifications and ignorance of the law.[26] Commentators complain that grand jurors are insufficiently experienced and untrained to determine whether there is probable cause for the alleged crime.[27]

*****

In summary, several reasons have been offered for the declines of the criminal, civil, and grand juries. Their falls are associated with beliefs that juries cannot reach non-biased, accurate decisions, and that they take too much time and money to constitute when better alternatives exist.

A New Theory for the Fall of the Juries

Despite the repeated themes of cost, incompetence, inaccuracy, and inefficiency, the jury occupies a prominent role in the Constitution in the original text and three different Amendments. So the fall of the jury remains puzzling. Even if costly, incompetent, inaccurate, and inefficient, the jury is constitutionally required. The executive, the legislature, the judiciary, and the states have also been criticized as being costly, incompetent, inaccurate, and inefficient[28] – but they have not declined in use like the jury has. Nor have those actors been disparaged as useless. And arguments for their abolishment have not enjoyed serious consideration.[29] Rather, as set forth in Chapter 2, these actors have taken substantial authority from the criminal, civil, and grand juries.

---

[25] *See* YOUNGER, *supra* note 20, at 145–46; Roger A. Fairfax, Jr., *Grand Jury Innovation: Toward a Functional Makeover of the Ancient Bulwark of Liberty*, 19 WM. & MARY BILL RTS. J. 339, 341–45 (2010).

[26] *See* YOUNGER, supra note 20, at 66, 69, 141; Ric Simmons, *The True Goals of the Modern Grand Jury – and How to Achieve Them*, in GRAND JURY 2.0, *supra* note 23.

[27] *See* Andrew D. Leipold, *Why Grand Juries Do Not (and Cannot) Protect the Accused*, 80 CORNELL L. REV. 260, 294–304 (1995).

[28] *See* Marco Battaglini & Stephen Coate, *Inefficiency in Legislative Policymaking: A Dynamic Analysis*, 97 AM. ECON. REV. 118 (2007); *cf.* Charles M. Blow, *The Do-Even-Less Congress*, N.Y. TIMES, Aug. 3, 2014 (citing research on the declining number of laws enacted by Congress, also mentioning little veto of laws by the President, and stating that Congress is sitting for fewer days than in the past).

[29] *See* WILLIAM L. DWYER, IN THE HANDS OF THE PEOPLE: THE TRIAL JURY'S ORIGINS, TRIUMPHS, TROUBLES, AND FUTURE IN AMERICAN DEMOCRACY 2 (2002).

To understand the fall of the jury and the continued rise of the executive, the legislature, the judiciary, and the states, we need to examine the relationships between the jury and the other actors, as well as the characteristics of each. Several features distinguish the jury. The first, which is the focus of the following section, concerns the treatment of the jury in relation to the other actors in the Constitution. The jury has been subjugated to a place of unequal footing with them. The other features, which are addressed at the end of the chapter, concern the inability of the jury to act on its own.

The Other "Branch"

The text of the Constitution in addition to evidence at the founding and at the ratification of the Fourteenth Amendment reveal commonalities among the roles that the jury, the executive, the legislature, the judiciary, and the states were to play. These bodies were constituted as separate, independent, powerful, and interrelated actors. However, the non-jury actors, led by the Supreme Court, have recognized only their own separate powers and independence. They have denied the jury's similar authority, and instead, have almost invariably appropriated its powers.

The Constitutional Text

An examination of the constitutional text reveals that the executive, the legislature, the judiciary, the states, the criminal jury, the civil jury, and the grand jury all have powers and limitations as well as interdependences.

The Executive   Article II establishes the powers and limitations of the executive. For example, the President can pardon defendants convicted of federal offenses, but cannot do so in impeachment cases. The President can make treaties, but only with the advice and consent of the Senate. The President can also appoint Supreme Court justices and all other officers of the United States, but also only with the advice and consent of the Senate. As a final example, the President is empowered to fill all vacancies that occur during the recess of the Senate. However, these commissions are limited as they expire at the end of the next session of the Senate.[30]

---

[30] U.S. Const. art. II.

The Legislature   Similar to Article II, Article I establishes the powers and limitations of the legislature. Such powers include the Senate's authority to try all impeachments. The legislature can enact laws on only certain subjects and is explicitly prohibited from passing a bill of attainder or ex post facto law. A majority in the House of Representatives and the Senate must approve a bill, and the President must sign it in order for the bill to become law. Without presidential approval, two-thirds of each of the House of Representatives and Senate must approve the bill for it to become a law.[31]

The Judiciary   Most of the express powers and limitations of the judiciary are established by Article III. Under this article, judges hold their office unless they have acted unlawfully, and Congress cannot decrease their compensation during their time in office. Moreover, Article III gives the judiciary jurisdiction over all cases, in law and equity that arise under the Constitution, the laws of the United States, and Treaties. Among other powers, it has authority over controversies between citizens of different states. Article III also limits the power of the judiciary by giving a different body – the jury – power to try all crimes except impeachment cases.[32]

The States   Article IV and the Tenth Amendment establish the powers and limitations of the states. Article IV guarantees that the acts of each state will be recognized by the other states. And the Tenth Amendment broadly grants power to states. It gives those powers not granted to the United States and those that the states are not prohibited from possessing to the states or the people.[33] Under Article I, states also can take certain actions such as imposing duties on imports or exports upon the consent of Congress.[34]

The Criminal Jury   Article III and the Sixth Amendment establish the powers and limitations of the criminal jury. Article III provides a jury trial for all crimes except impeachment cases. Additionally, the Sixth Amendment grants a person accused of a crime rights associated with the jury trial, including an impartial jury. No other constitutional provisions explicitly limit the criminal jury.[35] For example, under the previously mentioned

---

[31] U.S. Const. art. I.
[32] U.S. Const. art. III.
[33] U.S. Const. art. IV, amend. X.
[34] U.S. Const. art. I, § 10.
[35] U.S. Const. art. III, § 2 ("The Trial of all Crimes, except in Cases of Impeachment, shall be by Jury"); U.S Const. amend. VI.

articles and amendments, the executive, the legislature, the judiciary, and the states possess no express authority over the criminal jury.

The Civil Jury   The Seventh Amendment establishes the authority of the civil jury. It "preserve[d]" the right to a jury trial in "[s]uits at common law" where the value exceeds twenty dollars and grants the judiciary limited authority to re-examine facts tried by a jury "according to the rules of the common law." Pursuant to the Amendment, then, in cases above twenty dollars, the right to a jury trial at common law is preserved. Moreover, the judiciary is given express common law authority over facts tried by a civil jury.[36] Other than this common law authority, the executive, the legislature, the judiciary, and the states have no other explicit constitutional authority over the civil jury.

The Grand Jury   The Fifth Amendment establishes the grand jury requirement. With the exception of some cases that involve the military or state militia, it provides that a grand jury must present or indict in order for a person to be prosecuted "for a capital, or otherwise infamous crime." Thus, the grand jury has almost exclusive authority to initiate prosecutions for serious crimes.[37]

*****

In summary, in the constitutional text, specific authority is granted to the executive, the legislature, the judiciary, the states, the criminal jury, the civil jury, and the grand jury. Moreover, limitations are placed on all of those actors, often in relationship to one another.

The Founders and Ratifiers

In addition to the text of the Constitution, the Supreme Court has utilized evidence from the founding to limit the authority of the executive, the legislature, the judiciary, and the states in relationship to each other. It has

---

[36] U.S. CONST. amend. VII ("In Suits at common law, where the value in controversy shall exceed twenty dollars, the right of trial by jury shall be preserved, and no fact tried by a jury, shall be otherwise re-examined in any Court of the United States, than according to the rules of the common law.").

[37] U.S. CONST. amend. V ("No person shall be held to answer for a capital, or otherwise infamous crime, unless on a presentment or indictment of a Grand Jury, except in cases arising in the land or naval forces, or in the Militia, when in actual service in time of War or public danger"); U.S. CONST. art. I, § 8, cls. 14 & 16.

not similarly acted to limit their power in relationship to the jury.
The extent to which such evidence from the founding should have any
influence on the interpretation of the Constitution is debated and will be
addressed in Chapter 4. This section shows that the Supreme Court has
used such evidence to support limitations, employing the doctrine of
separation of powers among the executive, the legislature, and the judiciary and the concept of federalism between the federal government
and the states. At the same time, it has refused to use a similar doctrine
to limit the authority of the executive, the legislature, the judiciary, and
the states in relationship to the jury.

On the Executive, the Legislature, the Judiciary, and the States   The
Founders extolled the distinct responsibilities of the executive, the legislature, the judiciary, and the states and those actors' powers to keep one
another in check. These checks and balances were necessary to maintain
each actor's independence. Prior to the adoption of the Constitution,
James Madison stated

> [i]f it be a fundamental principle of free Govt. that the Legislative,
> Executive & Judiciary powers should be *separately* exercised; it is equally
> so that they be *independently* exercised.[38]

At that time, George Mason also stated that the three departments should
"be kept as separate as possible."[39]

After the Constitution was adopted, writing about the importance of
the division of the powers of the executive, the legislature, and the
judiciary in *The Federalist*, James Madison stated that

> [t]he accumulation of all powers, legislative, executive, and judiciary, in
> the same hands, whether of one, a few, or many, and whether hereditary,
> self-appointed, or elective, may justly be pronounced the very definition
> of tyranny.

"[T]he fundamental principles of a free constitution [would be] sub-
verted" if one department exercised all of the power of another department.[40] Madison emphasized that limits must be imposed on the powers
of these departments vis-à-vis the others. Accordingly, none of them

---

[38] 2 The Records of the Federal Convention of 1787, at 56 (Max Farrand ed., 1911);
see Bradford R. Clark, *Separation of Powers as a Safeguard of Federalism*, 79 Tex. L. Rev.
1321 (2001).

[39] 2 Farrand's Records, *supra* note 38, at 537.

[40] The Federalist No. 47, at 301–03 (James Madison) (Clinton Rossiter ed., 1961).

ought to possess, directly or indirectly, an overruling influence over the others in the administration of their respective powers. It will not be denied that power is of an encroaching nature and that it ought to be effectually restrained from passing the limits assigned to it.[41]

Additionally, the independence of the departments was emphasized.

In order to lay a due foundation for that separate and distinct exercise of the different powers of government, which to a certain extent is admitted on all hands to be essential to the preservation of liberty, it is evident that each department should have a will of its own; and consequently should be so constituted that the members of each should have as little agency as possible in the appointment of the members of the others.[42]

The mutual interrelationships made the division of their powers possible. As Madison stated:

[T]he defect must be supplied, by so contriving the interior structure of the government as that its several constituent parts may, by their mutual relations, be the means of keeping each other in their proper places.[43]

Madison illustrated these significant interrelationships.

The magistrate in whom the whole executive power resides cannot of himself make a law, though he can put a negative on every law; nor administer justice in person, though he has the appointment of those who do administer it. The judges can exercise no executive prerogative, though they are shoots from the executive stock; nor any legislative function, though they may be advised by the legislative councils. The entire legislature can perform no judiciary act, though by the joint act of two of its branches the judges may be removed from their offices, and though one of its branches is possessed of the judicial power in the last resort. The entire legislature, again, can exercise no executive prerogative, though one of its branches constitutes the supreme executive magistracy, and another, on the impeachment of a third, can try and condemn all the subordinate officers in the executive department.[44]

The Founders focused on the relationships between the departments because of their potential to overreach. At the federal convention, Governor Morris discussed the need for a "check" on the legislature, which posed the "greater danger" to "public liberty" than any other department.[45]

[41] THE FEDERALIST No. 48, *supra* note 40, at 308 (James Madison).
[42] THE FEDERALIST No. 51, *supra* note 40, at 321 (James Madison).
[43] THE FEDERALIST No. 51, *supra* note 40, at 320 (James Madison).
[44] THE FEDERALIST No. 47, *supra* note 40, at 303 (James Madison).
[45] 2 FARRAND'S RECORDS, *supra* note 38, at 75–76.

Executive power was also feared. George Mason discussed how it could turn into a "Monarchy."[46] Elbridge Gerry made similar comments about the judiciary, claiming it could be "oppressive."[47]

Similar to their discussion of this division of authority, the Founders examined the distinct powers of the states and the federal government in the governmental structure, although there was clear disagreement on the subject. "[I]t is widely recognized that 'The Federalist reads with a split personality' on matters of federalism."[48] As a general matter, Hamilton was very nationalistic in his interpretation of the Constitution, and Madison interpreted the powers of the states more broadly.[49]

Regardless of this difference, Hamilton and Madison agreed that divisions of power between the federal government and the states existed. When Hamilton discussed power held by the states, he emphasized corresponding constitutional limitations on the federal government's power. "[A]n attempt on the part of the national government to abridge them in the exercise of it would be a violent assumption of power, unwarranted by any article or clause of its Constitution." He emphasized that states would retain powers that they possessed before the Constitution was enacted. The states were limited in their authority only

> where the Constitution in express terms granted an exclusive authority to the Union; where it granted in one instance an authority to the Union and in another prohibited the States from exercising the like authority; and where it granted an authority to the Union to which a similar authority in the States would be absolutely and totally *contradictory* and *repugnant*.[50]

Consistent with the notion of the limited power of the union, Madison stated "[t]he powers delegated by the proposed Constitution to the federal government are few and defined. Those which are to remain in the state governments are numerous and indefinite." The power of the states extended to the aspects of "the ordinary course of affairs . . . and the internal order" of the state. And the states' powers were greatest in "times of peace and security," whereas the power of the federal

---

[46] 2 FARRAND'S RECORDS, *supra* note 38, at 35.

[47] 2 THE COMPLETE ANTI-FEDERALIST 6–7 (Herbert J. Storing ed., University of Chicago Press 1981).

[48] Printz v. United States, 521 U.S. 898, 915 n.9 (1997) (quoting DAAN BRAVEMAN ET AL., CONSTITUTIONAL LAW: STRUCTURE AND RIGHTS IN OUR FEDERAL SYSTEM 199 (3d ed. 1996)).

[49] See *Printz*, 521 U.S. at 915 n.9; THE FEDERALIST No. 45, *supra* note 40, at 292 (James Madison).

[50] THE FEDERALIST No. 32, *supra* note 40, at 198 (Alexander Hamilton).

government was primarily limited to externalities with its most extensive power in the rare events of war and danger.[51]

Madison discussed "the disposition and the faculty [the federal and state governments] may respectively possess to resist and frustrate the measures of each other." The natural emphasis on local interest would serve as a check on the power of the federal government because the officers would retain concerns about their own states. Also, if the federal government encroached on the states, the states would unite against the federal government.[52]

On the Criminal, Civil, and Grand Juries   As just described, the Founders of the Constitution emphasized the important interrelationships among the executive, the legislature, and the judiciary, as well as each actor's independence. The significant connection between the federal government and the states was also stressed along with their independence from one another. The Constitution's Founders and the Fourteenth Amendment's ratifiers similarly discussed the interrelationships between the jury and these other actors. The Founders and the ratifiers also understood that the American jury had an independent role like the executive, the legislature, the judiciary, and the states – specifically to protect against actions by them.

Early on, people who favored a greater role for states ("anti-federalists") expressed concern about the continued vitality of the jury's role because of the constitutional power over law and fact granted to the Supreme Court on appeal.[53] During this same period, Thomas Jefferson extensively discussed the importance of the people in every part of the government, including through the jury. The people elected the President, they selected legislators, and juries checked the judiciary. For example, juries could counter possible judicial bias.

> [W]e all know that permanent judges acquire an *Esprit de corps*; that being known, they are liable to be tempted by bribery; that they are misled by favor, by relationship, by a spirit of party, by a devotion to the executive or legislative power; that it is better to leave a cause to the decision of cross and pile, than to that of a judge biased to one side; and that the opinion of twelve honest jurymen gives still a better hope of right, than cross and pile does.

---

[51] The Federalist No. 45, *supra* note 40, at 292–93 (James Madison).

[52] The Federalist No. 46, *supra* note 40, at 294–300 (James Madison).

[53] *See* Edith Guild Henderson, *The Background of the Seventh Amendment*, 80 Harv. L. Rev. 289, 295 (1966).

Jefferson emphasized the power that the jury held in relationship to the judge – that a jury could decide the law in addition to the facts where the jurors believed the judge was biased.[54]

Similarly, James Wilson discussed the division of authority between judges and jurors. Recognizing the possibility that issues of law and fact sometimes intermix, he stated that in such circumstances juries must decide both the law and fact.[55] The Federal Farmer – an anti-federalist who wrote anonymously about the proposed Constitution – citing the support of English legal commentators Edward Coke, Matthew Hale, Sir John Holt, Blackstone, and Jean Louis De Lolme – acknowledged the civil jury's power specifically to determine both fact and law, including through a general verdict.[56] More generally, emphasizing the importance of the jury's possible role as law-finder, Jefferson stated that if people were to be excluded from a governmental department, it would be better that the people be left out of the legislature because "[t]he execution of the laws [of which the jury plays a role] is more important than the making" of the laws.[57] Referring to the jury as "the democratic branch of the judiciary power," the Maryland Farmer, another anti-federalist, agreed that the jury was more important than people in the legislature.[58]

John Adams also addressed the role of the jury as a check on the judiciary and compared its role in government to the legislature.

> As the constitution requires that the popular branch of the legislature should have an absolute check, so as to put a peremptory negative upon every act of the government, it requires that the common people, should have as complete a control, as decisive a negative, in every judgment of a court of judicature.[59]

---

[54] *See* THOMAS JEFFERSON, ON DEMOCRACY 62 (Saul K. Padover ed., 1939); *see* Letters from The Federal Farmer to the Republican No. 15, *reprinted in* 2 COMPLETE ANTI-FEDERAL-IST, *supra* note 47, at 321 (in the civil law, where there are no juries, judges are "often corrupted by ministerial influence, or by parties").

[55] *See* 2 JAMES WILSON, COLLECTED WORKS OF JAMES WILSON 1000–1001 (Kermit L. Hall et al. eds., Liberty Fund 2007).

[56] *See* Letters from The Federal Farmer to the Republican No. XV, *reprinted in* 2 COMPLETE ANTI-FEDERALIST, *supra* note 47, at 319–20.

[57] 3 THE WORKS OF THOMAS JEFFERSON 82 (H.A. Washington ed., John C. Riker 1884) (appearing to discuss both the criminal and civil juries).

[58] Essays by a Farmer No. IV, *reprinted in* 5 THE COMPLETE ANTI-FEDERALIST 38 (Herbert J. Storing ed., University of Chicago Press 1981).

[59] 2 THE WORKS OF JOHN ADAMS 253 (Charles Francis Adams ed., Charles C. Little & James Brown 1850).

Alexander Hamilton also discussed the interrelationship between the jury and the judiciary. He described the civil jury as "a security against corruption" of judges. Hamilton further explained the importance of the dual existence of the judiciary and the civil jury to the integrity of both institutions. He called the judiciary and the civil jury

> a double security; and it will readily be perceived that this complicated agency tends to preserve the purity of both institutions. By increasing the obstacles to success, it discourages attempts to seduce the integrity of either. The temptations to prostitution which the judges might have to surmount must certainly be much fewer, while the co-operation of a jury is necessary, than they might be if they had themselves the exclusive determination of all causes.

Hamilton also discussed the necessity of the criminal jury in light of possible judicial wrongdoing. He described fear of "judicial despotism" through the use of "arbitrary methods of prosecuting pretended offenses, and arbitrary punishments upon arbitrary convictions."[60]

In addition to addressing the division of authority between the jury and the judiciary, the Founders considered the relationship between the legislature and the jury. Those discussions reveal that the legislature was to hold no power over the jury beyond those expressly stated in the text of the Constitution. Thomas Jefferson insisted that the jury should remain separate and independent from the legislature. He stressed that the civil jury should be constitutionalized because the legislature should not be able to alter that "trust-worthy" governmental instrument that had helped secure the freedom to think and act, freedom with which the government had interfered.[61] Alexander Hamilton recognized that if a civil jury trial provision were not enacted, the legislature would be free to establish a jury trial or not to do so. He further acknowledged that by the creation of the jury trial in criminal cases, the legislature's "discretion . . . [was] abridged."[62] This quote suggests Hamilton's belief that if the Founders established a jury trial in the Constitution, the legislature would have no authority over it. Along similar lines, James Monroe affirmatively stated that the civil jury should be constitutionally established to prevent the legislature

---

[60] THE FEDERALIST NO. 83, *supra* note 40, at 499–501 (Alexander Hamilton); *see also* 2 FARRAND RECORDS, *supra* note 38, at 587 (At the Philadelphia convention, delegate Gerry said juries were necessary "to guard against corrupt Judges.").

[61] JEFFERSON, *supra* note 54, at 14, 47.

[62] *See* THE FEDERALIST NO. 83, *supra* note 40, at 496–97 (Alexander Hamilton).

from abolishing it.[63] And George Mason discussed the need for constitutional inclusion of the civil jury, because otherwise Congress could
have as much influence as it desired on the decisions of the jury.[64]

In proposing the civil jury right's inclusion in the Bill of Rights,
Madison discussed that, while the English's declaration of rights had
not limited the legislature, "a different opinion prevail[ed] in the United
States" on whether the legislature and other parts of the government
could be trusted. He highlighted why many states had proposed constitutional amendments or made declarations for certain rights, including
the jury right.

> [T]he great object in view is to limit and qualify the powers of Govern-
> ment, by excepting out of the grant of power those cases in which the
> Government ought not to act, or to act only in a particular mode. They
> point these exceptions sometimes against the abuse of the executive
> power, sometimes against the legislative, and, in some cases, against
> the community itself; or, in other words, against the majority in favor
> of the minority.

Madison further described the trial by jury as "a right resulting from a
social compact which regulates the action of the community," and stated
it was "as essential to secure the liberty of the people as any one of the
pre-existent rights of nature."[65]

The Founders also understood the civil jury to provide a mechanism
by which laws could be nullified. For example, "paper money and British
debt claims were the most prominently discussed civil jury trial issues
during the ratification debates." Juries gave debtors relief against the suits
by creditors, whose claims may have been inflated due to the past
excessive printing of currency by states.[66]

Similar to the Founders' discussion about the relationship between the
civil jury and the legislature, the interdependency between the criminal
jury and the legislature was discussed. Addressing the constitutionally

---

[63] *See* 3 THE DEBATES IN THE SEVERAL STATE CONVENTIONS, ON THE ADOPTION OF THE
FEDERAL CONSTITUTION 217–18 (Jonathan Elliot ed., Philadelphia, J.B. Lippincott Co.
2d ed. 1891).

[64] *See* 3 STATE DEBATES, *supra* note 63, at 431; *see also* Charles W. Wolfram, *The Constitutional History of the Seventh Amendment*, 57 MINN. L. REV. 639, 653, 707 n.186 (1973)
(amendment "was quite clearly to require juries to sit in civil cases as a check on what the
popular mind might regard as legislative as well as judicial excesses").

[65] 2 BERNARD SCHWARTZ, THE BILL OF RIGHTS: A DOCUMENTARY HISTORY
1028–29 (1971).

[66] Wolfram, *supra* note 64, at 673–705.

established criminal jury, James Wilson emphasized the jury's existing power to pass judgment on criminal defendants, and the related lack of power of the federal legislature to find people guilty of crimes through acts of attainder for treason or felony.[67]

The jury also provided a buffer between the executive and the people. The Declaration of Independence had described King George III as "depriving us in many cases, of the benefits of Trial by Jury."[68] So the significance of the jury derived in part from possible abuses of the executive. James Wilson had recognized "the oppression of government is effectually barred, by declaring that in all criminal cases, the trial by jury shall be preserved."[69] The history of the use of sedition laws appears to have motivated the Founders, as the Crown had attempted to prosecute people, including Peter Zenger for publishing material critical of the government. American juries checked the executive by refusing to convict under these laws. Juries also curbed the legislature by "virtually repeal[ing]" the law, and restrained the legislature and executive by not convicting defendants under other English trade and revenue laws.[70]

Civil juries were also expected to check the government. Discussing an improper search by a constable and a rendering of monetary damages by a jury against the government, anti-federalists recognized the civil jury was necessary in suits against the government.[71]

The grand jury served as another check on the executive. Discussing it, James Wilson stated "[i]n the annals of the world, there cannot be found an institution so well fitted for avoiding abuses, which might otherwise arise from malice, from rigour, from negligence, or from partiality, in the prosecution of crimes." He also said "[t]hey are not appointed for the prosecutor or for the court: they are appointed for the government and for the people." Moreover, "[a]ll the operations of government, and of its ministers and officers, [were] within the compass of their view

---

[67] *See* 2 WILSON, COLLECTED WORKS OF WILSON, *supra* note 55, at 1009.

[68] THE DECLARATION OF INDEPENDENCE (U.S. 1776).

[69] PAMPHLETS ON THE CONSTITUTION OF THE UNITED STATES 157 (Paul Leicester Ford ed., Da Capo Press 1968).

[70] *See* RANDOLPH N. JONAKAIT, THE AMERICAN JURY SYSTEM 23–24 (2003).

[71] Hampden emphasized the civil jury was necessary because of "abuse of private citizens" by "High Officers of State." Essays by Hampden, *reprinted in* 4 THE COMPLETE ANTI-FEDERALIST 200 (Herbert J. Storing ed., University of Chicago Press 1981); Akhil Reed Amar, *Fourth Amendment First Principles*, 107 HARV. L. REV. 757, 775–81 (1994) (describing connections between the Fourth Amendment and the Seventh Amendment).

and research."[72] The Zenger case illustrates the grand jury's check on the executive. There, the colonial grand jury had refused to indict when the Crown acted against Zenger for his criticism of it.[73]

The Founders warned of the possible shift in authority if the jury were to lose power. Indeed, the Maryland Farmer appeared to predict our present state of affairs regarding plea bargaining. He stated that with the elimination of juries, "[t]he judiciary power is immediately absorbed, or placed under the direction of the executive . . . Thus we find the judiciary and executive branches united, or the *former* totally dependent on the *latter* in most governments in the world."[74]

In addition to the Founders' more specific statements about jury authority in relationship to the executive, the legislature, and the judiciary, general language was also used to discuss the value of an independent jury to the government. Thomas Jefferson described "[t]rial by jury . . . as the only anchor ever yet imagined by man, by which a government can be held to the principles of its constitution." After the establishment of the civil and criminal jury trials, Jefferson named the jury trial among the "essential principles" of the government.[75] James Wilson stated that the jury, "this beautiful and sublime effect of our judicial system," promoted the principles of "an habitual courage, and dignity, and independence of sentiment and of actions in the citizens," which he thought "should be the aim of every wise and good government." He further acclaimed that "within its walls, strong and lofty as well as finely proportioned, freedom enjoys protection, and innocence rests secure."[76] Also, Hamilton believed that the criminal jury trial was "a valuable safeguard to liberty," while others more strongly considered it "the very palladium of free government."[77]

While recognizing the necessity of the jury to the Constitution, the Founders also acknowledged that the jury was not infallible. Thomas Jefferson conceded that the jury could do wrong, but he insisted that more wrong would be done without it.[78] Similarly, James Wilson

---

[72] 2 WILSON, COLLECTED WORKS OF WILSON, *supra* note 55, at 992, 995–96.

[73] *See* Kevin K. Washburn, *Restoring the Grand Jury*, 76 FORDHAM L. REV. 2333, 2343 (2008).

[74] Essays by a Farmer No. IV, *reprinted in* 5 COMPLETE ANTI-FEDERALIST, *supra* note 58, at 39.

[75] JEFFERSON, *supra* note 54, at 32–33, 160.

[76] 2 WILSON, COLLECTED WORKS OF WILSON, *supra* note 55, at 1009, 1011.

[77] THE FEDERALIST No. 83, *supra* note 40, at 499 (Alexander Hamilton).

[78] *See* JEFFERSON, *supra* note 54, at 47.

accepted that juries made mistakes, but asserted that such mistakes could "never grow into a dangerous system." Indeed a jury's mistakes generally could be corrected. If a grand jury indicted, a criminal jury might not convict. Even if the criminal jury convicted, a judge could order a new trial before a new jury. Also, mistakes could be avoided by the dismissal of jurors who showed bias against the defendant. Moreover, if a grand jury did not indict, another grand jury might still indict the defendant. Wilson emphasized the importance of this power to prevent or correct error, but also knew that regardless of the possibility of mistakes, the jury – not another tribunal – was the best body to decide cases.[79]

Along with the Founders viewing the jury as protection against the executive, the legislature, and the judiciary, the ratifiers of the Fourteenth Amendment saw the jury as an important safeguard against the states. Various people involved in the ratification discussed the importance of the first eight rights in the Bill of Rights, which included the criminal, civil, and grand juries. Representative Rogers stated that privileges in the Fourteenth Amendment that the states could not abridge included "the right to be a juror." Representative Bingham also asserted that the Fourteenth Amendment actually corrected for previous violations of the states of the rights that resided in the Bill.[80]

*****

In summary, the Founders recognized significant divisions of authority between the executive, the legislature, the judiciary, and the states, along with their independent governmental roles. The Founders of the Constitution and the ratifiers of the Fourteenth Amendment also acknowledged similar divisions of authority between the jury and the executive, the legislature, the judiciary, and the states. Moreover, they understood the criminal, civil, and grand juries' independent roles. The jury and these actors were related, and the Founders and the ratifiers intended that the jury play an important role to check the powers of those actors.

---

[79] 2 WILSON, COLLECTED WORKS OF WILSON, *supra* note 55, at 1001–1002, 1009. Wilson appears to be discussing the English common law practice and describing the possibility of new trials in any type of case, including felonies. However, there are other authorities that assert that new trials were not available for felonies. *See infra* Chapter 5.

[80] Cong. Globe, 39th Cong., 1st Sess. 2538, 2542 (1866). This evidence is considered without discussing the general debate on the incorporation of the Bill of Rights against the states and the proper method of incorporation. *See* Suja A. Thomas, *Nonincorporation: The Bill of Rights After* McDonald v. Chicago, 88 NOTRE DAME L. REV. 159, 162–65, 177–80 (2012).

The Interpretation of Power

As shown earlier, the constitutional text that establishes the executive, the legislature, the judiciary, and the states is similar to the constitutional text that creates the criminal, civil, and grand juries. Both grant power to those actors while simultaneously limiting their authority. Also as previously discussed, the Founders spoke about the relationships among the executive, the legislature, the judiciary, and the states as well as their respective powers very much like the Founders and the Fourteenth Amendment ratifiers expressed the relationships between the jury and those same actors as well as their particular powers. Although all of this – the constitutional text, evidence from the founding, and evidence at the Fourteenth Amendment's ratification – suggest that the executive, the legislature, the judiciary, and the states (referred to here as "the traditional constitutional actors" or "traditional actors") should interpret the jury's authority in the same manner as they interpret each other's power, the traditional actors have not done so. They have subjugated the jury while recognizing significant power in each other. Using Supreme Court case law, the following section first explores the authority that the traditional actors have recognized in each other and next explains how they have failed to acknowledge the jury's authority. Because the Court exercises final decision-making authority, and case law is the primary evidence of the interaction among the traditional actors as well as the interrelationship between the traditional actors and the jury, this case law is used to illustrate the respective, disparate treatments of the traditional actors and the jury.

The Executive, the Legislature, the Judiciary, and the States Under Separation of Powers and Federalism   Scholars and the courts regularly describe the traditional actors – excluding the states – as "branches."[81] The traditional actors, along with the states, are also often depicted as "constitutional actor[s]."[82] These terms, branch and constitutional actor, denote bodies that possess authority delegated by or recognized under the Constitution. These powers of the executive,

---

[81] *See, e.g.*, Mistretta v. U.S., 488 U.S. 361, 409, 412 (1989); Linda D. Jellum, *Which Is to Be Master, the Judiciary or the Legislature? When Statutory Directives Violate Separation of Powers*, 56 U.C.L.A. L. Rev. 837, 854–55 (2009).

[82] *See, e.g.*, Nixon v. U.S., 938 F.2d 239, 246 (1991); U.S. v. Linder, 2013 WL 812382, at *29 (N.D. Ill. 2013); Spencer Overton, *Political Law*, 81 Geo. Wash. L. Rev. 1783, 1788 (2013); Nelson Tebbe, *Government Nonendorsement*, 98 Minn. L. Rev. 648, 687 (2013).

the legislature, the judiciary, and the states are said to derive from different sources. They hold power that originated with the adoption of the Constitution; they are formally granted power that they possessed prior to the Constitution's adoption; or they are acknowledged as having certain authority not specifically bestowed by the Constitution.

The importance of the traditional actors as branches and constitutional actors has been recognized through the doctrines of separation of powers and federalism. Separation of powers governs the boundaries between the executive, the legislature, and the judiciary, while federalism polices the division between the federal government and the states. Although the Constitution does not specifically refer to separation of powers or federalism, the Supreme Court has deployed these doctrines to empower and limit the traditional actors, informed by the constitutional text, as well as the Founders' views of the interrelationships among the traditional actors and their particular powers.

An example of separation of powers is found in *Immigration and Naturalization Service v. Chadha*. There, the Supreme Court pushed back against Congress's effort to exert special authority against the Executive Branch. Through the Immigration and Nationality Act, Congress permitted the Executive to suspend alien deportations. However, one House of Congress could override the Executive's decision. The Supreme Court, in an oft-cited illustration of its exercise of separation of powers to prevent the aggrandizement of the power of the branches, described limited circumstances when one house could act without the other. It decided that Article I of the Constitution required both houses of Congress to pass on legislation. Adherence to these requirements constituted an essential check on the branches' powers. The Court described separation of powers not as "an abstract generalization in the minds of the Framers" but as "woven into" the Constitution. "Although not 'hermetically' sealed from one another, . . . the powers delegated to the three Branches [were] functionally identifiable." The Court insisted that "[t]o preserve those checks, and maintain the separation of powers, the carefully defined limits on the power of each Branch must not be eroded." The Court emphasized that the text of the Constitution sets forth certain requirements to check the branches' powers and that those requirements could not be circumvented based on considerations such as convenience and efficiency that a procedure might provide. Here, Congress had attempted to cede authority from the executive, and the Supreme Court intervened, invoking Congress's limited powers in particular, and separation of powers more generally, to maintain the branches' intended constitutional balance.[83]

Marbury v. Madison is another example of separation of powers where the judiciary blocked the legislature's attempted exertion of power over the executive. Discussing the limitations on the power of the legislature (as applied to the judiciary), the Court had declared

> [t]o what purpose are powers limited, and to what purpose is that limita-
> tion committed to writing, if these limits may, at any time, be passed by
> those intended to be restrained? The distinction, between a government
> with limited and unlimited powers, is abolished, if those limits do not
> confine the persons on whom they are imposed. . . . [84]

Youngstown Sheet & Tube Co. v. Sawyer is another example where the Supreme Court deployed separation of powers to restrain one traditional actor in relationship to another. Here, steel companies and their employees were engaged in a dispute regarding the terms of a new collective bargaining agreement (CBA). The union representing the employees indicated it would strike when the existing CBA expired. Because of the need for steel in war materials, the President issued an executive order that gave authority to the Secretary of State to seize the steel companies and continue operations. Thereafter, the President notified Congress, and Congress took no action. In its decision reviewing the President's action of seizing the mills, the Supreme Court emphasized that the President's power must derive either from an act of Congress or the Constitution. No congressional act had been passed granting the President the power to seize the mills, and the Constitution did not grant the Executive this authority. Concluding that the President's action was unconstitutional and that the legislature held the power that the President had tried to exercise, the Court stated that "[t]he Founders of this Nation entrusted the law making power to the Congress alone in both good and bad times." Here, the Court again emphasized the importance to the government of preserving limited powers in the different branches.[85]

The Supreme Court has also discussed the importance of the division of, and limits on, the constitutional powers of the federal government and the states. An early example of federalism that recognized the national government's power along with the states' limitations is

---

[83]   462 U.S. 919, 923–25, 944, 946, 951, 954–59 (1983).
[84]   5 U.S. (1 Cranch) 137, 176 (1803).
[85]   343 U.S. 579, 583–85, 589 (1952).

M'Culloch v. State of Maryland. In this case, which involved Congress's establishment of a national bank and the state of Maryland's attempted taxation of the bank, the Court stated "[t]his [federal] government is acknowledged by all, to be one of enumerated powers. The principle, that it can exercise only the powers granted to it, would seem too apparent." Although the government was not granted express power to create a corporation, Congress possessed power to make laws "necessary and proper" to the execution of its powers such as the power to raise revenue through a corporation. The key question was whether the state could tax the federal bank. The Court decided that although states had power to tax, granting states authority to tax the federal bank would empower the states to destroy the bank. Finding the Maryland law to tax the federal government unconstitutional, the Court discussed the limitation of state authority as related to the federal government's power.

> The sovereignty of a state extends to everything which exists by its own authority, or is introduced by its permission; but does it extend to those means which are employed by congress to carry into execution powers conferred on that body by the people of the United States? We think it demonstrable, that it does not.

Thus, the Court acknowledged the federal government's power to use means to execute its constitutional powers as well as the states' inability to interfere with that authority.[86]

The Supreme Court likewise has limited the federal government by holding many federal statutes unconstitutional based, at least in part, on violations of federalism. The trend of actively limiting the federal government began with *New York v. United States*, which involved the State of New York's challenge to the federal Low-Level Radioactive Waste Policy Amendments Act. The federal statute included three incentive provisions designed to encourage states to enact policies to manage waste generated within their borders. The Court held that Congress possessed authority to use two of the incentive provisions – monetary and disposal site access – to encourage states to plan for this waste disposal. But the Court determined that the Act's "take title" provision – forcing states to take ownership of radioactive waste if they were unable to provide appropriate disposal sites – was invalid. Congress lacked authority to compel states to enact legislation – the

---

[86] 17 U.S. 316, 405–29 (1819).

practical consequence of the Act's "take title" provision. The Founders had given Congress legislative authority over individuals but not states. While Congress could have required the states to choose between implementing their own regulatory programs and accepting a program created by Congress – an arrangement of "cooperative federalism" – the "take title" provision constituted an unconstitutional "commandeering" of state governments. The Court compared the protection under federalism to the protection under the separation of powers.[87]

> Just as the separation and independence of the coordinate branches of the Federal Government serves to prevent the accumulation of excessive power in any one branch, a healthy balance of power between the States and the Federal Government will reduce the risk of tyranny and abuse from either front.[88]

Here, the Supreme Court recognized the particular authority held by the federal government and the states and the importance of federalism to the proper functioning of the government.

At times, the Supreme Court and the other traditional actors act to limit their own authority. The most accessible examples occur when the Supreme Court acts to restrain itself. The Court has developed several doctrines limiting the judiciary's role under separation of powers. For example, the Court has defined the constitutional requirement that a federal court hear only "[c]ases" or "[c]ontroversies" as mandating: that a plaintiff have standing, that a case is not moot, that a case is ripe, and that a case does not involve a political question.[89] The Court has described these doctrines as "'founded in concern about the proper – and properly limited – role of the courts in a democratic society.'"[90]

Similarly, through the federalism-based doctrines of sovereign immunity, the judiciary has recognized specific limits on its power in relationship to the states. The Supreme Court has referred to sovereign immunity as "an essential component of federalism."[91] Under this doctrine, the judiciary's power to hear suits against states has been limited. The Court has emphasized that

---

[87] 505 U.S. 144, 149–53, 161, 165–67, 173–76 (1992).
[88] *Id.* at 181–82 (quoting Gregory v. Ashcroft, 501 U.S. 452, 458 (1991)).
[89] *See* Allen v. Wright, 468 U.S. 737, 750 (1984).
[90] *Id.* (quoting Warth v. Seldin, 422 U.S. 490, 498 (1975)).
[91] Pennhurst State Sch. & Hosp. v. Halderman, 465 U.S. 89, 100 n.10 (1984) (quoting Nevada v. Hall, 440 U.S. 410, 430–31 (1979) (Blackmun, J., dissenting)).

each State is a sovereign entity in our federal system . . . [and] '[i]t is inherent in the nature of sovereignty not to be amenable to the suit of an individual without its consent.'[92]

While federal courts may order prospective enforcement of federal laws against the states, sovereign immunity sets limitations on the power of the federal courts to order states to pay damages.[93]

The other traditional actors also sometimes restrain themselves in relationship to competing traditional actors when they believe they do not hold authority. Evidence of such self-restraint is not always apparent because it typically involves inaction – for example, Congress not enacting a statute that is beyond its power. Louis Fisher has argued that Congress attempts to stay within its legislative boundaries. He provided the example of the legislature's 1789 debate over the President's power to remove executive officials without legislative action.[94] Another example of the self-restraint exercised by the traditional actors occurs where a legislator votes for an official or judicial nominee that the President has recommended because of the legislator's view of the Constitution's requirements.[95] And a final example is the interpretation of the states that the federal government has the power and responsibility to secure the borders.[96]

*****

Although separation of powers and federalism form a barrier against incursions on the traditional actors' powers, these doctrines do not provide impenetrable boundaries. The traditional actors can intrude upon each others' turf. When this happens, the actor whose authority has been infringed upon may have no recourse if it cannot successfully oppose the intrusion on its own or challenge the action in court. For example, the executive has circumvented the legislature in times of international crisis. The President has acted without Congress despite

---

[92] Seminole Tribe of Fla. v. Florida, 517 U.S. 44, 54 (1996) (quoting Hans v. Louisiana, 134 U.S. 1, 13 (1890)).

[93] See Ex parte Young, 209 U.S. 123 (1908).

[94] See Louis Fisher, Constitutional Interpretation by Members of Congress, 63 N. Car. L. Rev. 707, 709–11 (1985).

[95] See Nicole Allan, Lyndsey Graham Dramatically Casts His Vote for Elena Kagan, The Atlantic, July 20, 2010.

[96] See U.S. Const. art. IV, §4; cf. Jason L. Riley, Perry's Immigration Pose, Wall St. J., July 23, 2014 (discussing the decision of Texas Governor Rick Perry to send Texas National Guard to the border after his call to President Obama to secure the border).

the power of Congress to declare war set forth in Article I. Moreover, the United States Supreme Court has initially granted authority to a state and later overruled its decision in favor of federal power. For example, in *Garcia v. San Antonio Metropolitan Authority*, it found constitutional a federal congressional act forcing state and local governments to pay their employees minimum wage and overtime.[97]

Despite these limitations, the Supreme Court has employed separation of powers and federalism to provide significant protection for the traditional actors to maintain their authority, and the traditional actors themselves have acted to restrain their own power. Moreover, the traditional actors have the ability to test the boundaries of their own authority even if their authority has been questioned by another traditional actor. A recurring example occurs in the context of abortion. After *Roe v. Wade*,[98] states have continued to enact statutes that restrict abortion procedure that may or may not be within the bounds of *Roe*. While these statutes may be reviewed by the Court, the ability of the states to push back gives them at least temporary authority and also raises these issues in public fora.

A Missing Constitutional Role for the Jury?   The jury and the traditional actors hold similar roles in the Constitution. Just as the text of the Constitution divides and limits powers among the traditional actors, it divides and limits the powers of the traditional actors in relationship to the powers of the criminal, civil, and grand juries. Also, just as the Founders planned empowering and restraining lines among the traditional actors, the Founders of the Constitution and the ratifiers of the Fourteenth Amendment intended these types of divisions and limitations to preserve the jury's realm. Despite these similarities, the Supreme Court and scholars generally recognize the traditional actors as branches or constitutional actors, but, as shown in this section, do not acknowledge such an authoritative role for criminal, civil, and grand juries. Consequently, they have not analyzed the authority of the criminal, civil, and grand juries under doctrines similar to separation of powers and federalism, which, as demonstrated earlier, have played a significant role in securing the traditional actors' powers.

The Supreme Court's differing treatment of the traditional actors and the jury and the deference to the traditional actors has contributed to the

---

[97] *See* 469 U.S. 528 (1985).
[98] *See* 410 U.S. 113 (1973).

jury's decline. The Court has examined issues related to jury authority in a disjointed, piecemeal fashion that neither recognizes the jury as an essential part of the governmental structure in the Constitution nor acknowledges that it serves roles to protect against power grabs by the traditional actors. The Court has often initially recognized authority in the jury and then, changed its decision to grant power instead to a traditional actor. A review of some of the primary cases where the Court has diminished the jury's authority while it has granted power to the traditional actors exhibits the different treatment of the jury and the traditional actors. Specifically, it shows how the omission of a separation of powers and federalism-type doctrine from the Court's jury jurisprudence has contributed to the jury's decline.

Although there have been substantial shifts in authority from the jury to other parts of the government, one area where there has been a shift in favor of jury power should be acknowledged first. In the last decade or so, in a series of decisions, the Court has recognized that the jury holds authority regarding factual decisions related to sentencing. For example, the Court held unconstitutional provisions of the Federal Sentencing Act that permitted a judge, instead of a jury, to decide certain sentencing facts.[99] In one of the decisions on the jury's role in sentencing, the Court referred to the criminal jury as "a fundamental reservation of power in our constitutional structure." It emphasized that "the very reason the Framers put a jury-trial guarantee in the Constitution is that they were unwilling to trust government to mark out the role of the jury."[100]

Outside of this sentencing area (where, by the way, there remains some debate on the importance of these changes), there is little recognition of the jury as an important part of the constitutional structure and government. The Court has failed to acknowledge any specific authority in the jury or any necessity to guard that authority. Instead, the Supreme Court permits the traditional actors to decide many matters instead of juries. Moreover, it ultimately has held constitutional almost every modern

---

[99] *See* United States v. Booker, 543 U.S. 220 (2005).

[100] Blakely v. Washington, 542 U.S. 296, 306–08 (2004); *cf.* Wellness Int'l Network v. Sharif, 135 S. Ct. 1932, 1961 n.1 (2015) (Thomas, J., dissenting) (stating that while "[t]here is some dispute whether the guarantee of a jury trial protects an individual right, a structural right, or both, . . . [i]t is a 'fundamental reservation of power in our constitutional structure'" – the violation of which an individual cannot approve).

procedure before and after a jury deliberation that has eliminated or reduced jury authority.

One example shows the Court initially valued the role that the grand jury could play against the government but changed its view over time. In the late nineteenth century, in *Ex parte* Bain, the Court considered whether a person could be convicted for a crime upon a grand jury's indictment that the government subsequently changed without the grand jury's consent. Upon the prosecutor's request, the judge had changed the indictment. The Supreme Court focused on the Fifth Amendment's language that requires a person not to answer for certain crimes "unless on a presentment or indictment of a grand jury," and cited the common law, under which an indictment could not be amended. Despite what the Court described as the present general trustworthiness of the government, the Court decided that the indictment could not be changed in this manner. It quoted a previous decision and emphasized that the grand jury checked governmental power.

> In this country, from the popular character of our institutions, there has seldom been any contest between the government and the citizen which required the existence of the grand jury as a protection against oppressive action of the government. Yet the institution was adopted in this country . . . , and is designed as means, not only of bringing to trial persons accused of public offenses upon just grounds, but also as a means of protecting the citizen against unfounded accusation, whether it comes from government, or be prompted by partisan passion or private enmity.

The Court discussed the present importance of the grand jury, including the possibility of bad behavior on the part of the executive.

> [I]t remains true that the grand jury is as valuable as ever in securing, in the language of Chief Justice SHAW in the case of *Jones v. Robbins*, 8 Gray, 329, 'individual citizens from an open and public accusation of crime, and from the trouble, expense, and anxiety of a public trial before a probable cause is established by the presentment and indictment of such a jury; and in case of high offenses it is justly regarded as one of the securities to the innocent against hasty, malicious, and oppressive public prosecutions.'

Emphasizing the intentions of the Framers, who

> had for a long time been absorbed in considering the arbitrary encroachments of the crown on the liberty of the subject, and were imbued with the common-law estimate of the value of the grand jury as part of its system of criminal jurisprudence,

the Court stated that the indictment could not be changed, because a court held no power to hear the case except upon a grand jury's indictment.[101]

But in 2002, in *United States v. Cotton*, the Supreme Court overruled this decision. In *Cotton*, the government failed to allege in the original indictment the amount of the drug that influenced the ultimate sentence that was imposed. The Court insisted that the previous decision of *Bain* was "a product of an era in which this Court's authority to review criminal convictions was greatly circumscribed." Concepts of jurisdiction had changed, and a defective indictment did not prevent a court from proceeding against a criminal defendant. Emphasizing the evidence presented in the trial, the Court stated "[s]urely" the grand jury would have indicted on the amount of cocaine under these circumstances where it had indicted on the conspiracy. Moreover, the defendant did not object to the indictment at trial so he waived the grand jury. Although the Court recognized the grand jury "as a check on prosecutorial power," this served as window dressing, because, at the same time, it shifted power to the courts and the executive.[102]

The ability of a judge to try a criminal case, a power absent from the Constitution, is another power about which the Court changed its mind and transferred authority from the jury to the judiciary. In the late nineteenth century, in *Thompson v. Utah*, the Supreme Court originally determined that a defendant could not waive the required trial of twelve jurors. There, quoting an earlier case that cited Blackstone and emphasizing that the jury was the mechanism by which a criminal defendant was to be tried under the Constitution, the Court decided the Constitution required a unanimous jury of twelve.

> The natural life, says Blackstone, cannot legally be disposed of or destroyed by any individual, neither by the person himself, nor by any other of his fellow creatures, merely upon their own authority. . . . The public has an interest in his life and liberty. Neither can be lawfully taken except in the mode prescribed by law.[103]

Later in *Patton v. United* States, a case considering, among other questions, whether a judge could try a case instead of a jury, the Court rejected that the jury constituted a fundamental part of the governmental structure.

---

[101] *Ex parte Bain*, 121 U.S. 1, 11–13 (1887). Note that the U.S. Reporter actually states "the presentment and indictment of a grand jury" instead of "such a jury," but this book uses the Westlaw database for U.S. case citations.

[102] 535 U.S. 625, 628–29, 633–34 (2002).

[103] 170 U.S. 343, 354–55 (1898).

Examining the question "[i]s the effect of the constitutional provisions in respect of trial by jury to establish a tribunal as a part of the frame of government, or only to guarantee to the accused the right to such a trial," the Court dismissed any notion that history supported a role for the jury as a part of the constitutional structure.

> The record of English and colonial jurisprudence antedating the Constitution will be searched in vain for evidence that trial by jury in criminal cases was regarded as a part of the structure of government, as distinguished from a right or privilege of the accused. On the contrary, it uniformly was regarded as a valuable privilege bestowed upon the person accused of crime for the purpose of safeguarding him against the oppressive power of the King and the arbitrary or partial judgment of the court.

After accepting that the jury trial was nothing more than a right that a defendant could exercise, the Court decided that judges had authority to try defendants through Congress's creation of the district courts.[104] In permitting judges to try cases instead of juries, the Court acted differently from how it had acted with respect the traditional actors. Although the Constitution specifically gave certain types of cases to juries and judges, the Court ignored this text. It also failed to recognize Blackstone's express warnings about trial by judge. Moreover, the Court did not acknowledge that the jury could not check the government if the government itself, through the judge, decided the case. Finally, the Court fundamentally failed to recognize its own interest in the case. In contrast to its treatment of the traditional actors, perceiving them as mutual checks in the government, the Court took power from the jury and placed it in its own hands without any appreciation for the check that the jury was to play with respect to the judiciary.

More than trials by judges, plea bargaining is a primary reason cited for the decline of criminal jury trials. Although the Supreme Court has not thoroughly evaluated the constitutionality of plea bargaining, it officially legitimized it in *Bordenkircher v. Hayes*.[105] In doing so, it again ignored the type of evidence that it has recognized when it has granted power to the traditional actors. There, the prosecutor offered the defendant five years of the possible sentence of two to ten years to plead guilty to the indicted offense. The state simultaneously informed the defendant that it would seek an indictment for a crime that could result in defendant's life

---

[104] 281 U.S. 276, 293, 296–302 (1930).

[105] Bordenkircher v. Hayes, 434 U.S. 357 (1978); *see also* Timothy Lynch, *The Case Against Plea Bargaining*, REGULATION (Fall 2003) (arguing plea bargaining is unconstitutional).

imprisonment if the defendant insisted on a jury trial and refused to plead guilty. When the defendant refused to take the plea, the prosecutor obtained an indictment on the new charge. A jury then convicted the defendant on this charge, resulting in life imprisonment. The defendant argued that the action of the prosecutor to seek this other charge as punishment for the defendant's exercise of his right to a jury trial was unconstitutional under the due process clause of the Fourteenth Amendment. The appeals' court decided that the prosecutor had acted vindictively to punish the defendant for exercising his right to a jury trial and invalidated the subsequent charge and conviction under the due process clause. Reviewing the decision, the Supreme Court emphasized "that the guilty plea and the often concomitant plea bargain are important components of this country's criminal justice system." Finding no constitutional infirmity with the prosecutor's action, the Court stated:

> [i]t follows that, by tolerating and encouraging the negotiation of pleas, this Court has necessarily accepted as constitutionally legitimate the simple reality that the prosecutor's interest at the bargaining table is to persuade the defendant to forgo his right to plead not guilty.[106]

The Court failed to discuss the Article III criminal jury power and the Sixth Amendment, and any possible role of the jury as a check on the government. Instead, it prioritized the executive's interest and did not consider the constitutional text and historical evidence that it had considered when it granted power to the traditional actors in other cases.[107]

The Supreme Court also has treated the civil jury differently than the traditional actors. Again, the jury's diminution has occurred after the Court previously recognized jury authority. In the early twentieth century, in *Slocum v. New York Life Insurance Company*, the Court considered whether after a jury verdict in a civil case, a judge could decide that the evidence was insufficient, reverse the verdict, and direct a judgment for the side that had lost before the jury. During the trial, after all of the evidence was presented, the court had denied the defendant's request that the court direct a verdict in its favor. After the jury found for the plaintiff, the Court of Appeals later reversed and found for the

---

[106] 434 U.S. at 358–59, 361, 364.

[107] Dissenting, Justice Blackmun, joined by Justices Brennan and Marshall, agreed with the appeals' court that the behavior of the prosecutor violated the due process clause and also suggested that overcharging the defendant in order to plea bargain also was unconstitutional behavior. *See* 434 U.S. at 365–70, 368 n.2 (Blackmun, dissenting). Justice Powell also dissented. *See id.* at 368–73 (Powell, dissenting).

defendant. The Supreme Court acknowledged that it must examine the English common law to determine the meaning of the Seventh Amendment. At common law, another jury trial was the only method by which the determination of the first jury could be re-examined. Deciding that the Court of Appeals acted improperly when it circumvented the jury in ruling in the defendant's favor, the Court emphasized the importance of both the judge and the jury and the relationship between them.

> In the trial by jury, the right to which is secured by the 7th Amendment, both the court and the jury are essential factors. To the former is committed a power of direction and superintendence, and to the latter the ultimate determination of the issues of fact. Only through the co-operation of the two, each acting within its appropriate sphere, can the constitutional right be satisfied. And so, to dispense with either, or to permit one to disregard the province of the other, is to impinge on that right.

In its decision, the Court distinguished the demurrer to the evidence and the nonsuit, procedures at common law in England that differed from the procedure employed by the appellate court.[108]

Just over twenty years later, in *Baltimore & Carolina Line, Inc. v. Redman*, however, the Court took a different view of the roles of the judiciary and the jury. In that case, after evidence was presented at trial, the defendant asked the judge to decide in its favor on the basis that the plaintiff had not presented sufficient evidence in support of his case. The court deferred consideration of the motion, and after a jury verdict for the plaintiff, decided that the evidence in favor of the plaintiff was sufficient. The Court of Appeals determined differently that the evidence was insufficient, ordered a new trial, and cited *Slocum* in support of its decision. Reviewing the decision of the appeals' court to order a new trial instead of a judgment for the defendant, the Supreme Court first recognized that the Amendment was "to retain the common-law distinction between the province of the court and that of the jury," including that "issues of law are to be resolved by the court and issues of fact are to be determined by the jury." It went on to take authority from the jury by incorrectly characterizing the sufficiency of the evidence as a common law issue of law that it could decide. It attempted to distinguish *Slocum* on the ground that the issue of the insufficiency of the evidence was not reserved for the court before the case was sent to the jury and claimed

---

[108] 228 U.S. 364, 377–78, 382, 388–98 (1913).

that the Court of Appeals in this case employed a practice similar to the common law practice, whereby such issues of law could be reserved for the court during trial. The Court concluded that a judge could decide the opposite of what the jury decided. Where the jury had found for one party, the judge could later dismiss the case in favor of the other party without ordering a new jury trial. According to the Court, parts of *Slocum* went beyond the proper confines of the case and therefore did not apply, and in any event, the *Redman* decision "qualified" its holding in *Slocum*.[109]

The final case that shifted significant authority to the judge from the civil jury was decided soon after *Redman*. In *Galloway v. United States*, after the parties presented evidence at trial, the trial court decided that the evidence was "legally insufficient" and ruled in favor of the government. The Supreme Court considered the question of whether a judge could decide that the evidence was insufficient at trial and find for one party without sending the case to a jury. Deciding that the procedure did not violate the Seventh Amendment, the Court also stated that "[t]he objection therefore [came] too late." This argument was "foreclosed by repeated decisions made [in the Court] consistently for nearly a century," and the "approv[al] explicitly in the promulgation of the Federal Rules of Civil Procedure." Despite its previous statement in *Redman* about the authority of the jury to find fact, the Court asserted that "[t]he jury was not absolute master of fact in 1791," and it cited the demurrer to the evidence and the new trial in support of this assertion. Moreover, not acknowledging its prior statements about the demurrer to evidence in *Slocum*, the Court attempted to favorably compare the directed verdict – the present procedure – to the demurrer to the evidence. It also discussed how the Seventh Amendment did not tie the judiciary to any specific procedure that occurred at the time of the adoption of the Seventh Amendment, and that the common law was continuously changing, even when the Amendment was adopted. The Court emphasized that the procedures of the demurrer to the evidence and the new trial were inconsistent, and that differences between the common law procedures and the modern directed verdict were inconsequential.[110]

The Supreme Court also failed to recognize the authority of the jury in relationship to traditional actors in shifting authority from the jury to

---

[109] 295 U.S. 654, 656–57, 660–61 (1935).
[110] 319 U.S. 372, 373, 389–95 (1943).

the executive in *National Labor Relations Board v. Jones & Laughlin Steel Corp*. There, the Supreme Court considered whether the Seventh Amendment applied in circumstances in which Congress had established an executive agency to investigate and determine whether employers or employees engaged in unfair labor practices. The NLRB – the agency – had ordered the employer to pay monetary damages to employees as the result of unfair labor practices by the employer. The employer argued that a jury should decide the damages issue. Labeling the proceeding as "statutory," the Supreme Court said that the matter was not a common law suit under the Seventh Amendment. Because Congress established this claim, there was no jury trial right.[111] The Court failed to discuss the authority of the jury to decide damages, any related inability of the legislature itself to decide who determines damages, and the shift of authority from the jury to the executive.

Finally, "nonincorporation" of the civil and grand jury provisions provides evidence of how the Court has shifted power from the jury to the states. In 1916 and 1884, respectively, the Supreme Court decided not to incorporate the Seventh Amendment civil jury provision and the Fifth Amendment grand jury clause against the states. When the Court did so, these cases were consistent with the other Supreme Court jurisprudence on whether parts of the Bill of Rights should be incorporated. Subsequently, the Court changed its decisions on the incorporation of the Bill of Rights, most recently in 2010 when it required states to recognize the Second Amendment right to bear arms. However, the Court has not acted similarly to require states to recognize the civil jury and the grand jury provisions under the Seventh and Fifth Amendments respectively.[112]

The Missing "Branch" in the Supreme Court's Jurisprudence

The Supreme Court presently does not acknowledge the jury's independent constitutional function and its role to check the powers of the traditional actors. On the other hand, the Court does recognize the traditional actors' independent constitutional functions to restrain one another through the use of the doctrines of separation of powers and federalism. Scholars and the Court generally agree that these doctrines are essential to the proper functioning of the government. The absence of doctrine affirming the jury's relative independent constitutional role plus the historical transfer of authority from the jury to the traditional actors suggest one conclusion.

---

[111] 301 U.S. 1, 22, 48 (1937).
[112] *See* Thomas, *supra* note 80, at 166, 173–204.

Depriving the jury of its proper equal status – effectively as a branch or constitutional actor – among the traditional actors has contributed to its decline and its loss of power to the traditional actors.

The closest reference to the jury as a branch or constitutional actor is in the context of the grand jury. The Supreme Court has referred to the grand jury as "a constitutional fixture in its own right," "belong[ing] to no branch of the institutional Government," and independent of them.[113] In somewhat similar fashion, as previously mentioned, in a decision granting the criminal jury power, the Court described it as "a fundamental reservation of power in our constitutional structure."[114] But, such designations by the Court are sparse, and some have been rejected by the Court in later decisions.

Nonetheless, several scholars have recognized that the jury holds an important, branch-like role in the government. Notably, Akhil Amar has identified the jury as an important part of the constitutional structure. As he describes it, "[t]he dominant strategy [of the Constitution] to keep agents of the central government under control was to use the populist and local institution of the jury." The jury helped balance two of the branches. The grand jury counterbalanced prosecutors in the executive branch, while the civil jury equalized judges in the judicial branch. In these roles, juries could, for example, check abuses by the executive and determine compensation for people when the government took their property. Juries also provided knowledge about the government to jurors.[115] Another scholar, Nancy Marder, has affirmatively referred to the jury as "a coordinate branch of government" that checks all of the branches.[116]

Others have also emphasized a significant role for grand, criminal, and civil juries to check the government. Roger Fairfax stated "the grand jury is its own constitutional entity, which checks each of the three branches of government." The grand jury is a barrier that must be crossed before the judge sentences a criminal defendant. Similar to its role to check the judiciary, the grand jury can act as a restraint on the executive by preventing it from proceeding with a prosecution. It can also act as a check on the legislature by refusing to indict on a

---

[113] United States v. Williams, 504 U.S. 36, 47–50 (1992).

[114] Blakely v. Washington, 542 U.S. 296, 306 (2004); *see also* Wellness Int'l Network v. Sharif, 135 S. Ct. 1932, 1961 n.1 (2015) (Thomas, J., dissenting)

[115] Akhil Reed Amar, The Bill of Rights: Creation and Reconstruction 83, 88, 93–94, 111 (1998); *see* Akhil Reed Amar, America's Constitution: A Biography 237 (2006).

[116] Marder, *supra* note 10, at 11.

particular charge out of disagreement with a law. Finally, local citizens can act against the federal government through their roles on the grand jury checking federal laws.[117]

Rachel Barkow has described the criminal jury as a check on the executive and the legislature due to its ability to nullify prosecutions or laws. She has also described the criminal jury as possessing powers similar to the traditional actors, to act and not act.

> The constitutional system of criminal justice protects the discretionary judgments of all key actors not to proceed criminally. That is why the executive has discretionary pardon and charging power, why the legislature has the freedom not to criminalize conduct, and the jury has the unreviewable power to acquit.[118]

Randy Jonakait has depicted the civil jury as serving the same function as the criminal jury – "as a check on government," and also referred to the civil jury as a check on "the powerful," public or private.[119] Renee Lettow Lerner similarly has discussed the civil jury as a political institution with the purpose of checking the legislature, the executive, and the judiciary.[120]

The Right to a Trial by Jury versus Power in the Jury   Despite these perspectives, the Supreme Court considers the jury neither an independent powerful actor nor a check on the governmental structure. As described previously, while the Court originally recognized that the jury occupied this important position, over time, it has become less enamored with the jury. The jury is now viewed only in terms of a right to a jury – relevant only when a party chooses to have their case decided by a jury. For example, a criminal defendant can simply waive his jury trial right, and a judge can try the case, or the defendant can plea and in turn receive a lesser sentence.

Under this view, the jury may not have fallen so much as it is merely an individual right that plaintiffs and defendants can waive. Moreover, in some circumstances, because no right may exist, the jury may not fall. For example, courts believe there is no jury right in civil cases when a judge decides no reasonable jury could find for one party.

---

[117] Roger A. Fairfax, Jr., *Does Grand Jury Discretion Have a Legitimate (and Useful) Role to Play in Criminal Justice?*, in GRAND JURY 2.0, *supra* note 23, at 67–69.

[118] Rachel E. Barkow, *Separation of Powers and the Criminal Law*, 58 STAN. L. REV. 989, 1042, 1048–49 (2006).

[119] JONAKAIT, *supra* note 70, at 38.

[120] *See* Lerner, *supra* note 13, at 828–31.

But constitutional text and evidence present a different perspective. The Fifth Amendment states a person cannot be convicted for serious crimes ("capital, or otherwise infamous") without a presentment or indictment by a grand jury unless special specific circumstances arise. There is no reference to a "right" to jury trial in the Amendment, and it gives the grand jury alone (absent the stated special circumstances) the power to initiate proceedings against defendants accused of serious crimes. No other constitutional text provides the executive, judges, or any other traditional actor authority to initiate a proceeding against defendants accused of serious crimes.

James Wilson acknowledged the power of the grand jury to both bring presentments of its own accord and act on charges brought by the prosecutor. He discussed this as the "right" and "duty" of the grand jury to act "diligently" and "present truly."[121] He also emphasized the great power of the jury in comparison to the judiciary.[122]

Like the Fifth Amendment grand jury provision, Article III gives the jury affirmative authority. It grants the jury power to try all crimes except impeachment cases. The Sixth Amendment, however, refers to a right – "the right to a speedy and public trial, by an impartial jury" in the area where the crime was committed. So, the question becomes what power, if any, does the jury possess given the use of the term "right" in the Sixth Amendment? More specifically, does "right" in the Sixth Amendment limit the power of the criminal jury in Article III? There is no evidence that the Sixth Amendment limits or qualifies the jury power set forth in Article III. Moreover, the Sixth Amendment, other rights in the Bill of Rights, and the original Constitution do not grant authority to any institution other than the jury to try crimes (outside of impeachment).

At the time of the founding, language describing the criminal jury also referred or related to power. For example, James Wilson specifically described the criminal jury as "[a] man, or a body of men, habitually clothed with a power over the lives of their fellow citizens."[123] The Federal Farmer also acknowledged the power of people on juries.

---

[121] 1 Wilson, Collected Works of James Wilson 325 (Kermit L. Hall et al. eds., Liberty Fund 2007).

[122] See 2 Wilson, Collected Works of Wilson, *supra* note 55, at 996–1002.

[123] 2 Wilson, Collected Works of Wilson, *supra* note 55, at 1008–1009; *see also* Laura I. Appleman, Defending the Jury: Crime, Community and the Constitution 13–36 (2015).

Few could be elected to the legislature but they could be part of juries. Both provided "their true proportion of influence."

> Their situation, as jurors and representatives, enables them to acquire information and knowledge in the affairs and government of the society; and to come forward, in turn, as the centinels and guardians of each other.[124]

The civil jury under the Seventh Amendment – unlike the grand jury under the Fifth Amendment and the criminal jury under Article III – denotes a "right" of trial by jury. However, evidence at the founding does not show a difference in the discussion of the roles of the three juries. At the time of the Constitution's original enactment, many people had also wanted a guarantee of a civil jury trial. Moreover, there is evidence that the intentions for the civil jury trial were similar to the intentions for the jury trial for crimes – that is, to check the government.[125] Add to this, in the time between the Constitution's enactment and the enactment of the Bill of Rights, there is no evidence that intentions regarding the civil jury trial changed. This suggests that "right" in the Seventh Amendment does not limit power granted to the civil jury.

The text of the Seventh Amendment further informs the meaning to be given to the civil jury trial. The text refers to the preservation of the right in suits at common law. At common law, almost invariably juries heard cases in which monetary damages were alleged. So the text suggests that juries were to continue to hear such cases. Also, the text states the specific conditions under which judges can be involved once a jury tries a case – thus setting forth limitations on the power of the judiciary as well as the authority of other traditional actors, which are granted no power at all.

At times, the Founders referred to the civil jury's power in a similar manner to the grand and criminal juries. Discussing the civil jury trial, the Federal Farmer, an anti-federalist, emphasized the importance of the jury as an institution through which the people could be educated and by which the people could exercise power to protect rights. He wrote that

> [t]he body of the people, principally, bear the burdens of the community; they of right ought to have a controul [sic] in its important concerns, both in making and executing the laws.

---

[124] *See* Letters from The Federal Farmer to the Republican No. IV, *reprinted in* 2 COMPLETE ANTI-FEDERALIST, *supra* note 47, at 249–50.

[125] *See* JONAKAIT, *supra* note 70, at 38.

The legislature and the jury

> are the means by which the people are let into the knowledge of public
> affairs – are enabled to stand as the guardians of each others rights, and to
> restrain, by regular and legal measures, those who otherwise might
> infringe upon them.[126]

There is, however, some evidence that the civil jury amendment provided a right rather than a power. For example, when Massachusetts ratified the Constitution, it recommended "[i]n civil actions between citizens of different States, every issue of fact arising in actions at common law, shall be tried by jury, if the parties, or either of them, request it."[127]

Finally, assume that the Seventh Amendment created only a right that can be waived. In some circumstances, no waiver of the right occurs, and power shifts from the civil jury to traditional actors. The traditional actor affirmatively acts to usurp power that the jury previously held, such as when a judge reduces a jury verdict after a jury trial through the use of remittitur, a procedure that did not exist at English common law.[128] Thus, although the Seventh Amendment's text denotes a "right," it nonetheless establishes the jury's power to decide certain cases and issues, in relationship to the traditional actors' corresponding limited powers.

To serve the role that it is supposed to play as a check on the power of the traditional actors, the jury itself must possess power. For example, through its choice of charges under the law, the executive can threaten a criminal defendant with more significant penalties to incentivize the defendant to waive the jury trial. Without any recognition of corresponding jury authority, these actions of the legislature and the executive go unchecked. As another example, a federal judge can dismiss a case seeking civil remedies for a federal officer's improper search of an individual's home. Again, without any recognition of corresponding authority in the jury to decide the case, the government's effort to stymie the constitutional check of its power goes unexamined.[129]

---

[126] Letters from The Federal Farmer to the Republican No. XV, *reprinted in* 2 COMPLETE ANTI-FEDERALIST, *supra* note 47, at 320.

[127] Debates and Proceedings in the Convention of the Commonwealth of Massachusetts 80 (1856).

[128] *See* Suja A. Thomas, *Re-Examining the Constitutionality of Remittitur Under the Seventh Amendment*, 64 OHIO ST. L.J. 731 (2003).

[129] *See* AMAR, AMERICA'S CONSTITUTION, *supra* note 115, at 237.

Other Arguments Against the Jury as a "Branch"   In addition to the argument that the jury holds no separate power, other arguments can be made against the jury as an independent body. Many regard the jury as solely part of the judicial branch and thus related to the judiciary alone. The Founders make many references to the jury as part of the judicial branch. For example, James Wilson stated that the people retained "part of the judicial authority" through its power to decide criminal cases.[130] Also, as previously described, some scholars believe the jury is part of some or all of the branches.

This book does not argue that the jury has never been characterized as part of a branch. It asserts that regardless of such descriptions, the constitutional text and other evidence show an independent, inter-related relationship between the jury and the traditional actors, similar to the relationship among the traditional actors, to the extent that the jury is functionally a branch with significant authority like the traditional actors.

A final argument against the jury as a branch recognizes the criminal jury, civil jury, and grand jury as very different entities that cannot be grouped together as one branch or constitutional actor. But ascribing "the branch" to the grand, criminal, and civil juries is not to aggregate them as indistinguishable. Instead, the reference to the jury as a branch is to point out a common history of diminution in power, the similar roles each was to play in opposition to the traditional actors, and the comparable reason for the declines of each.

Alexis de Tocqueville supported the view of the jury as a separate independent actor. In the early nineteenth century, after the adoption of the Constitution and Bill of Rights, Tocqueville characterized the jury as its own independent body. He referred to both criminal and civil juries, as "before all else a political institution." In fact, he distinguished the role of the jury as a judicial institution – its role in trials – from its political role. In discussing the importance of the political role of the jury, he equated its importance to voting. He stated "the institution of the jury puts the people themselves, or at least a class of citizens, on the judge's bench. So the institution of the jury really puts the leadership of society into the hands of the people or of this class." Similar to some others previously mentioned, Tocqueville believed that the importance of the jury was particularly to those on the jury. "I do not know if the jury is

---

[130]   2 WILSON, COLLECTED WORKS OF WILSON, *supra* note 55, at 1008.

useful to those who have legal proceedings, but I am sure that it is very useful to those who judge them. I regard it as one of the most effective means that a society can use for the education of the people."[131] This view of the jury, as well as the view of the jury as a check on the traditional actors, has been lost.

*****

So, why has the jury declined in authority? Comparison of the jury to the traditional actors provides insight. The Constitution grants authority to the traditional actors, as well as to the criminal, civil, and grand juries. Through the use of the doctrines of separation of powers and federalism, the Supreme Court has acknowledged that the traditional actors possess significant authority and are restrained by important limitations. Their power under this regime is evident. The President carries out activities. The legislature makes laws. Courts issue opinions. And states enact laws and carry out other activities. No significant decline in the authority of any of the traditional actors from the founding to the present time has been recognized – outside of a debated decline in state authority.[132]

The traditional actors' status contrasts with the jury's status. The jury is not considered to have power as a part of the constitutional structure or government. It hears few cases, and when it tries a case, its authority can be usurped. The similarities between the traditional actors and the jury along with the jury's dissimilar decline show the failure to give the jury branch-like status has contributed to the jury's decline. While it is difficult to disprove that cost, incompetence, inaccuracy, or inefficiency have caused the decline of the jury, as mentioned previously, the traditional actors are also criticized for having similar characteristics. However, they thrive.

---

[131] ALEXIS DE TOCQUEVILLE, 2 DEMOCRACY IN AMERICA 443–48 (Eduardo Nolla ed., Liberty Fund 1835); see also JOHN GASTIL ET AL., THE JURY AND DEMOCRACY: HOW JURY DELIBERATION PROMOTES CIVIC ENGAGEMENT AND POLITICAL PARTICIPATION (2010); Vikram David Amar, Jury Service as Political Participation Akin to Voting, 80 CORNELL L. REV. 203 (1995); Laura Gaston Dooley, Our Juries, Our Selves: The Power, Perception, and Politics of the Civil Jury, 80 CORNELL L. REV. 325 (1995); Andrew Guthrie Ferguson, The Jury as Constitutional Identity, 47 U.C. DAVIS L. REV. 1105 (2014).

[132] See, e.g., Roger C. Cramton, The Supreme Court and the Decline of State Power, 2 J. L & ECON. 175 (1959).

Further Assessing the Decline of the Criminal, Civil, and Grand Juries

As discussed, then, in contrast to its treatment of the traditional actors, the Supreme Court has denied the jury doctrine that establishes and protects its authority in the constitutional structure. If the jury was prescribed such doctrine analogous to separation of powers or federalism, the divisions of authority between the jury and the traditional actors could be better assured.

So why have the traditional actors not recognized the jury as part of the constitutional structure, and not established doctrine for it similar to separation of powers and federalism? This underlying question is difficult to answer. Different possibilities persist, including some of the reasons proffered in the first part of this chapter – for example, democratization of the jury or the rise of the administrative state through the establishment of administrative agencies. First, a related question is how the traditional actors were able to take authority from the jury.

Unique Characteristics of the Jury

The traditional actors could shift power from the jury to themselves because of certain characteristics of the jury. While the relationships among the traditional actors and between the traditional actors and the jury share some qualities, the unique characteristics of the jury can cause its relationships to function differently. Using the relationship between the judiciary and the jury as an example, the judiciary reviews the authority of the jury, just as it examines the power of the traditional actors. When the judiciary hears a case, it can compete for authority with traditional actors as it can with the jury. The judiciary may need to decide whether it, another traditional actor, or the jury has authority with regard to some matter. For example, the federal judiciary can decide whether a federal court or a state court hears a case, exercising final decision-making power as to this question. Also, the judiciary can determine whether a congressional act that takes authority from the judiciary is unconstitutional, and if it so finds, the law can no longer apply. Moreover, the judiciary can determine whether a federal rule authorizing a judge to appropriate power from the jury is constitutional, and if so, the rule empowers the judge and disempowers the jury.

In these competitive relationships, the jury differs from the traditional actors in ways that contribute to its non-branch-like status and its comparative decline. First, the jury cannot sit or otherwise perform without the action of the judiciary. The judiciary must constitute the jury before it can act. Contrast this with examples of the power of traditional actors to exercise power on their own: the legislature enacts laws; the President takes action as the Commander in Chief of the Army and Navy; and states enact legislation. Indeed, the judiciary's review of the power of traditional actors often takes place after a traditional actor acts in the first instance. Unlike its authority over the traditional actors, the judiciary can prevent the jury from acting at all. No jury is convened unless the judiciary facilitates the creation of one.

The second characteristic of the jury that differs from the traditional actors that has contributed to its decline is the significant interrelationship between its authority and the judiciary's. While the jury competes with the judiciary for authority like the traditional actors do, in contrast to the traditional actors, the judiciary's reviews of the jury's power most often involve the judiciary's review of its own competing authority. If the judiciary resolves a question of jury authority favorably toward the jury, the judiciary denies itself power.

Third, unlike the jury, the traditional actors have power to counter impingement on their own authority by the judiciary or another actor. When a law is deemed unconstitutional, Congress is not without remedy. It can enact another piece of legislation testing the boundaries of its authority. Furthermore, the judiciary or another traditional actor may exercise self-restraint because of the power that the other traditional actors can exercise against them. Judges may act in a certain manner because legislators can impeach them or increase their salaries. Judges may take certain action because the President can promote them. States can influence the other traditional actors through voting.[133] The legislature can block the executive's choice of judges through filibuster or a vote of no confirmation. The legislature also can block the executive's appointments to the executive administrative agencies – for example, the National Labor Relations Board or the Consumer Protection Bureau. At the same time, through regulation, the executive can attempt to add law that Congress will not pass, for example, environmental rules. These interrelationships can affect the actions of the traditional actors. An actor

---

[133] Herbert Wechsler argued that while scholarship had been focused on the distribution of authority to states, the influence of the states on the national government through selection of Congress and the President was actually more important to the balance between the states and the federal government under federalism than the particular authority distributed to the states. *See* Herbert Wechsler, *The Political Safeguards of Federalism: The Role of the States in the Composition and Selection of the National Government*, 54 COLUM. L. REV. 543, 544 (1954).

may be more reticent to take action against another actor when they know the actor can affect them negatively.

In contrast, the jury has little ability to affect the power of judges or the other traditional actors. The criminal jury can nullify through its verdict after a judge constitutes the jury and gives the case to the jury. However, under modern rules, the judge can still acquit if a jury convicts. Because the jury can provide no benefit to the traditional actors that the actors cannot derive on their own, the jury also has no implicit effect on the traditional actors' authority against it. No mutual relationship incentivizes the traditional actors to aid the jury; for example, Congress has no incentive as a result of its relationship with the jury to create legislation granting the jury authority that has not been recognized under the Constitution.

Even if the other traditional actors want to help the jury, they do not have the power to fully counter the Supreme Court's impingement of the jury's authority. Arguably, Congress can legislate a jury trial right for crimes or claims that the Court has deemed not to require a jury trial right. But once a jury trial right exists, the Court retains significant power to affect that right through mechanisms that it deems constitutional.

At times the other traditional actors work with the judiciary against jury authority instead of helping the jury counter the judiciary. Congress can enact criminal statutes with significant mandatory sentences. Prosecutors can use those statutes to charge defendants and incentivize pleas. The courts then decide whether the pleas are knowing and voluntary. The end result is juries are eliminated from the process.

The Supreme Court's Shifting Opinions of the Jury

These differences between the jury and the traditional actors provide only a partial explanation of why the Court and other traditional actors have not acknowledged the jury as part of the constitutional structure, and have taken its authority. If these were the sole causes of the jury's decline, the Court or the traditional actors would have taken authority from the jury continuously after the enactment of the Constitution. However, the Supreme Court has recognized significant authority in the jury at different times, including in the late nineteenth century. As a result, there must be some other reason or reasons for the shift in authority to the traditional actors and the decline of the jury.

Decisions of the Supreme Court first recognizing authority in the jury and later shifting authority away from the jury offer reasons for the decline. I have found nine circumstances in which the Supreme Court

Figure 1 PRO-JURY AND ANTI-JURY CASES, 1866–2007

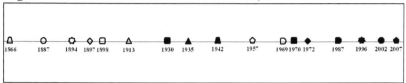

No fill = pro-jury
Solid fill = anti-jury

originally granted authority to the grand, criminal, or civil jury and later, decided against such authority. Some of these shifts have been described in this chapter as well as in Chapter 2. In these decisions illustrated by the symbols in Figure 1, the Court recognized significant authority in the jury in the late nineteenth century through the early twentieth century from 1866 to 1913.

By the 1930s, the Court had changed its mind and shifted authority from the jury to itself and other non-jury tribunals. In this specific set of cases, the trend of shifting authority away from the jury remained consistent from the 1930s onward except for two times in 1957 and 1969, when the Court recognized significant authority in the jury but later changed its mind in 2007 and 1987 respectively.[134]

Commentaries do reveal significant restrictions on jury authority prior to the shifts of authority from the jury to the traditional actors that are illustrated in Figure 1. Scholars have written about constraints on the jury's authority that judges and legislatures have imposed since the founding and have emphasized the influence of legal elites. William Nelson has written that distrust of juries to find law came with economic development and differences in "ethical values and assumptions" among people in states such as Massachusetts in the nineteenth century. In this time period, states began to set aside jury verdicts that judges deemed

---

[134] *Compare Ex parte* Milligan, 71 U.S. 2 (1866) and *Ex parte* Quirin, 317 U.S. 1 (1942); *Ex parte* Bain, 121 U.S. 1 (1887) and United States v. Cotton, 535 U.S. 625 (2002); City of Lincoln v. Power, 151 U.S. 436 (1894) and Gasperini v. Center for Humanities, 518 U.S. 415 (1996); American Pub. Co. v. Fisher, 166 U.S. 464 (1897) and Apodaca v. Oregon, 406 U.S. 404 (1972); Thompson v. Utah, 170 U.S. 343 (1898) and Patton v. United States, 281 U.S. 276 (1930) and Williams v. Florida, 399 U.S. 78 (1970); Slocum v. New York Life Ins. Co., 228 U.S. 364 (1913) and Baltimore & Carolina Line v. Redman, 295 U.S. 654 (1935); Conley v. Gibson, 355 U.S. 41 (1957) and Bell Atlantic Corp. v. Twombly, 550 U.S. 544 (2007); O'Callahan v. Parker, 395 U.S. 258 (1969) and Solorio v. United States, 483 U.S. 435 (1987).

contrary to the weight of the evidence. Nelson concluded that "the law came to be a tool by which those interest groups that had emerged victorious in the competition for control of law-making institutions could seize most of society's wealth for themselves and enforce their seizure upon the losers."[135] Morton Horwitz also wrote that judges "regularly" set aside verdicts for being contrary to law. They also began to characterize other matters as matters of law, on which they could rule. This included ordering new trials for jury decisions they deemed contrary to the weight of the evidence. State legislatures also removed some damages issues from the jury's purview. Horwitz wrote about the alliance between the bar and corporate interests as well as the alliance between the bar and the judiciary in this period. He stated that a measure of the alliance was the "swiftness with which the power of the jury [was] curtailed after 1790." This was accomplished through the use of procedures that gave judges authority to decide questions that effectively took the cases away from the jury. Horwitz wrote about the growing relationship between judges and companies and stated

> [o]ne of the great American transformations in the relations between judge and jury arose out of marine insurance cases at the beginning of the nineteenth century, when courts forged new procedural weapons that enabled them to reverse damage awards by juries.[136]

In the first period from 1866 to 1913 in Figure 1 when the Court decided several cases in favor of jury authority, there were also some cases in which the Court did not favor jury authority. For example, the Court decided several cases that supported the judge's power to direct the jury to find in a certain way if the judge thought the evidence supported that decision.[137] In this period, the Court also decided that juries could not find law.[138]

In the period from 1930 to 2007, when we see the Court decide several cases that disfavor jury authority, there were also other cases that favored jury authority. The so-called four horsemen, known for their conservative decisions, even decided cases that granted authority to the jury at times.

---

[135] WILLIAM E. NELSON, AMERICANIZATION OF THE COMMON LAW 165–70, 174 (1975). Juries continued to have some ability to find the law and fact in criminal cases. *See id.* at 257 n.37.

[136] *See* MORTON J. HORWITZ, THE TRANSFORMATION OF AMERICAN LAW 1780–1860, at 28–29, 84–85, 141–43, 228 (1977).

[137] *See Slocum*, 228 U.S. 364, 369 (1913) (citing several cases).

[138] *See* Sparf v. United States, 156 U.S. 51 (1895).

Barry Cushman points out, however, that it could have been to support the corporate greed of defendants who committed crimes.[139] Additional examples of cases favoring jury authority in the period 1930 to 2007 include a recent series of criminal cases about fact finding for sentencing.

The Supreme Court's historical treatment of the jury clearly varies with some decisions in favor and against jury authority in the nineteenth century and some decisions in favor and against jury authority in the twentieth century. With this said, examining decisions in which the Court changed its view of the jury's authority and reviewing the associated time periods may reveal some information on why the jury has declined over time.

In the decisions discussed earlier in which authority changed from pro-jury to anti-jury, the Court altered its characterization and corresponding treatment of the jury to deny it an essential role in government. In these cases, the Court proffered different reasons for the changes – none of which is sufficiently explanatory. It said that a previous case contained only dicta on an issue.[140] It also overruled decisions.[141] And it asserted that the facts encompassed by a past case were different from the ones in the case at hand.[142]

Public Opinion About the Jury

Additional information on the shift against jury authority may be derived from public articles written in the time period when the Supreme Court changed its mind on several issues concerning the jury. There is much scholarly literature on how the Supreme Court reacts to public opinion. Barry Friedman has argued that the Supreme Court is influenced by public opinion.[143] Studying this influence, Epstein and

---

[139] See Barry Cushman, *The Secret Lives of the Four Horsemen*, 83 Va. L. Rev. 559, 579–80 (1987).

[140] See Patton, 281 U.S. 276, 293 (1930) (regarding *Thompson*); Redman, 295 U.S. 654, 660 (1935) (regarding *Slocum*); Williams, 399 U.S. 78, 90–91 (1970) (regarding *Thompson*); Apodaca, 406 U.S. 404, 408–09 & n.4 (1972) (regarding *Fisher*).

[141] See Solorio, 483 U.S. 435, 436–46 (1987) (regarding *O'Callahan*); cf. Redman, 295 U.S. at 660 (regarding *Slocum*); Twombly, 550 U.S. 544, 562–63 (2007) (regarding *Conley*).

[142] See Quirin, 317 U.S. 1, 45–46 (1942) (regarding *Milligan*).

[143] See Barry Friedman, The Will of the People: How Public Opinion Has Influenced the Supreme Court and Shaped the Meaning of the Constitution (2009). Michael Link has written that the Supreme Court follows the public mood on certain issues more than others. See Michael W. Link, *Tracking Public Mood in the Supreme Court: Cross-Times Analyses of Criminal Procedure and Civil Rights Cases*, 48 Pol. Res. Q. 61 (1995).

Martin stated "[w]hat is surprising is that even after taking into account ideology, public mood continues to be a statistically significant and seemingly non-trivial predictor of outcomes." "When the 'mood of the public' is liberal (conservative), the Court is significantly more likely to issue liberal (conservative) decisions." They do not know why. It could be that the Court is following public opinion or, as members of the public, their opinions are similarly affected. They conclude that there is some association between public opinion and the decisions of the Court but cannot say definitely whether public mood influences decisions.[144] Lawrence Baum and Neal Devins add to this literature through their argument that the Court is more influenced by legal elites than by the public.[145]

Accepting that public opinion influences the Court, I analyzed public opinion in the time period surrounding the cases that were decided when the Supreme Court recognized jury authority (1866–1913) and when it began to change its decisions to not recognize such authority (1930–1942). I reviewed *New York Times* articles from 1851 (the date when the *New York Times* was established) to 1945 to encompass a time period before and after the time period in question. I specifically examined the articles that contained the term "juries." The *New York Times* has been intended to appeal to a more cultured, intellectual readership,[146] and thus these articles present information about public sentiment – though often the elite public sentiment – about the jury at the time. Indeed, this elite public sentiment could be different from public sentiment more generally.

These articles revealed much information about opinions regarding the jury. Beliefs about the jury were mixed. From the 1850s, criticism of the criminal, civil, and grand juries abounded. The jury was said to be too sympathetic, swayed by emotion. It was too easy on criminals.[147]

---

[144] Lee Epstein & Andrew D. Martin, *Does Public Opinion Influence the Supreme Court? Possibly Yes (But We're Not Sure Why)*, 13 U. Pa. J. Const. L. 263, 264, 279–80 (2010).

[145] *See* Lawrence Baum & Neal Devins, *Why the Supreme Court Cares About Elites, Not the American People*, 98 Geo. L.J. 1515 (2010).

[146] *See* Susan E. Tifft & Alex S. Jones, The Trust: The Private and Powerful Family Behind The New York Times (1999); *see also The New York Times*, Encyclopaedia Brittanica Online Academic Edition, Sept. 25, 2014.

[147] A correspondent for the *Cincinnati Gazette* criticized the result in a Cincinnati criminal case decided by a jury by describing that "the passions, prejudices and sympathies of the jury are clearly studied and brought to influence the decision; all the resources of eloquence and of ingenuity are exhausted in the endeavor, not to clear up obscurities and ascertain *the truth*, but to swerve the minds of the jury, and induce them to render a

Some complained that grand juries would not find an indictment when a person was guilty.[148] New York juries were referred to as "an infallible protection of lawlessness and license," and people who avoided jury service were blamed for this situation.[149] Moreover, workingmen were criticized as not having the qualifications to serve as jurors, and businessmen were viewed as the best jurors.[150]

In the wake of such criticism, efforts to reform the jury were attempted. These attempts included broadening the membership of the jury to include more businessmen by taking away exemptions and discouraging bribery to avoid service, not requiring unanimity, which "puts it in the power of one stupid or prejudiced person to block the course of justice altogether,"[151] and eliminating cast-iron jurymen, who were controlled by officials who chose them.[152]

Not only were juries criticized. Judges were called corrupt.[153] In this arena, the jury was recognized as the best method for resolving disputes. One article described the jury in the following manner:

> [a]t its best estate, trial by jury is only tolerable because no better way of approximating to the truth of guilt, or innocence, has been invented. That

verdict, in violation of their oath, on *other grounds* than those of fact – on grounds of prejudice, of sympathy, or of some other sentiment, honorable and just it may be, but utterly out of place in a judicial determination of matters of fact." *Criminal Trials*, N.Y. TIMES, May 5, 1854; *Sympathy for Criminals*, N.Y. TIMES, Mar. 27, 1858; *see Charge to a Grand Jury by a Philadelphia Judge*, N.Y. TIMES, Apr. 6, 1869 ("It is time that the bad should be made to feel the power of the law.").

[148] *The Grand Jury*, N.Y. TIMES, Nov. 28, 1871; *The Courts and the People*, N.Y. TIMES, Oct. 14, 1871.

[149] *Our Juries*, N.Y. TIMES, Mar. 11, 1873; *see* Civis, Letter to the Editor, *The Ethics of the Bar*, N.Y. TIMES, Mar. 11, 1873; Henry L. Clinton, Letter to the Editor, *Law Reforms*, N.Y. TIMES, Dec. 28, 1872.

[150] *Service on Juries*, N.Y. TIMES, May 10, 1867; *see The Jury System and its Defects*, N.Y. TIMES, Sept. 25, 1867 (discussing cost of repeated criminal trials when juries disagree and difficulty of obtaining sufficiently knowledgeable jurors for civil cases).

[151] *Trial by Jury*, N.Y. TIMES, June 1, 1871; *Working of the New Jury Law*, N.Y. TIMES, Oct. 18, 1870.

[152] For many years in the federal courts, the officials who selected jurors (who were thus able to give them pay) controlled them; the same people were selected time and time again for grand and criminal juries. The jurors were referred to as "cast-iron jurymen." While this changed, at times, criticisms were lodged that the same type of corruption continued to occur in certain cases. *See Our Jury System*, N.Y. TIMES, Feb. 6, 1873; *Juries in the Federal Courts*, N.Y. TIMES, Nov. 12, 1867; *Cast Iron Juries*, N.Y. TIMES, Oct. 23, 1860.

[153] *See "Let Him Go,"* N.Y. TIMES, Jan. 4, 1871.

it abounds with defects, and results too frequently in serious injustice, is the experience and opinion of the highest legal authorities.[154]

Around this time, Wisconsin abolished grand juries, and Justice Miller of the United States Supreme Court criticized this action. He stated "'that, could the fathers of this Republic see today the Grand Jury abolished, they would think us a very degraded people.'"[155]

The late nineteenth century brought more reasons to fault the jury. Railway ticket scalpers asserted that they did not fear the law because at least one juror would "refuse to allow wrong to be done."[156] An African-American congressman proposed a bill to have the federal courts try those accused of lynchings because southern juries would not convict.[157] In this period, there were also complaints from labor organizations that workingmen were not selected for grand juries and that the people selected "represented wealth or property."[158]

Confidence in the jury system nonetheless persisted. In the late nineteenth century, Joseph Choate, the president of the American Bar Association, gave a speech before the ABA that extolled the virtues of the jury system and its immortality. He said

> he had no fears for the safety of the jury system in this country. The 'learned essayists and philosophers,' whom he described as its enemies [who describe the jury as 'rotten' and 'out of date'], are never likely to become numerous or powerful enough to menace its existence. All the evils of the system are in the practice, not in the principle of it, and these are trivial, indeed, as compared with its benefits.[159]

[154] *Disagreeing Juries*, N.Y. TIMES, Jan. 16, 1856; *see How to Stop the Slave-trade*, N.Y. TIMES, Dec. 10, 1858 (recognizing juries would not convict slave-dealers but that "it does, in the long run, and on the whole, more good and less harm than any other system that has ever been devised, and we can only improve it by improving the public itself"); *Sentence of Another Slave-Trader*, N.Y. TIMES, Nov. 17, 1862 (describing change to convictions under "Anti-Slave-trade laws, which were before considered little else than a dead letter on the statute book").

[155] *The Abolition of Grand Juries in Wisconsin*, N.Y. TIMES, July 10, 1871.

[156] *Scalpers and Juries*, N.Y. TIMES, May 21, 1897

[157] *See The Trial of Lynchers*, N.Y. TIMES, Nov. 29, 1899.

[158] *"Labor" and the Grand Jury*, N.Y. TIMES, Dec. 2, 1896. The article discounted the complaint, stating that there was no showing that justice had not been accomplished under grand juries as constituted. *See id.*

[159] *Mr. Choate on the Jury System*, N.Y. TIMES, Aug. 19, 1898. He remarked that the instructions of judges were as responsible for jury disagreement as the incompetence of jurors. *Id.*

Around this same time period, a call for reform from the business community received praise. "It is an extremely encouraging sign that the scheme for securing jury reform is being taken up by the Chamber of Commerce and other business organizations." The Chamber represented those who were "deeply interested in good juries and that suffer most from the present imperfect and unequal system for obtaining juries." The article insisted that juries should be populated with these classes of people because of their intelligence, experience, and responsibility.[160] Special juries, which included people selected for their intelligence and experience, were established in New York in this time period, and later were criticized as intended to convict.[161]

In the early twentieth century, sentiments toward the jury remained mixed. Judge O'Sullivan of a New York state court spoke of his change of mind from observing juries over time, that though the system could be improved, juries should be trusted in both criminal and civil cases.[162] On the other hand, others, including some lawyers, continued to distrust juries.[163] Civil juries could hold prejudice against corporations.[164] One former juror wrote that the jurors on the jury on which he sat expressed opinions that the corporation should pay regardless of its fault and that judges were biased in favor of the corporations so their instructions should be ignored.[165] At the same time, there were allegations that jurors and judges were paid by corporations to find in their favor.[166] Criminal juries likewise could be biased. In the opinion of the former attorney general of Massachusetts, criminals in Boston did not fear conviction because juries could be bribed.[167] Moreover, southern

---

[160] *Good Juries*, N.Y. TIMES, Jan. 6, 1898; *cf.* EDWARD A. PURCELL, JR., LITIGATION AND INEQUALITY 202–03 (1992) (in 1870, federal judge recognizing that insurance companies tried to avoid juries).

[161] *See* Fay v. New York, 332 U.S. 261, 269 (1947); *"Blue-Ribbon" Jury Held Un-American*, N.Y. TIMES, Jan. 17, 1939 (criticized as "un-American and indefensible"); *Stryker Condemns Blue Ribbon Juries*, N.Y. TIMES, July 2, 1939. Those selected "represent[ed] the upper stratum of economic and social life in the County of New York," were conservative, and convicted more often. *Fay*, 332 U.S. at 290.

[162] *See Is Our Jury System a Failure?*, N.Y. TIMES, July 8, 1906.

[163] *See id.*; *English Recorder's View. Tells Grand Jury the British Trust Juries More Than Americans Do*, N.Y. TIMES, Apr. 14, 1907.

[164] *See Juries and Corporations*, N.Y. TIMES, June 5, 1901.

[165] *See* Letter to Editor, *Business Men at Fault*, N.Y. TIMES, Apr. 19, 1905. He said that sufficient business men generally were on juries and this ensured proper results but that business men should not avoid jury service because of these consequences. *See id.*

[166] *See Hired to Swing Juries in Car Suits, He Says*, N.Y. TIMES, Jan. 25, 1906.

[167] *See Says Boston Juries Have Proved Corrupt*, N.Y. TIMES, Sept. 12, 1923.

juries might not convict someone of murder of an African-American because of bribery or friendship.[168] Around this time period, at a meeting of the Committee on Law Enforcement of the American Bar Association, American juries were criticized as too lenient on crime, in comparison to juries in England and Canada. It was said that in most areas of the country, in capital cases, juries included "a large proportion of sentimental or imbecile jurymen." And as a result, changes in the composition of juries were advocated.[169]

In the late 1920s, the intensity of the criticism of the jury increased. Public officials spoke affirmatively in favor of a shift in authority from juries to judges to promote justice and democracy. In 1928, at a meeting of the New York branch of the Federal Bar Association, Charles Evans Hughes, a former and future United States Supreme Court justice, advocated greater power for judges and diminished authority for juries.

> Our hope for the progress of the administration of justice . . . lies not with juries, but with conscientious, able, industrious judges in the control of the business of their courts. Give the judge all the power he has and more, too. Of course, you must have able, conscientious men on the bench, but you will not get better judges by curtailing their functions and making them mere moderators of juries.

He urged "[g]et[ting] rid of jury trials as much as possible" and said "[o]ften it is almost impossible to get a satisfactory one." He called "the judge, the best servant in our democracy." Fifteen years earlier Justice Hughes was one of the justices in dissent in Slocum, one of the last significant pro-jury cases. The toastmaster of the event in which Hughes spoke, the United States Attorney Charles H. Tuttle, echoed Hughes' comments, recommending that Congress pass legislation passing more authority from the jury to the judge.[170] While Tuttle discussed independent investigation by the grand jury, he also suggested that minor felonies should not require a grand jury indictment.[171] The fact that Hughes and Tuttle held significant authority respectively in the Supreme Court and in the Executive, in addition to their obvious authority by their selection to address the New York branch of the Federal Bar Association, suggests that their anti-jury attitudes were not uncommon among other influential members of the bar. Hughes' subsequent election as the President of

[168] See Grand Juries and Bribery, N.Y. TIMES, July 7, 1901.
[169] Criminal Justice, N.Y. TIMES, June 3, 1922.
[170] See Fewer Jury Trials Urged by Hughes, N.Y. TIMES, Dec. 7, 1928.
[171] See Grand Jury Revives an Ancient Function, N.Y. TIMES, Aug. 26, 1928.

the American Bar Association in 1925 also suggests that his views may have been common to the legal community.[172]

In this same time period, a lawyer gave a speech in favor of "retention of the jury system," because "without it the United States would become corrupt."[173] This speech arguing for keeping the jury shows that there was a strong tide occurring against jury power. This same year, Justice McCook of the New York state courts advocated judges over juries.

> 'The jury is far from an efficient body, and never can be made so,' . . . 'Also, a Judge should be preferred to a jury because of the time saved to the public and to the citizen compelled to serve. The jury represents democracy applied to legal problems. Of these it often makes a mess, just as the voters often do of *political problems*.'[174]

Again, that this justice advocated publicly against jury authority and in favor of his own authority suggests that there was significant sentiment against the jury in important circles.

In this time frame, there is evidence that the jury acted against the law. Through the jury, the community was said to react against harsh sentences for violations of liquor laws, with decisions to acquit or verdicts of guilt of a lesser charge.[175] At the same time, the business community continued to push for reform. The Merchants' Association released statistics that showed "clerks and salesmen predominate on the juries of New York County, and that merchants, bankers and manufac-turers rarely are talesmen." It asserted more convictions for crimes would occur if more executives served.[176] The importance of juries to companies is further demonstrated by Macy's decision to pay its employees while they served on juries. The Executive Vice President of Macy's explained that

> '[t]he Merchants' Association report reveals that from one-half to two-thirds of those drawn for jury duty in 1927 successfully evaded it' . . . 'This unwillingness on the part of a class best qualified to serve [merchants,

---

[172] *See* American Bar Association 2014–2015 Leadership Directory 287 (ABA 2014).

[173] *Steuer Says Juries Usually are Right*, N.Y. TIMES, Dec. 28, 1928.

[174] *Justice Decries Juries*, N.Y. TIMES, Mar. 2, 1928. In a letter to the editor in this period, the author discusses the civil congestion due to trial by jury, most of which are negligence cases. He states that although companies insist on jury trials, judges could decide the cases better than juries and in less time. *See* Henry Waldman, Letter to the Editor, *Trials Without Juries*, N.Y. TIMES, Nov. 25, 1935.

[175] *See Liquor Laws and Juries*, N.Y. TIMES, Jan. 22, 1929, at 23.

[176] *Jury Duty Falls Mostly to Clerks*, N.Y. TIMES, July 12, 1928.

bankers, and manufacturers] interferes seriously with the administration of justice in our courts.'[177]

Some years later in the 1930s, past concern that juries would be biased against business persisted. An article discussed the increase in car insurance premiums because juries rendered "sympathetic and excessive verdicts."[178] Also elsewhere there was continued reference to "[i]f we are to retain the jury," an intimation that there continued to be opinion expressed that juries should decide fewer cases.[179]

At the same time that juries were criticized because they did not include sufficient businessmen, juries became more diverse in other ways. While African-Americans and women had served on juries in some parts of the country in the past, the rights of these groups became more firm in this period. The right of women to serve on juries was debated and upheld in certain localities.[180] The Supreme Court also decided that African-Americans could not be excluded from juries based on race or color.[181]

In the 1940s, different interest groups continued their efforts to diversify the jury by eliminating exemptions[182] and to include more women and African-Americans. However, judges had significant discretion to choose jurors.[183] During the war, when many men were away, it became more difficult to find jurors deemed qualified.[184] And in some places, only four jurors sat in civil cases.[185] At the same time,

---

[177] *Macy's to Pay Employees While They Serve on Juries*, N.Y. TIMES, Aug. 10, 1928.

[178] C.L. Mosher, *Fake Claims Bring High Rates*, N.Y. TIMES, Nov. 8, 1936; *see also* Vincent T. Russo, Letter to Editor, '*Sympathy Decisions*,' N.Y. TIMES, Nov. 4, 1936 (decisions by judges and jurors increase cost for insurance).

[179] Letter to the Editor, *Juries and Questions of Law*, N.Y. TIMES, Sept. 11, 1936.

[180] *See Women on the Juries: A Continuing Debate*, N.Y. TIMES, Mar. 15, 1931 (debate in New York state); *States that Admit Women Jurors*, N.Y. TIMES, Jan. 17, 1937; *Women 'Juries' Differ in Trying Same Case*, N.Y. TIMES, Sept. 23, 1937 (first women selected for criminal and grand juries in federal courts in state of New York); *Woman Juries Upheld*, N.Y. TIMES, Aug. 9, 1939; *Grand Jury Group Bars Women As Members in Westchester County*, N.Y. TIMES, Mar. 8, 1939; *Frees Women From Juries*, N.Y. TIMES, Feb. 15, 1939; *Law Expert Doubts Women's Right To Serve on Grand Juries Here*, N.Y. TIMES, Sept. 28, 1938.

[181] *See Norris v. Alabama*, 294 U.S. 587 (1935); *see also High Court States Negro Rights Anew*, N.Y. TIMES, May 14, 1935; *The Scottsboro Case*, N.Y. TIMES, Jan. 25, 1936 (describing unfair jury selection process that resulted in no African-Americans on the jury). The Supreme Court ordered a new trial of an African-American man convicted of murder of a white man by a jury that had excluded African-American membership. *See Court Saves Negro Doomed by Whites*, N.Y. TIMES, Dec. 9, 1947.

[182] *See Sheriff's Juries*, N.Y. TIMES, Mar. 12, 1945.

[183] *See Ask Women to Serve on Federal Juries*, N.Y. TIMES, Nov. 30, 1942.

[184] *See 'Twelve Good Men and True*,' N.Y. TIMES, Oct. 31, 1943.

[185] *See Ohio Courts Cut Jurors to 4*, N.Y. TIMES, Jan. 22, 1942.

blue-ribbon juries – "generally drawn from a social and economic class different from that of the accused" – continued to be criticized as insufficiently representative of the community.[186]

While grand juries continued to serve important roles, for example, in one instance issuing a report regarding bribery by public officials that involved the construction industry,[187] criticisms persisted, including allegations that the grand jury failed to indict when it should.[188] A measure to give juries additional power to recommend life sentences in all first-degree murder cases in New York carried few votes. One legislator stated that the jury "would 'pass the buck'" and judges would join in this recommendation.[189]

There was further emphasis that judges could better decide cases than jurors. "[A] judge, at worst, is apt to be more often right than a jury, and the poison of politics is a thing of the past, or almost so. It is not as much to be feared as bias among jurymen, especially in these times."[190] Also, in this time period, the selection of jurors in the United States was referred to as "so often" "the long farce" and was unfavorably compared to the proper selection of jurors in England.[191]

The articles reviewed here do not discuss the executive. At the time, the executive aided by the legislature also demonstrated a desire to shift matters from the jury to other tribunals over which it had control. These shifts coincide with the beginning of the rise of the administrative state around the time of the New Deal in the 1930s.[192] For example, on the labor side, Congress gave authority to the executive agency of the National Labor Relations Board to decide certain damages issues that arguably juries should have had authority to decide.

The articles reveal growing resistance to the jury's authority over time. The public statements of judges against jury authority and in favor of judicial authority in the late 1920s coincide with the shift in the case law against jury authority in the 1930s, illustrated in Figure 1. Moreover,

---

[186] *Bars Blue-Ribbon Jury*, N.Y. Times, Feb. 26, 1941.

[187] *See Amen Juries Warn of Graft in City*, N.Y. Times, June 12, 1942.

[188] *See Hudson Vote Frauds are Linked to Juries*, N.Y. Times, May 27, 1943; *Grand Jury Laxity Held Weakening Motor Law*, N.Y. Times, Aug. 14, 1943 (in New Jersey).

[189] *State Senate Kills Mercy Verdict Bill*, N.Y. Times, Apr. 2, 1941.

[190] Letter to the Editor, *Jury Trials Decreasing: Trend Discovered in England as Early as 1854*, N.Y. Times, Sept. 2, 1941.

[191] *An Old Right Suspended*, N.Y. Times, Aug. 30, 1941.

[192] *See, e.g.*, Gary Lawson, *The Rise and Rise of the Administrative State*, 107 Harv. L. Rev. 1231 (1994).

criticisms that the jury did not include sufficient businessmen occurred around this time period, as did legislative efforts to include businessmen on juries. Also, as the jury continued to be more diverse in gender and race, the jury was less desirable to judges and corporations. It appears that the legal elites opposed jury authority and acted against it, ultimately succeeding in influencing the Supreme Court.[193]

These articles are consistent with the theory that over time legal elites and corporations sought to shift authority from the jury to the traditional actors. For example, in reaction to the *Slocum* case in which the Supreme Court decided that the procedure of judgment notwithstanding the verdict violated the Seventh Amendment, a committee of the American Bar Association was empanelled to draft federal legislation to permit judges to direct a judgment. Some state legislatures themselves actually enacted such procedures. This activity culminated in the *Redman* decision in which the Court changed its decision in favor of jury authority to find against jury authority. This result was praised as consistent with the value of efficiency.[194]

*****

The traditional actors led by the Supreme Court have treated the jury differently than they have treated each other by denying any place for the jury in the constitutional structure. This has shifted jury authority to the traditional actors. As discussed here, why this shift has occurred, particularly in the 1930s, is a difficult question. While many reasons have been offered for the decline of the jury, such as the democratization of the jury, the question remains why has that "reason" contributed to the fall. For example, why has jury authority declined with the democratization of the jury? Previous literature, as well as public articles from the time period, reveal that the Supreme Court likely has been influenced by legal elites as well as by corporations to reduce jury authority over time.[195] There have been relationships between these

---

[193] Indeed, connected to this idea of the influence of elites on the jury, the New Deal has been said to "possess an ideological character, a moral perspective, and a set of political relationships among policy elites, interest groups, and electoral constituencies that decidedly shaped American political life for forty years." THE RISE AND FALL OF THE NEW DEAL ORDER 1930–1980, at xi (Steve Fraser & Gary Gerstle eds., 1989).

[194] *See* Lerner, *supra* note 13, at 876–88.

[195] *See also* BURNS, *supra* note 8, at 91–97; Marc Galanter, *A World Without Trials?*, 2006 J. DISP. RESOL. 1, 13; Edward J. Devitt, *Federal Civil Jury Trials Should Be Abolished*, 60 A.B.A. J. 570 (1974) (Chief Judge of the United States District Court for Minnesota arguing for abolishing jury trial).

actors and all of them have something to gain when the jury loses authority. They acquire power.

Conclusion

Over the years, many different reasons have been offered for the declines of the criminal, civil, and grand juries, and their falls have not been connected. Primarily blamed are their purported incompetency, inaccuracy, inefficiency, and cost. The falls have not been associated with the previously unrecognized phenomenon of the traditional actors' usurpation of the jury's authority.

While the Supreme Court has protected and limited the traditional actors' powers under the doctrines of separation of powers and federalism, it has not recognized a similar doctrine to protect and limit the separate power of the jury despite similar empowering text in the Constitution and the like intentions of the Founders of the Constitution and ratifiers of the Fourteenth Amendment. Instead, the Court has often originally acknowledged the jury's power, only to later deny the same. Deprived of doctrine legitimizing the jury as a separate power, the jury has lost significance with each decision in which the Court shifted its authority to a traditional actor. This doctrinal void along with the jury's unique characteristics as unable to combat infringements on its authority place the jury in a precarious position in the constitutional structure. The cause of this treatment of the jury and thus its decline likely includes the influence of legal elites and corporations on the Supreme Court.

PART II

The Future Jury

4

Interpreting Jury Authority

The American jury today resembles neither its English predecessor nor the jury envisioned by many of the Founders. Thus far, the book has assumed that the jury that existed in England in the late eighteenth century and the jury discussed by the Founders form the model for the jury under Article III, the Seventh Amendment, and the Fifth Amendment. This Chapter explores whether the Supreme Court and the other traditional actors – the executive, the legislature, the other courts, and the states – should interpret the jury provisions based on this jury of the past.

How Should the Traditional Actors Interpret the Jury Provisions?

The fall of the criminal, civil, and grand juries is linked to several related factors discussed in Chapter 3. First, the Supreme Court has failed to treat the jury in a similar manner to the traditional actors. Despite parallels in the constitutional text and the likeness of the Founders' discussion of the traditional actors and the jury, the Court has not recognized doctrine analogous to separation of powers or federalism to protect the jury's authority. Second, it appears that no such doctrine has been established for the jury, at least in part because of the self-interest of the traditional actors, who benefit from shifts in authority from the jury to themselves. Third, the unique characteristics of the jury have contributed to its fall. The jury cannot decide cases without a traditional actor permitting the jury to do so. The jury also has no ability to affect the power of the traditional actors and thus, has no opportunity to influence those decision-makers to act more favorably toward it. Fourth, legal elites and companies appear to have influenced the decline.

The traditional actors' future recognition of the jury as essentially a "branch" of the government under a protective doctrine analogous to separation of powers or federalism could help restore the jury's power. Of course, the Supreme Court must be willing to change its jurisprudence.

And even if doctrine similar to the separation of powers or federalism were established for the jury, it could still remain at a disadvantage to the traditional actors due to the jury's lack of ability to act independently and its insufficient influence on the traditional actors. Thus, for the jury to be able to exercise the constitutional authority granted to it – whatever that is – the traditional actors may need to defer to the jury. While at times the traditional actors already act in this manner toward one another – whether they try to operate within constitutional bounds or whether they need to do so in order for their fellow traditional actors not to act against them – the question here concerns whether the Constitution actually requires the traditional actors to employ doctrine and create additional safeguards to protect the jury's authority.

Originalism and the Constitution

In interpreting the jury provisions, the Supreme Court has purported to apply some type and degree of originalism – a debated methodology by which interpretation of the Constitution occurs based on the original meaning of the Constitution. Some have argued that the Framers intended for the Constitution to be interpreted according to originalism.[1] Others have contended that regardless of the Framers' intention regarding originalism, an originalist interpretation of the Constitution is the only way that the Constitution's meaning will not change according to the particular inclinations of the justices interpreting the Constitution. Additional justifications – not discussed here – have also been offered for originalism.[2]

Many, however, oppose originalism, arguing that it stifles the meaning of the Constitution when society continues to change. Under this view, originalism does not adequately account for evolving values and circumstances. Instead, the use of living constitutionalism, which attempts to take into account these concerns, is a better way to interpret the Constitution.[3]

---

[1] *See* RAOUL BERGER, GOVERNMENT BY JUDICIARY 4 (2d ed. 1997). *But see* H. Jefferson Powell, *The Original Understanding of Original Intent*, 98 HARV. L. REV. 885 (1985).

[2] For extensive discussions of the normative justifications of originalism, *see* THE CHALLENGE OF ORIGINALISM: THEORIES OF CONSTITUTIONAL INTERPRETATION (Grant Huscroft & Bradley W. Miller eds., 2011).

[3] *See* DAVID A. STRAUSS, THE LIVING CONSTITUTION 1 (2010) ("A 'living constitution' is one that evolves, changes over time, and adapts to new circumstances, without being formally amended"); *see also* ROBERT W. BENNETT & LAWRENCE B. SOLUM,

For originalists, the prevailing view of originalism refers to the original public meaning of the Constitution, as opposed to, for example, the intentions of the Framers or ratifiers. Under this form of originalism, regardless of the Founders' different reasons for adopting the constitutional text, the text was adopted, and the original public meaning of that text best captures the Constitution's meaning.[4]

While justices of the Supreme Court agree that originalism plays some role in constitutional interpretation, they have disagreed about how much influence it should have.[5] Dependent upon the beliefs of different justices who have sat on the Court over time or the particular issues that have come to the Court, originalism has had more or less influence in the Court's decisions.[6]

A Brief History of the Origins and Interpretation of the Seventh Amendment

To decide how the jury provisions should be construed, including whether they should be interpreted through the use of originalism, the Seventh Amendment is arguably the best place to start. It is the only provision in the entire Constitution to refer explicitly to originalism – there, by its use of "common law" and "preserved" – terms that the Supreme Court has stated are tied to originalism. It provides

CONSTITUTIONAL ORIGINALISM (2011) (debating originalism and living constitutionalism). Recently, the presumed incompatibility of originalism and living constitutionalism has been challenged. JACK M. BALKIN, LIVING ORIGINALISM (2011).

[4] See Lawrence B. Solum, *What Is Originalism? The Evolution of Contemporary Theory* in THE CHALLENGE OF ORIGINALISM, *supra* note 2, at 22–24, 30–32. There are many versions of originalism. Lawrence Solum has discussed originalists' disagreement on how "fixation" occurs, on the form of the constraint, the extent to which context affects the text's meaning, and the intensity of any "construction zone," which involves ambiguous text, vague text, contradictory text, and textual gaps in the Constitution. *See, e.g.*, Lawrence B. Solum, *Originalism and Constitutional Construction*, 82 FORDHAM L. REV. 453 (2013). This book does not enter into the scholarly debate about Solum or others' descriptions of originalism.

[5] See Stephen E. Sachs, *Originalism as a Theory of Legal Change*, 38 HARV. J. L & PUB. POL'Y 817, 830–32 (2015). Sachs stated "[m]ost everyone accepts that some kind of original meaning is legally relevant sometimes; the only live disputes are what kind of original meaning, how much it contributes, and whether and when other sources can validly supplement or supplant that meaning." *See id.*

[6] For example, originalism as a theory of interpretation became significant in the 1980s, when Judge Robert Bork and then-Judge Antonin Scalia promoted the theory. *See* Keith E. Whittington, *Originalism: A Critical Introduction*, 82 FORDHAM L. REV. 375, 375–76 (2013).

[i]n Suits at common law, where the value in controversy shall exceed twenty dollars, the right of trial by jury shall be preserved, and no fact tried by a jury, shall be otherwise re-examined in any Court of the United States, than according to the rules of the common law.[7]

The meaning of the Seventh Amendment is unclear from its text and the actual records surrounding its adoption.[8] As a result, it has been the subject of much research and debate. There was little discussion of the civil jury trial in the federal convention. Although one delegate argued that the jury was necessary to protect against "corrupt Judges," others recognized difficulty in expressing the cases in which a civil jury trial was warranted, and some argued that the legislature could be "trusted" to determine the cases in which juries were required. Thereafter, a proposal to add language to Article III stating "a trial by jury shall be preserved as usual in civil cases" failed. Delegates stated that differences in the states' jury trials made what was "*usual*" impossible to determine. They emphasized that "such a clause in the Constitution would be pregnant with embarrassments."[9]

Significant concern mounted after the Constitution was adopted, granting the Supreme Court appellate jurisdiction over law and fact but providing no jury trial for civil cases.[10] Congress subsequently passed the United States Judiciary Act of 1789, which among other things, granted power to juries to try "issues in fact, in the district courts, in all causes except civil causes of admiralty and maritime jurisdiction." The Act also gave the judiciary certain authority over the facts that juries tried, presenting it power to order new trials "for the reasons for which new trials ha[d] usually been granted in the courts of law."[11] Just a day after

---

[7] U.S. Const. amend. VII.

[8] *See* Charles W. Wolfram, *The Constitutional History of the Seventh Amendment*, 57 Minn. L. Rev. 639, 652 (1973) ("[T]he original understanding can be only imperfectly perceived today.").

[9] J. Madison, *Debates in the Federal Convention*, *in* 2 The Records of the Federal Convention of 1787, at 587–88, 628 (Max Farrand ed., 1911) (Mr. Gerry, Mr. Gorham, and Col. Mason).

[10] *See* Edith G. Henderson, *The Background of the Seventh Amendment*, 80 Harv. L. Rev. 289, 295 (1966); Wolfram, *supra* note 8, at 667–73, 678–79, 693–94.

[11] Judiciary Act of 1789, ch. 20, §§ 9, 17, 1 Stat. 73 (Sept. 24, 1789) (An Act to Establish the Judicial Courts of the United States). The authority of juries over facts was also expressed elsewhere in the Act. "[T]he trial of issues in fact in the circuit courts shall, in all suits, except those of equity, and of admiralty, and maritime jurisdiction, be by jury." *Id.* at § 12. "[T]he trial of issues of fact in the Supreme Court, in all actions at law against citizens of the United States, shall be by jury." *Id.* at § 13; *see also id.* § 7.

the Act was passed, Congress proposed the Seventh Amendment to the states,[12] and it was subsequently adopted in 1791.

In interpreting the Seventh Amendment, the Supreme Court has decided two issues. First, it has determined when a jury trial is required, and second, it has decided whether a procedure that affects the jury trial is constitutional. In these evaluations, the focus has been on the Amendment's "common law" language. In the Seventh Amendment, "common law" – which governs the types of cases in which the jury trial is "preserved" and also how the judiciary can re-examine facts tried by a jury – could refer to a variety of practices. It could refer to the practice of the English common law courts, to the practice of the state courts, or to the practice of the federal courts. Common law could be those practices in 1791 when the Amendment was adopted; thus, the term could mean the English common law in 1791, state common law in 1791, or federal common law in 1791. Alternatively, it could refer to the English common law, the individual practices of the state courts, or the law of the federal courts at any point in time. Other possible interpretations could include the statutory law of England, the states, or the federal government.

In the early nineteenth century, Justice Story stated that "common law" in the Seventh Amendment could not mean the law of the individual states. "[B]eyond all question" common law meant the English common law. He explained that

> the common law here alluded to is not the common law of any individual state, (for it probably differs in all), but it is the common law of England,

---

[12] The history of the language of the Amendment is not completely clear because of the lack of record keeping. Madison proposed the first version to the House of Representatives on June 8, 1789, as "[i]n suits at common law, between man and man, the trial by jury, as one of the best securities to the rights of the people, ought to remain inviolate," along with "nor shall any fact triable by jury, according to the course of common law, be otherwise re-examinable than may consist with the principles of common law." 1 ANNALS OF CONG. 435 (1789). On August 17, 1789, a committee of the House considered "nor shall any fact, triable by jury according to the course of the common law, be otherwise re-examinable than according to the rules of the common law." 1 ANNALS OF CONG. 755 (1789). On August 18, 1789, the proposal for "'[i]n suits at common law, the right of trial by jury shall be preserved,' was considered and adopted" by the House. 1 ANNALS OF CONG. 760 (1789). The House adopted this version on August 21, 1789. 1 ANNALS OF CONG. 767 (1789). On September 7, the Senate added an amount in controversy requirement. 1 ANNALS OF CONG. 76 (1789). On September 25, 1789, the Senate adopted the language "[i]n suits at common law, where the value in controversy shall exceed twenty dollars, the right of trial by jury shall be preserved; and no fact, tried by a jury, shall be otherwise re-examined in any court of the United States, than according to the rules of common law." 2 BERNARD SCHWARTZ, THE BILL OF RIGHTS: A DOCUMENTARY HISTORY 1165 (1971).

the grand reservoir of all our jurisprudence. It cannot be necessary for me
to expound the grounds of this opinion, because they must be obvious to
every person acquainted with the history of the law.[13]

Soon thereafter, the Supreme Court adopted Justice Story's interpretation of common law.[14] Although the Court did not refer specifically to
England and 1791, it mentioned past practices, and the Court subsequently confirmed that the common law in the Seventh Amendment
meant the English common law in 1791.[15]

In its decisions, the Court has recognized that the English common
law in 1791 influences the extent of the jury trial right under the first
clause of the Amendment. It has also used this common law to determine
whether new procedures that affect the jury trial right, under the first and
second clauses, are constitutional.

At English common law, cases with monetary damages almost invariably rested with juries.[16] Consistent with this, the Court has interpreted
the jury trial right to extend to causes of action with monetary remedies,
including ones that existed in England, and ones that did not exist in
England, at the time of the Amendment's adoption. Under this jurisprudence, the Court generally has found a jury trial right if the new claims
are similar in nature to those at English common law.[17] For example, a
jury trial right existed in a housing discrimination suit in which the
plaintiff alleged monetary damages because housing discrimination cases
were comparable to torts cases.[18] On the other hand, the Court has
approved congressional decisions to place certain matters that involve
money damages with administrative law judges instead of juries.[19] Moreover, in its Seventh Amendment jurisprudence to decide whether a case
goes to a jury, the Court has ventured beyond the historical analysis and
assessed "the practical abilities and limitations of juries."[20]

---

[13] United States v. Wonson, 28 F. Cas. 745, 750 (No. 16, 750) (C.C.D. Mass. 1812).
[14] See Parsons v. Bedford, 28 U.S. 433, 446–48 (1830).
[15] See Dimick v. Schiedt, 293 U.S. 474, 476–85 (1935) (examining English common law case
law and treatises before and after the adoption of the Seventh Amendment); see Wolfram,
supra note 8, at 642 (citing Thompson v. Utah, 170 U.S. 343 (1898), the first case
mentioning the specific date).
[16] See Suja A. Thomas, A Limitation on Congress: "In Suits at common law," 71 OHIO ST. L.J.
1071 (2010).
[17] See City of Monterey v. Del Monte Dunes at Monterey, Ltd., 526 U.S. 687, 715 (1999).
[18] See Curtis v. Loether, 415 U.S. 189 (1974).
[19] See NLRB v. Jones Laughlin Steel Corp., 301 U.S. 1 (1937).
[20] Ross v. Bernhard, 396 U.S. 531, 538 n.10 (1970).

Over time, the Court has taken a similar approach when assessing whether new procedures that affect the jury trial are constitutional. As described in other chapters, originally, the Court found that they did not exist in late eighteenth-century England and therefore, were unconstitutional.[21] But later, in other decisions, the Court interpreted the Seventh Amendment more broadly. Although it reasonably stated that the "'substance'" of the jury trial right at English common law, not its form, must be preserved,[22] the substance of the right was loosely defined. The substance concerned decisional authority. Judges were said to decide law and juries facts.[23] However, certain issues, previously designated as factual and for juries at common law, were re-characterized as legal questions for judges.[24] The Court also began to raise consideration of the past practices of some state courts along with the English common law practices to determine whether a procedure was constitutional.[25] Under its analyses, the Supreme Court found constitutional almost all of the new procedures that it examined,[26] including procedures previously deemed unconstitutional under the original test. So, the Court has made the historical test softer over time, and this has shifted authority from the jury to the traditional actors, which have been given authority that they did not hold in late eighteenth-century England.

The Future Interpretation of the Seventh Amendment

How should the traditional actors interpret the Seventh Amendment? As previously discussed, the Seventh Amendment expressly functions to grant and limit the judiciary's and jury's authority. Also, recall that the

---

[21] *See* Slocum v. New York Life Ins. Co., 228 U.S. 364 (1913).

[22] Colgrove v. Battin, 413 U.S. 149, 155–56 (1973) (quoting Baltimore & Carolina Line v. Redman, 295 U.S. 654, 657 (1935)).

[23] *See* Suja A. Thomas, *The Seventh Amendment, Modern Procedure, and the English Common Law*, 82 WASH. U. L.Q. 687, 696–702 (2004) (discussing cases).

[24] *See* Gasperini v. Center for Humanities, Inc., 518 U.S. 415, 435 (1996).

[25] The significance of this particular change invoking state practices is unclear. In dicta, in *Markman*, Justice Souter, who wrote for the Court, raised the issue of the relevance of state common law. He stated "the historical test do[es] not deal with the possibility of conflict between actual English common law practice and American assumptions about what the practice was, or between English and American practices at the relevant time. No such complications arise in this case." *See* Markman v. Westview Instruments, Inc., 517 U.S. 370, 376 n.3 (1996). Although the Supreme Court has compared these practices, there has never been a case when the state practice differed in such a manner that the English common law was not followed at least in name. Wolfram, *supra* note 8, at 641.

[26] *See Gasperini*, 518 U.S. at 436 & n.20 (1996).

jury itself cannot prevent or act against any incursions on its authority. Using originalism to interpret the Amendment would establish significant boundaries on the authority of the judiciary and the jury. The following section describes an interpretation of the Amendment according to originalism. After that description, the next section explores the possibility of a different, evolving, or living constitution method of interpretation of the Amendment.

Original Public Meaning of the Seventh Amendment

As already mentioned, how to interpret the Constitution according to originalism is debated, but the original public meaning is a generally accepted methodology. An example of the use of the original public meaning to interpret a provision of the Constitution is found in *District of Columbia v. Heller*. There, the Court described originalism based on the original public meaning as

> '[t]he Constitution was written to be understood by the voters; its words and phrases were used in their normal and ordinary as distinguished from technical meaning.' . . . Normal meaning may of course include an idiomatic meaning, but it excludes secret or technical meanings that would not have been known to ordinary citizens in the founding generation.[27]

Among other sources used to determine the original public meaning of terms in the Second Amendment were the 1773 edition of Samuel Johnson's *Dictionary of the English Language*, the 1771 edition of Timothy Cunningham's *A New and Complete Law Dictionary*, state laws, Blackstone's treatise, other treatises, and works of the Founders. In the following section, the original public meanings of the major terms of the Seventh Amendment are explored using these guides.[28]

"**common law**" In the first clause of the Seventh Amendment, "common law" is used to describe the cases in which a right to jury trial is preserved. In the second clause, it is used to limit the authority of the judiciary to re-examine facts tried by juries in those common law suits. Samuel Johnson's dictionary defined common law as "[c]ustoms which have by long prescription obtained the force of laws; distinguished from the statute law, which owes its authority to acts of

---

[27] 554 U.S. 570, 576 (quoting United States v. Sprague, 282 U.S. 716, 731 (1931)).
[28] *See* 554 U.S. 570 (2008); *see also* Solum, *What Is Originalism?*, *supra* note 4, at 30–31.

parliament."[29] In his description of the history of the term, Timothy Cunningham stated that the law applied to "the whole kingdom" as opposed to "only several parts thereof" and "was therefore properly called the *Common law*, because it was *common* to the whole nation." He also stated that there were three important characteristics of the common law.

> [F]irst, it is taken for the laws of this realm simply, without any other law joined to it; . . . Secondly, For [sic] the *King's court*, as the *King's Bench* or *Common Pleas*, only to shew [sic] a difference between them and the base courts. . . . Thirdly, and most usually, By [sic] the *Common law* is understood such laws as were generally taken and holden for law, before any statute was made to alter the same.[30]

In his treatise, Blackstone stated that these legal customs could be found "in the records of the several courts of justice, in books of reports and judicial decisions, and in the treatises of learned sages of the profession, preserved and handed down to us from the times of highest antiquity." He further described that "they receive their binding power, and the force of laws, by long and immemorial usage, and by their universal reception throughout the kingdom."[31] All of these English sources emphasized one long existing law that derived from courts – not from the legislature – that applied to the whole nation. There was one such law in existence in the late eighteenth century – the English common law.

William Stoebuck has analyzed the extent to which the colonies adopted the English common law. He said that over time, especially in the late seventeenth century into the eighteenth century, the English common law had a growing, significant influence due to several factors. In this time period, more American lawyers became trained in the law, some in England. As the colonies stabilized, additional, mature legal systems based on what was known – the English common law – were established. Although England had interest in the colonies in this period, which caused some additional influence of the English common law, England did not dictate that the common law be applied in the colonies, so any adoption of the English common law by states was voluntary. Stoebuck concluded that

---

[29] 1 SAMUEL JOHNSON, A DICTIONARY OF THE ENGLISH LANGUAGE (5th ed. 1773).

[30] 1 TIMOTHY CUNNINGHAM, A NEW AND COMPLETE LAW DICTIONARY (2d ed. 1771).

[31] 1 WILLIAM BLACKSTONE, COMMENTARIES ON THE LAWS OF ENGLAND 63–64 (University of Chicago Press 1979) (1765).

the [English] common law was applied in substantially the same fashion when the Revolution began as it was in the first days of the Republic. . . . reading the post-Revolutionary cases perceives that the bench and bar were using long-accustomed processes, mental and judicial, for deciding cases. The whole tenor of the opinions is quite convincing that except for some statutes, the judges were applying the same body of law they had long known.[32]

In eighteenth-century material, references to common law often are explicitly to the English common law, including in legal documents that applied to all of the colonies. For example, in 1774, representatives of the colonies who met in Philadelphia drafted the Declaration and Resolves of the First Continental Congress, which was sent to England. The fifth right specifically referred to the privilege of trial by jury according to the English common law. It stated "[t]hat the respective colonies are entitled to the common law of England, and more especially to the great and inestimable privilege of being tried by their peers of the vicinage, according to the course of that law."[33] The English common law was also explicitly adopted in certain state statutes. For example, in 1786, the Constitution of New York stated that the law in New York generally included the common law of England.

> And this Convention doth further, in the Name and by the Authority of the good People of this State, ORDAIN, DETERMINE AND DECLARE, That such Parts of the common Law of *England*, and of the Statute Law of *England* and *Great-Britain*, and of the Acts of the Legislature of the Colony of *New-York*, as together did form the Law of the said Colony on the *Nineteenth* Day of *April*, in the Year of our Lord, one Thousand Seven Hundred and Seventy-five, shall be and continue the Law of this State; subject to such Alterations and Provisions as the Legislature of this State shall, from Time to Time, make concerning the same.[34]

Further, in 1787, the Statutes of the state of Vermont also adopted the English common law. It set forth

> An act adopting the common & statute law of England . . . That so much of the common law of England as is not repugnant to the constitution, or to any act of the legislature of this state, be, and is hereby adopted, and

---

[32] William B. Stoebuck, *Reception of English Common Law in the American Colonies*, 10 WM. & MARY L. REV. 393, 396–426 (1968).

[33] DECLARATION AND RESOLVES OF THE FIRST CONTINENTAL CONGRESS (Oct. 14, 1774).

[34] 1 LAWS OF THE STATE OF NEW YORK COMPRISING THE CONSTITUTION AND THE ACTS OF THE LEGISLATURE SINCE THE REVOLUTION, FROM THE FIRST TO THE TWELFTH SESSION, INCLUSIVE 12, 281 (1789).

shall be and continue to be, law within this State. And whereas the statute law of England is so connected and interwoven with the common law, that our jurisprudence would be incomplete without it: Therefore, . . . That such statute laws and parts of laws, of the Kingdom of England and Great-Britain, . . . for the explanation of the common law, . . . shall be, and continue to be, law within this State.[35]

In some other places, it seems apparent that the English common law applied although it was not specifically mentioned. For example, when Congress used common law to describe the judicial proceedings in the Northwest Ordinance in 1787, the English common law was the most familiar and relevant law.

The Inhabitants of the said territory shall always be entitled to the benefits of the writ of habeas corpus, and of the trial by Jury; of a proportionate representation of the people in the legislature, and of judicial proceedings according to the course of the common law.[36]

No common law existed for these areas so some other common law was intended. Given the differences of the common law in the states, states' common law could not have been referenced. On the other hand, the English common law is the most likely because of the history of this common law to America.

Similar to this congressional designation of "common law" without a specific tie to the English common law, several states likewise used "common law" in their individual laws. Again the states were likely referring to the English common law, because of the influence of this law on the states and the relative youth of the states' own laws.[37]

---

[35] STATUTES OF THE STATE OF VERMONT 28 (1791).

[36] An ordinance for the government of the territory of the United States, North-west of the river Ohio.

[37] In 1788, the Laws of the state of New-York stated that the African-Americans and other slaves accused of capital crimes should have the privilege of trial by jury "according to the course of the common law." LAWS OF THE STATE OF NEW-YORK, PASSED BY THE LEGISLATURE OF SAID STATE, AT THEIR ELEVENTH SESSION 77 (1788). In 1788, the perpetual laws, of the Commonwealth of Massachusetts also refer to common law, which again must reference the common law of England especially given that it states "no punishments shall be inflicted but such as have been known and accustomed at common law," again a reference to law that has existed for some time. THE PERPETUAL LAWS, OF THE COMMONWEALTH OF MASSACHUSETTS, FROM THE ESTABLISHMENT OF ITS CONSTITUTION TO THE FIRST SESSION OF THE GENERAL COURT 234 (1788). Similarly, South Carolina used "the rules of the common law" with respect to what would happen regarding wills and estates. ACTS, ORDINANCES, AND RESOLVES, OF THE GENERAL ASSEMBLY OF THE STATE OF SOUTH-CAROLINA 25 (1789).

Looking at only the language of "common law" in the Amendment, the original public meaning of common law appears to be the English common law. This common law was the one enduring common law that existed that the united colonies/states and individual colonies/states used.

"In Suits at common law" Common law is accompanied by other words in the Seventh Amendment. In the first clause of the Seventh Amendment, it states "[i]n Suits at common law, . . . the right of trial by jury shall be preserved." For the common law to be defined as the late eighteenth-century English common law continues to be logical in the context of that clause. Courts of "public and general jurisdiction" existed in England at the time of the adoption of the Seventh Amendment: the courts of common law and equity, the ecclesiastical courts, the military courts, and the maritime courts. A jury trial existed in the common law courts.[38] This division between common law courts in which juries sat and other courts, in which juries did not, also existed in the colonies. It was recognized, for example, by the distinction in the Judiciary Act between cases in which juries tried facts and other – admiralty and maritime – cases in which juries did not sit.

Another phrase of the Seventh Amendment – "where the value in controversy shall exceed twenty dollars" – also supports that the common law is the late eighteenth-century English common law. While Chapter 5 will fully describe the division of authority between the jury and the judiciary at that time, the general distinction upon which a jury trial existed in England was whether the plaintiff sought money damages. Common law courts and equity courts worked in conjunction with one another. Common law courts (with juries) heard claims with monetary damages, and equity courts decided claims that sought other types of relief such as specific performance of a contract and an injunction of an action. When the common law courts could not provide adequate protection to litigants, equity courts acted. In rare cases, when an equity court otherwise properly heard a case, the judge in this court might order damages, but this exercise of jurisdiction was quite controversial. Also, only in cases of trusts and then, a select few of these cases, did equity courts have exclusive jurisdiction to decide monetary damages. The general difference between common law courts

---

[38] *See* 3 WILLIAM BLACKSTONE, COMMENTARIES ON THE LAWS OF ENGLAND 30, 59–60 (University of Chicago Press 1979) (1768).

and equity courts was the remedy not the cause of action; juries in common law courts heard damages.[39]

"preserved"   "[P]reserved" in the Seventh Amendment also supports that common law means the English common law in 1791. The Amendment states "[i]n Suits at common law, . . . the right of trial by jury shall be preserved." Samuel Johnson defined "to preserve" as "[t]o save; to defend from destruction or any evil; to keep."[40] In the late eighteenth century, in many statutes and treatises, "preserved" is used in this same manner, consistent with this definition.[41]

The Seventh Amendment refers to the past tense of preserve – "preserved." So, common law must refer to a law that already existed – that was "preserved." The meaning of common law as the English common law in 1791 is reasonable given this idea of "preserved" and the definition of preserved. The Amendment would save, defend from destruction, or keep the jury trial right that existed in late eighteenth-century England. In contrast and as discussed later, an evolving or changing common law right is inconsistent with preserving – saving, defending from destruction, or keeping – any right.

"rules"   The final significant word in the Seventh Amendment is "rules." The Amendment states "no fact tried by a jury shall be otherwise re-examined in any Court of the United States, than according to the rules of the common law." Johnson defines "rule" as "2. An instrument by which lines are drawn. 3. Canon; precept by which the thoughts or actions are directed."[42] In other words, "rules" in this context refers to certain mechanisms that limit how courts can re-examine facts. The use of the English common law in the late eighteenth century could serve as

---

[39] *See* Thomas, *supra* note 16, at 1083–1101.

[40] 2 SAMUEL JOHNSON, A DICTIONARY OF THE ENGLISH LANGUAGE (4th ed. 1775). Cunningham's law dictionary does not define "preserved" or "preserve."

[41] *See, e.g.*, ACTS AND LAWS OF THE STATE OF CONNECTICUT, IN AMERICA 261, 264 (1786); AN ACT FOR PUNISHING MUTINY AND DESERTION; AND FOR THE BETTER PAYMENT OF THE ARMY AND THEIR QUARTERS 18 (1774); 1 BLACKSTONE, *supra* note 31, at 120; 1 EDWARD WYNNE, EUNOMUS: DIALOGUES CONCERNING THE LAW AND CONSTITUTION OF ENGLAND 29 (1785).

[42] 2 JOHNSON, *supra* note 40. It also states "1. Government, empire; sway; supreme command. . . . 4. Regularity; propriety of behavior. Not in use." *See id.* Cunningham's law dictionary does not define "rule."

such a restriction because under that law, there were limited ways by which courts could review jury verdicts.[43]

*****

A principle of constitutional interpretation is logic, which requires a reasonable meaning between words.[44] The Seventh Amendment's text dictates that juries try certain cases. It also gives one actor – the judiciary – limited power over the jury. Borrowing from the previous definitions, common law refers to a common, long-standing practice that could refer to the English common law. Moreover, juries sat in common law cases in the late eighteenth century so "[i]n Suits at common law" could refer to the late eighteenth-century English common law. "[P]reserved" refers to saved, defended from destruction, or kept. A practice must exist to be saved, defended from destruction, or kept. Again, such a practice could be the English common law in 1791. "[R]ule" refers to a particular mechanism used for control. Such a mechanism could be the English common law in 1791, under which judges had limited mechanisms to control the jury.

As previously mentioned, "common law" could refer to practices of the English courts, American state courts, or the federal courts. It also could refer to the statutory law. Having already examined the English common law, the possibility of "common law" meaning the American state common law, the federal common law, or the statutory law is analyzed here.

As for an alternative to the English common law, the state common law is not a logical choice. There were no common and long-standing state practices to govern whether a jury trial right existed and how courts could govern juries. Moreover, the Seventh Amendment dictated that the common law was to be "preserved." In states that were anticipated to form in the future, there was no such common law to preserve.[45] In other words, "common law" in the Seventh Amendment cannot be the common law of the individual states that did not exist because there would be no "common law" that could be "preserved." Finally, there was no federal court practice that could be preserved.[46]

---

[43] See Thomas, *supra* note 23, at 704–48.

[44] *Cf.* District of Columbia v. Heller, 554 U.S. 570, 577 (2008) ("logic demands . . . link between the stated purpose and the command").

[45] Henderson, *supra* note 10, at 336.

[46] James Wilson recognized that there was no federal common law. PAMPHLETS ON THE CONSTITUTION OF THE UNITED STATES 157 (Paul Leicester Ford ed., Da Capo Press 1968)

The next alternative is that the phrase "common law" means statutory law. First, this possible definition contrasts with the accepted definition of common law. Second, other parts of the Constitution also do not support such a meaning. The Supreme Court has used other parts of the Constitution to aid its interpretation of a constitutional provision – for example, comparing the use of words in the Second Amendment with those same words elsewhere in the Constitution.[47] The term "rules" is used in places in the Constitution outside of the Seventh Amendment. In Article I and Article IV, Congress itself is granted specific authority to create certain rules.[48] On the other hand, the term "rules" as used in the Seventh Amendment provides no grant of authority to Congress. Instead, it explicitly grants authority to "any Court of the United States" – or the judiciary – to re-examine facts according to "rules of the common law." Contrasting these parts of the Constitution that grant authority to Congress or the judiciary along with using the meaning of the term "common law" show that the Founders intended for the judiciary to make these rules as opposed to Congress.

The use of rules in the Seventh Amendment, which limits the authority of one constitutional actor (judiciary) in relationship to another constitutional actor (the jury), also differs significantly from the use of this term in Articles I and IV. In Articles I and IV, rules are not explicitly limited in any way and are not tied to one actor that is competing with another for authority. Thus, Congress can change the rules associated with these articles as it so desires.[49] On the other hand, a reasonable

---

(stating that trial by jury cannot be "'as heretofore'" because "there has never existed any foederal [sic] system of jurisprudence").

[47] *See* District of Columbia v. Heller, 554 U.S. 570, 576–600 (2008).

[48] "Each House may determine the Rules of its Proceedings . . ." U.S. Const. art. I, § 5, cl. 2. "The Congress shall have Power . . . [t]o . . . make Rules concerning Captures on Land and Water." U.S. Const. art. I, § 8, cl.11. "The Congress shall have Power . . . [t]o make Rules for the Government and Regulation of the land and naval Forces." U.S. Const. art. I, § 8, cl.14. "The Congress shall have Power to dispose of and make all needful Rules and Regulations respecting the Territory or other Property belonging to the United States." U.S. Const. art. IV, § 3, cl. 2.

[49] The phrase "rules of the common law" is used many times in the eighteenth century in statutes in Ireland, statutes in England, in the states, and in treatises. *See* An Abridgement of All the Statutes in Ireland, In the Reigns of Queen Anne, and King George. In Force and use. 185 (1718); An act for making the exemplification of the settlement made upon the marriage of James Lord Annesley with the Lady Elizabeth Manners 2 (1712) (referring to "the strict Rules of the Common-Law"); Acts, ordinances, and resolves, of the General Assembly of the state of South-Carolina, passed in March, 1789 25 (1789); Sir Robert Atkyns, Parliamentary and Political Tracts 96 (1734) (distinguishing "ordinary

meaning of the different use of "rules" in the Seventh Amendment prohibits the judiciary from having the authority to change the rules. Otherwise, the judiciary could exercise limitless authority against the competing actor of the jury.

Logic dictates that for the Seventh Amendment's language – "common law" – to have a sensible meaning, the common law must be an existing common, long-standing practice of the courts. The English common law in 1791 is such a common, long-standing practice that could be kept and could govern the extent of the authority of the jury and the judiciary, as well as govern the control that the judiciary has over the jury. The use of the late eighteenth-century English common law would grant authority to the jury in certain cases at the same time that it would grant the judiciary related power.[50]

An Originalist or an Evolving Interpretation of the Seventh Amendment

Through the adoption of the English common law, the Supreme Court has supported the use of an originalist methodology to interpret the Seventh Amendment. By permitting significant changes to eighteenth-century jury procedures, however, its approach is only loosely based on the substance of the common law. In the scholarly literature, there is significant support for a pliable method of interpretation similar to the Court's. Edith Henderson argued that some flexibility in the interpretation of the common law was necessary. She supported the Court's course to "preserv[e] the substance of the common law trial by jury and particularly the jury's power to decide serious questions of fact, while allowing rational modifications of procedure in the interests of efficiency." Under this method, Henderson would permit judicial intervention even if it was forbidden in the past. If practices proscribed in the original states were not permitted, the jury trial could be based on "historical accident," and "rational development" of procedures might

---

Rules of the Common law" with the Law of the High Court of Parliament). Even equity was governed by the rules of the common law. SAMUEL BURROUGHS, THE HISTORY OF THE CHANCERY; RELATING TO THE JUDICIAL POWER OF THAT COURT, AND THE RIGHTS OF THE MASTERS 9 (1726); 1 SIR EDWARD COKE, THE REPORTS OF SIR EDWARD COKE (1777).

[50] Quoting Judge Coke, John Hawles stated "it is a most dangerous Thing to shake or alter any of the Rules or fundamental Points of the Common Law, which, in truth, are the main Pillars and Supporters of the Fabrick of the Commonwealth." SIR JOHN HAWLES, KNIGHT, THE ENGLISHMAN'S RIGHT: A DIALOGUE BETWEEN A BARRISTER AT LAW AND A JURYMAN 7–8 (1763).

be prevented. Henderson also would give the judiciary the authority to decide what issues involve "serious questions of fact" and would enable it to permit incursions on jury authority based on justifications of efficiency. Her approach was informed by her belief that the Founders did not formulate the Seventh Amendment to create a particular relationship balancing the jury and the judiciary or apparently the jury and other traditional actors.[51] Her conclusion is belied, however, by the text and evidence at the founding. First, the text of the Amendment gives the judiciary limited authority to hear certain cases and restricted authority to re-examine facts tried by juries. Second, material from the founding shows that the Seventh Amendment was intended to restrain the authority of the judiciary, the legislature, and the executive.[52] Henderson's evolving approach does not account for these limitations, but rather, permits courts to determine what facts are serious and allows courts to make changes based on efficiency. This ability results in significant judicial power to decide its own authority as well as the other traditional actors' authority in relationship to the jury.

In an earlier article, Austin Wakeman Scott also argued for a flexible standard to preserve the "substance" of the jury trial at English common law. He argued for "a spirit of open-mindedness" to decide "what requirements are fundamental and what are unessential." Similar to the Court and Henderson, Scott concluded that the issue of whether there was a jury trial right rested on whether there was a disputable fact to be tried by a jury. He also emphasized efficiency, stating that the jury trial "must be an efficient instrument in the administration of justice."[53]

Outside of the flexible use of the English common law for the interpretation of the Seventh Amendment, another possibility is the flexible use of the law of the states or federal courts. The Court has stated that state court law should inform the interpretation of the Seventh Amendment, though the significance of the Court's actual consideration of such law in the Amendment's interpretation is unclear. Akhil Amar has argued that the Seventh Amendment should be interpreted based on an evolving state and federal common and statutory law. He has contended that the Seventh Amendment right in

---

[51] Henderson, *supra* note 10, at 290, 336.

[52] *See supra* chapter 3.

[53] Austin Wakeman Scott, *Trial by Jury and the Reform of Civil Procedure*, 31 HARV. L. REV. 669, 671, 690–91 (1918).

the federal courts is "rooted in federalism concerns." It is based on the jury right in the states where the federal court sits, and Congress can alter the right to provide more than the right provided by the state. In support of this argument, Amar cited sources that stated jury rights in the states varied at the time that the Amendment was adopted and other sources that showed various Founders disagreed about the civil jury right.[54]

The use of state law is not the best interpretation of the Amendment for several reasons.[55] First, with widely differing state practices that would have resulted in varied practices in the federal courts, one common law would not exist – an essential component of the general definition of common law. Second, the statutory law of the individual states is unlikely because this law had been explicitly expressed elsewhere by Congress but was not stated in the Seventh Amendment. In the First Session of Congress on September 24, 1789, just one day before the passage of the Seventh Amendment, Congress passed an act regarding the substantive rules applicable in trials at common law. In the act, Congress differentiated between state practices and the common law. It stated "[t]hat the laws of the several states . . . shall be regarded as rules of decision in trials at common law in the courts of the United States in cases where they apply."[56] These separate references to state practices and common law suggest that the term "common law" in the Seventh Amendment did not incorporate state practices. Also, if Congress had desired to do so, it could have included state practices in the Seventh Amendment, as it had done in the act.[57] On September 29, 1789, just days after the passage of the Seventh Amendment, Congress passed an act regarding certain procedures in the federal courts, which included the language "in suits at common law," and again differentiated between state practices and the common law. It stated

> the forms of writs and executions, except their style, and modes of process and rates of fees, except fees to judges, in the circuit and district courts, in

---

[54] AKHIL REED AMAR, THE BILL OF RIGHTS: CREATION AND RECONSTRUCTION 89–93, 222 (1998).

[55] See also Suja A. Thomas, Nonincorporation: The Bill of Rights After McDonald v. Chicago, 88 NOTRE DAME L. REV. 159, 194–96 (2012).

[56] Judiciary Act, supra note 11, at § 34.

[57] But see AMAR, supra note 54, at 89 (arguing that the Seventh Amendment "parallels" the Rules of Decision Act (with some exception) to place certain procedural issues in state hands).

suits at common law, shall be the same in each state respectively as are now used or allowed in the supreme courts of the same.[58]

The reference to the practice of each "state" separate from the reference to "in suits at common law" suggests that "in suits at common law" itself does not refer to state practices in this statute. Again, in this act, Congress had expressed the notion of adopting different state practices. If it had desired to do so in the Seventh Amendment, it could have similarly done so. It did not, suggesting that Congress did not intend to adopt state practices. As mentioned previously, another reason that an interpretation of the Amendment according to state practice does not work is future anticipated states – which had no common law that could be preserved – would have no common law to govern the jury trial. The fourth reason against the state practice interpretation concerns the plain meaning of the Amendment's text. The Amendment is governed by common law as opposed to statutory law so state statutory law or federal statutory law simply cannot apply.

The evolving law that Amar proposes also is not the best interpretation. Law that changes is not preserved or saved, defended from destruction, or kept. States could decide to change the jury right at will or states not in existence at the founding could decide to forgo adoption of jury trial rights. In either circumstance, no right would be preserved. Amar attempted to argue that "preserved" in the Seventh Amendment should be treated similarly to "reserved" to the states in the Tenth Amendment.[59] Congress chose not to use "reserved" in the Seventh Amendment versus its decision to use it in the Tenth. Thus, instead of a similarity, "reserved" in the Tenth Amendment and "preserved" in the Seventh Amendment show an intentional difference – that state law does not apply to the Seventh Amendment.

Looking also at the words in the context of what the Amendment is doing – granting authority to the jury and limiting the authority of the judiciary – the law cannot evolve for a few reasons. The judiciary – which is being limited – cannot be given the power to determine the authority that it has at any point in time. Also, certain specific words in the Amendment are inconsistent with an evolving interpretation. The Amendment states that the facts cannot be "otherwise re-examined" than

---

[58] An Act to Regulate Processes in the Courts of the United States, ch. 21, § 2, 1 Stat. 93 (Sept. 29, 1789).

[59] AMAR, *supra* note 54, at 90.

according to common law rules. If the rules could be any rules, then "otherwise" is superfluous.

Charles Wolfram was in favor of yet another evolving approach. Wolfram did reject the Court's jurisprudence that propounded that the civil jury trial right could be evaluated according to functionality – whether the jury or judge could better decide a question – as contrary to the goal of the Amendment.[60] But he believed that the common law that was prescribed in the Seventh Amendment was intended to be flexible. He described the common law as "the distinctive common-law process of adjudication and law-making that then and now, in England and in the United States, was recognized as flexible and changing." Although Wolfram recognized that his "dynamic" interpretation of the common law could permit significant judicial and legislative discretion contrary to the wishes of anti-federalists in the ratification debates, he argued that this problem would be eliminated by a generous interpretation toward jury authority. He advocated the "tendency" to recognize only "post-1791 changes in common-law remedies and practices that would have the effect of enlarging the occasions for civil jury trial and the perogatives [sic] of the civil jury." He qualified this statement and stated that this jury-enhancing result was not always necessary. For example, concern over trial judges' rejection of jury findings was unwarranted because appellate judges could effectively police trial judges through the use of trial transcripts. Despite the lack of an analogous historical practice for judges to question jury findings in the late eighteenth century, the use of such transcripts on appeal were, when he wrote in the 1970s, "universally established" and, in his opinion, effective. Through this application of his evolving method of interpretation, Wolfram did not recognize the precarious constitutional division of authority between the judiciary and the jury. Moreover, taking this particular example, trial transcripts do not show witness demeanor or other important information that the jury evaluated.[61]

---

[60] *See* Wolfram, *supra* note 8, at 746. Additional commentary on the "common law" in the Seventh Amendment is extensive, with many theories on how a court should interpret this phrase. *See, e.g.,* Patrick Woolley, *Mass Tort Litigation and the Seventh Amendment Reexamination Clause*, 83 Iowa L. Rev. 499, 516–17 & n.90 (stating that courts must focus on the "fundamental purpose" of the re-examination clause of "ensuring the proper balance of power between the federal judiciary and local juries"; "[C]ourts must give due consideration to history, but need not attempt to replicate rigidly the balance of power that existed between local juries and the federal judiciary.").

[61] Wolfram, *supra* note 8, at 745–46.

More recently, William Nelson took a broad stance in favor of an evolving interpretation of the Seventh Amendment that was tied to an evolving interpretation of the rest of the Constitution. He stated that "a progressive Constitution that changes in response to changing societal needs" as opposed to an originalist conception should govern the United States. Specifically, with respect to the Seventh Amendment, the originalist interpretation through the use of the common law in 1791 should not govern. Nelson compared the Seventh Amendment to the Contracts Clause in Article I, Section 10 of the Constitution, which he stated had appropriately become "largely a dead letter." He argued that the Seventh Amendment was adopted due to anti-federalist concerns that federal judges might ignore jury findings and force a national law on localities. Because he believed that the policy behind the Seventh Amendment – that of protecting "local self-rule" – no longer existed, the jury trial was "a legal siding" that should not be permitted to cause the "wreck" that would result from eliminating commonly used modern procedures that did not exist at common law. In connection to his proposed limited role for the jury, Nelson discussed the need of businesses for knowledge, predictability, and consistency in relationship to litigation outcomes.

> Entrepreneurs need to know the background norms against which they are being asked to invest resources; otherwise, they cannot negotiate the terms of investment and will refuse to invest. Investors also need assurance that the rule of law will preclude discrimination against them on account of their being outsiders. Finally, cross-jurisdictional uniformity of rules is useful in reducing the transaction costs of investment, thereby facilitating its flow.

He concluded this line of thought to state that "[j]uries . . . are not tightly bound to the rule of law" and therefore will not be good for entrepreneurs and investors. Nelson thus argued that the reason for the Seventh Amendment no longer existed, and the jury could not adequately protect corporate interests. For these reasons, he propounded that the common law in 1791 should not govern what procedures were constitutional under the Seventh Amendment.[62]

Previously, Wolfram performed an extensive study of the history behind the ratification of the Seventh Amendment. His conclusions regarding the reasons for the adoption of the Seventh Amendment

---

[62] William E. Nelson, *Summary Judgment and the Progressive Constitution*, 93 Iowa L. Rev. 1653, 1653–64 (2008); *see also* William E. Nelson, *The Lawfinding Power of Colonial American Juries*, 71 Ohio St. L.J. 1003 (2010).

somewhat conflict with Nelson's view. According to Wolfram, the reasons supporting the establishment of the Seventh Amendment went beyond the protection of local self-rule. The reasons were "the protection of debtor defendants; the frustration of unwise legislation; the overturning of the practices of courts of vice-admiralty; the vindication of the interests of private citizens in litigation with the government; and the protection of litigants against overbearing and oppressive judges." The "weighty premise" behind each of these arguments "was to achieve results from jury-tried cases that would not be forthcoming from trials conducted by judges alone." Moreover, Congress could not or would not protect the jury trial, and as a result the jury trial right had to be constitutionalized.[63]

Even if local self-rule was the primary reason behind the adoption of the Seventh Amendment, Nelson may be wrong about its supposed lack of continued importance. People sitting on juries in different states such as New York and Texas can represent divergent values and can so respond to federal laws.[64] Moreover, Nelson gives no constitutional support for why corporate interests should govern the interpretation of the Seventh Amendment. Finally, with a process by which the Constitution can be amended,[65] in the absence of such an amendment, opinions on whether a constitutional provision is irrelevant or harmful should have no relevance.

Although many scholars have argued for an evolving common law, such a law is difficult to reconcile with the words of the Seventh Amendment. The original public meaning of the words (common law, In Suits at common law, preserved, rules, and others) strongly suggests the common law is the English common law. Moreover, the context of the Amendment granting and limiting the authority of the judiciary and the jury suggests a significant restraint on the authority of the judiciary (and other traditional actors), which an evolving law does not provide. Thus, the one obvious reading of common law is the English common law in 1791. In the early nineteenth century, the Court originally recognized this reading, as opposed to an evolving common

---

[63] Wolfram, *supra* note 8, at 664–65, 670–710.

[64] *See, e.g.*, Dan Balz, *Pew poll: In polarized United States, we live as we vote*, WASH. POST, June 12, 2014 ("Conservatives and liberals . . . like to live in different places, associate with like-minded people . . ."); Dan Balz, *Texas, California embody red–blue divide*, WASH. POST, Dec. 28, 2013 (describing difference between states).

[65] U.S. CONST. art. V.

law. Later, it again emphasized that common law in the Seventh Amendment referred to the established late eighteenth-century English common law, not a flexible one.

> It is said that the common law is susceptible of growth and adaptation to new circumstances and situations, and that the courts have power to declare and effectuate what is the present rule in respect of a given subject without regard to the old rule; and some attempt is made to apply that principle here. The common law is not immutable, but flexible, and upon its own principles adapts itself to varying conditions. . . . But here we are dealing with a constitutional provision which has in effect adopted the rules of the common law in respect of trial by jury as these rules existed in 1791. To effectuate any change in these rules is not to deal with the common law, qua common law, but to alter the Constitution. The distinction is fundamental, and has been clearly pointed out by Judge Cooley in 1 Const. Limitations (8th ed.) 124.[66]

Despite the Supreme Court's initial adoption of the English common law, over time, as described in this and other chapters, the Court loosened its interpretation of the English common law to the result that its own authority and the traditional actors' authority has not been limited to the power that they held in the past. Others have criticized the Court's use of a soft historical test to determine the scope of the civil jury trial right.[67]

*****

The use of the late eighteenth-century English common law will limit the authority of the judiciary and the other traditional actors. Assuming the acceptance of this originalist understanding of the Seventh Amendment, the next question is what, if any, changes to the English common law are constitutional. The Court has stated that the substance of the

---

[66] *See* Dimick v. Schiedt, 293 U.S. 474, 487 (1935).

[67] *See* Martin H. Redish & Daniel J. La Fave, *Seventh Amendment Right to Jury Trial in Non-Article III Proceedings: A Study in Dysfunctional Constitutional Theory*, 4 Wm. & Mary Bill Rts. J. 407, 417–29, 442–53 (1995) (arguing jurisprudence can be justified only on the basis of "functionalism" over constitutional theory and arguing that only if Court overruled case law such that the Seventh Amendment did not apply to causes of action created after the adoption of the Amendment could congressional enactments giving authority to other bodies to decide damages be deemed constitutional); Renee Lettow Lerner, *The Failure of Originalism in Preserving Constitutional Rights to Civil Jury Trial*, 22 Wm. & Mary Bill Rts. J. 811, 815, 845 (2014) (discounting any possible difficulty of determining the practices at the time of the framing, because the procedures that surrounded the jury at that time were known and are known and also stating courts and legislatures have "chip[ped] away at [the] civil jury trial").

practice in England in 1791 should be satisfied, and I have previously agreed with this assessment. Joan Larsen has stated that "[n]ot even the purest originalist would likely claim that all attributes of the jury trial were fixed in the late eighteenth century – that juries must forever consist of twelve hungry men." On the other hand, she has stated "not everything about jury trials can be up for grabs."[68] The question concerns the line that must be drawn. How can the right be preserved? In the different context of the criminal jury, the Court has striven to avoid "'gross denial'" or "'erosion.'"[69] Although Wolfram somewhat distanced himself from his own proposal, his original idea – that is, only changes from the late eighteenth-century English common law practice that enhance jury authority should be permitted because such restrictions will limit the authority of the competing actors – is appealing. Chapter 5 begins to explore the jury trial according to this interpretation of originalism.

Interpreting the Criminal and Grand Jury Provisions: A New Theory of Relational Originalism

Although the Article III criminal jury and the Fifth Amendment grand jury provisions do not refer to "common law" like the Seventh Amendment civil jury right,[70] the Supreme Court has also used the English common law from the late eighteenth century, along with other sources,

---

[68] Joan L. Larsen, *Ancient Juries and Modern Judges: Originalism's Uneasy Relationship with the Jury*, 71 Oʜɪᴏ Sᴛ. L.J. 959, 962–63, 984–88, 994–97 (2010) (discussing the importance of text to originalists and how an originalist would find that a twelve-person jury was integral to trial by jury).

[69] Apprendi v. New Jersey, 530 U.S. 466, 483 (2000) (quoting Jones v. United States, 526 U.S. 227, 247–48 (1999)) (discussing Framer's fear regarding jury authority disappearing).

[70] Early on, the Supreme Court emphasized the importance of the text and also appeared to recognize that some significance attached to the original public meaning of the text for the interpretation of the Constitution. It stated

> [t]he framers of the constitution employed words in their natural sense; and, where they are plain and clear, resort to collateral aids to interpretation is unnecessary, and cannot be indulged in to narrow or enlarge the text; but where there is ambiguity or doubt, or where two views may well be entertained, contemporaneous and subsequent practical construction is entitled to the greatest weight.

McPherson v. Blacker, 146 U.S. 1, 27 (1892); *cf.* Barry Friedman & Scott B. Smith, *The Sedimentary Constitution*, 147 U. Pᴀ. L. Rᴇᴠ. 1, 9–33 (1998) (discussing use of originalism and living constitutionalism by the Supreme Court).

to interpret those jury sections.[71] The late eighteenth-century English common law has also been used to interpret many other parts of the Constitution, which do not refer to common law.[72] The question is whether the Court should interpret the criminal and grand jury provisions using the late eighteenth-century English common law in the absence of the phrase "common law" in those jury provisions. A related issue is whether originalism governs the interpretation of the criminal and grand jury clauses.

If an originalist interpretation of the Constitution was equivalent to the use of the "common law" to interpret the Constitution, arguably just the Seventh Amendment should be interpreted according to originalism, because only it refers to "common law" and "preserved." Under this reading of the Constitution, common law would govern only the meaning of the Seventh Amendment, and not the interpretation of other constitutional text.

Alternatively, the common law could be used to interpret other constitutional provisions that do not explicitly include the term "common law." However, if the common law was used to govern the rest of the Constitution in the same manner as it governs the Seventh Amendment, the reference to "common law" in the Seventh Amendment would be superfluous. So, if common law is used to interpret other constitutional text, it appears that it should be used in a different manner. Discussing this idea in a dissent in a case regarding the interpretation of the Eleventh Amendment, Justice Souter stated

> [t]he Seventh Amendment . . . was adopted to respond to Antifederalist concerns regarding the right to jury trial. . . . Indeed, that Amendment vividly illustrates the distinction between provisions intended to adopt the common law (the Amendment specifically mentions the "common law" and states that the common-law right "shall be preserved") and those provisions, like the Eleventh Amendment, that may have been inspired by a common-law right but include no language of adoption or specific reference.[73]

An originalist interpretation of the Constitution could include more than the use of the common law. It could refer to the use of additional

---

[71] *See, e.g.,* United States v. Booker, 543 U.S. 220, 238–44 (2005).

[72] *See, e.g.,* McDonald v. Chicago, 561 U.S. 742, 767–70 (2010).

[73] Seminole Tribe v. Florida, 517 U.S. 44, 164 n.59 (1996) (Souter, J., dissenting); *cf.* District of Columbia v. Heller, 554 U.S. 570, 579–80 (2008) (The use of words in parts of the Constitution can help inform the meaning of the same words in other parts.).

sources of original public meaning. Although the originalist interpretation of various constitutional provisions has occurred through the use of more than the English common law – for example, American statutes – the English common law has been a main source on which the Supreme Court and many scholars have relied to define the original public meaning of provisions in the Constitution.[74] In other words, use of the common law has been significant to an originalist interpretation of a constitutional provision.

The reason for which common law was included in the Seventh Amendment and not in other parts of the Constitution, including the other jury provisions, may help determine how, if at all, common law should be used to interpret the other jury provisions. Not much is known about the particular wording used in the Amendment. The decision to include common law possibly was related to the ease or difficulty with which the Founders could express authority in the Constitution. If authority could be easily expressed, then a reference to material outside the Constitution may not have been necessary. On the other hand, if authority was more difficult to express, an outside reference might help establish such authority. The decision to include common law in the Seventh Amendment also may have been related to the ability of the traditional actors to go beyond their own authority and the inability of the jury to protect its authority.

Common law could have been included in only the Seventh Amendment because the constitutional authority of other constitutional actors could be easily expressed. The wordings of the constitutional provisions that set forth the authority of these actors are consistent with this idea. The powers of the legislature, the executive, and the judiciary are delineated in Articles I, II, and III. The authority of the states is broadly set forth in the Tenth Amendment. Similarly, the authorities of the grand and criminal juries are set forth in the Fifth Amendment and Article III including specific exceptions to their authorities.[75]

---

[74] *But see, e.g.*, Kurt T. Lash, *Originalism All the Way Down?*, 30 CONST. COMMENT. 149, 156–59 (2015) (reviewing JOHN O. McGINNIS & MICHAEL B. RAPPAPORT, ORIGINALISM AND THE GOOD CONSTITUTION (2013)) (disputing McGinnis's & Rappaport's claim that Framers and ratifiers accepted English common law, including as represented by Blackstone).

[75] The exceptions respectively apply "in cases arising in the land or naval forces, or in the Militia, when in actual service in time of War or public danger" and in "impeachment" cases. *See* U.S. CONST. amend. V, U.S. CONST. art. III.

To the contrary, there is evidence of the difficulty in explicitly defining the authority of the civil jury, exemplified by the discussion of congressional members in the federal convention and the discussion by Hamilton in the *The Federalist*. The ultimate result was tying the authority of the civil jury to an outside reference. The Seventh Amendment set forth that a jury trial was preserved in certain types of suits – "in [s]uits at common law" – and courts could not re-examine facts other than in accordance with certain types of rules – "rules of the common law." Both of these references to common law restrained the judiciary and the jury. Juries, not judges, could hear common law suits, and judges could not affect the factual determination of the jury except according to common law rules. So, the Founders used "common law" to leave instructions on the authority that the judiciary and the jury held in relationship to one another. There had been difficulty expressing the authority of the civil jury; the judiciary and the jury shared authority; and the judiciary and possibly other traditional actors could otherwise usurp the jury's authority.

Because "common law" and "preserved" are found only in the Seventh Amendment, arguably the past common law should not strictly govern other parts of the Constitution.[76] So, how if at all should the traditional actors use the past common law to interpret the other constitutional provisions, including the grand and criminal jury provisions? If text is ambiguous, some sources are necessary to interpret it. Because the Court has used common law to interpret the Constitution from the time of its adoption, this provides good reason that there was an intention for the common law to have some influence on the interpretation of the constitutional text.

The unique characteristics of the jury could also influence the application of the common law beyond the interpretation of the Seventh Amendment. Because the Founders decided that common law restrained the power of the judiciary in relationship to the authority of a competing actor – the jury in civil cases – the use of the common law in a similar circumstance to influence the interpretation of the power of competing, dominant, traditional actors in relationship to the criminal and grand

---

[76] *Cf.* John F. Manning, *The Eleventh Amendment and the Reading of Precise Constitutional Texts*, 113 YALE L.J. 1663 (2004) (discussing how precise constitutional text should be interpreted). On the other hand, for a discussion of arguments by Akhil Reed Amar, Gary Lawson, and Michael Stokes Paulsen that originalism is mandated by other constitutional text, *see* Henry Paul Monaghan, *Supremacy Clause Textualism*, 110 COLUM. L. REV. 731, 739 & n.44 (2010).

juries is arguably justifiable. As previously discussed, the jury's unique position in the Constitution – as unable to act without the assistance of a traditional actor and unable to influence those actors because of its inability to affect their authority – results in the vulnerability of the jury.

Another factor in interpreting the jury's authority concerns how issues related to jury authority arrive at the Supreme Court. Unlike many reviews of the authority of the traditional actors, the Court considers the authority of the jury not when the jury purportedly has taken power from another actor, but rather, only when another actor purportedly has taken authority from the jury. One actor – the traditional actor – competes with and takes authority from another actor – the jury, the dependent actor. Because of this one-way power grab, to the extent that the common law should influence the interpretation of other parts of the Constitution, it could be used to restrain the traditional actors in relationships with the grand jury and criminal jury. When the constitutional text is ambiguous or the traditional actor grants itself power in circumstances in which the jury competes for authority, the common law could be used to limit the traditional actor's authority.

This book advances the notion that this "relational originalism" is the best method to reconcile the use of the phrase "common law" only in the Seventh Amendment. This proposed application of originalism is premised on relationships among the actors with authority in the Constitution. A constitutional actor may have a relationship(s) with another constitutional actor(s) such that it solely depends upon the other actor(s) in order to act. Here, the dominant constitutional actor should interpret the authority of the dependent actor using originalism and defer to the competing authority of the dependent actor when the meaning of the text is not clear and either actor could arguably possess authority. The criminal and grand jury have these relationships with the traditional actors, making them vulnerable to power grabs. While the respective governing amendments do not specifically require originalism, applying it to protect the authority of the jury is logical, given that the jury may have no authority, if not protected. Under this theory,[77] the traditional actors should use originalism to limit their own constitutional authority in relationship to the constitutional authority of the jury.

---

[77] See Suja A. Thomas, *Introducing Text-Bound Originalism (and Why Originalism Does Not Strictly Govern Same Sex Marriage)*, 2015 U. Ill. L. Rev. Slip Ops. 61 (discussing new theory of "text-bound originalism," use of originalism for jury provisions, and less decisive use of originalism elsewhere).

While the traditional actors will independently act based on their assessments of their own authority in relationship to the jury's, the judiciary often reviews whether another traditional actor has properly taken authority from the jury. The fact that the traditional actors depend upon one another for authority, including possessing the ability to curb each other's power, must be taken into account. The judiciary, for example, which can receive additional compensation from the legislature, is incentivized to give authority to the legislature. So, where the judiciary interprets the authority of the other traditional actors in relationship to the competing power of the jury, the judiciary should also use the common law. It should use it to determine the authority of the jury and defer to the competing authority of the jury when the meaning of the text of the Constitution is not clear and either actor could arguably possess authority.

Efficiency, Costs, and the Constitution

Much of the criticism of the jury and the justifications to place fewer matters with juries over time center around concerns that the jury is inefficient or a related issue that the cost of jury trials is too high. As discussed here, the Court has used efficiency and costs as an explicit or implicit consideration for whether a jury hears a case or whether a procedure that affects the jury trial right is constitutional. Several scholars have agreed that this is a valid consideration. The Court and these scholars have assumed that the economic incentives of the courts and interested parties play a legitimate role in this jurisprudence. The assumption has been that sufficient resources do not exist for juries to try many cases and the use of juries can impose unnecessary costs. These costs can include costs to parties, court time, and payment to jurors. The question is whether the efficiency, costs, and the related capabilities of the judiciary, the legislature, the executive, and juries should be considered in the decision of whether a jury or another body hears a case or re-examines facts tried by a jury. Thus far, whether these considerations are appropriate in relationship to the Constitution has never been generally evaluated.[78]

---

[78] *See* Granfinanciera, S.A. v. Nordberg, 492 U.S. 33, 61 n.16 (1989) ("Although enhanced efficiency was likely Congress' aim once again, neither Justice WHITE nor Justice BLACKMUN points to any statement from the legislative history of the 1984 Amendments confirming this supposition with respect to preference actions in particular. More

In criminal cases, efficiency and cost have been justifications to shift matters away from juries to other bodies. Plea bargaining has been the primary mechanism for such efficiency and cost-saving in the criminal system. The Court has emphasized that the efficiency and cost-saving nature of plea bargaining is necessary to the criminal justice system.

> The disposition of criminal charges by agreement between the prosecutor and the accused . . . is an essential component of the administration of justice. . . . If every criminal charge were subjected to a full-scale trial, the States and the Federal Government would need to multiply by many times the number of judges and court facilities.

Moreover, plea bargaining is fast and generally final; it "leads to prompt and largely final disposition of most criminal cases."[79] In this context, the Court has also placed value on efficiency and cost-savings over giving full information to defendants in order for them to decide whether to take a trial or plea. The Court decided that, as part of a plea, prosecutors could ask defendants to waive their right to see exculpatory evidence. To be required to give this evidence to defendants "could require the Government to devote substantially more resources to trial preparation prior to plea bargaining, thereby depriving the plea-bargaining process of its main resource-saving advantages."[80]

The legislature and executive are also integrally involved in these efficiency and cost considerations in plea bargaining. Through sentencing law – the legislature – and through plea-bargaining decisions – the executive – each makes choices based on efficiency and cost. Creating incentives to forgo jury trials decreases costs and increases efficiency. Darryl Brown has stated that "[i]n virtually every instance, the choice is for rules that reduce the process costs of reaching judgments, despite the harm to other interests . . . [which include] jury decision-making."[81]

Langbein compared the nontrial criminal system as similarly efficient to the nontrial civil system of settlement but argued that in contrast to the civil system, the criminal system was unfair in practice. The criminal jury

---

important, they offer no evidence that Congress considered the propriety of its action under the Seventh Amendment.").

[79] Santobello v. New York, 404 U.S. 257, 260–61 (1971).

[80] United States v. Ruiz, 536 U.S. 622, 632–33 (2002) (government need not disclose "material impeachment evidence prior to entering a plea agreement" nor disclose information about defendant's affirmative defenses). In addition to potential cost-savings, non-jury mechanisms may help increase the rate of convictions. Jed S. Rakoff, *Why Innocent People Plead Guilty*, THE NEW YORK REVIEW OF BOOKS, Nov. 20, 2014.

[81] Darryl Brown, *The Perverse Effects of Efficiency*, 100 VA. L. REV. 183, 189, 207, 217 (2014).

has been improperly eliminated through the threat of greater prison sentences implemented by the executive, the legislature, and the judiciary.

> Unlike the settlement dynamics in a civil case, which turn principally on the parties' efforts to discount the likelihood of success at trial in light of what has been learned in the pretrial about the facts and the law, the main determinant of plea bargaining is the severity of the threatened sentence if the defendant insists on trial.

The disparity in resources in these criminal settings, which includes the prosecutor with the state backing him, forcing the often publicly defended defendant into a plea without a finding of guilt, makes the circumstances even more unfair.[82]

Outside of plea bargaining, the Court has made efficiency part of the criminal system through the use of the reasonable jury standard. Before a jury verdict or after a jury finds against the defendant, the judge can decide that a reasonable jury would not convict the defendant. This decision eliminates the jury.[83] So, judges can decide what reasonable juries would find and eliminate juries in some contexts, arguably decreasing cost and increasing efficiency.

While many scholars argue that the criminal jury has been improperly replaced, the general sentiment for the grand jury is not the same. Once again, efficiency considerations control. For example, Andrew Leipold has argued that grand juries do not have the capability to decide whether there is probable cause to believe the suspect committed the alleged crime, and judges more effectively answer similar questions on motions such as for acquittal.[84]

As briefly discussed earlier, the Supreme Court has examined efficiency and cost in its analysis of the right to a civil jury trial. Significant evidence of the increasing importance of this concern is found especially at the beginning of the twentieth century. In 1913, in *Slocum v. New York*

---

[82] John H. Langbein, *The Disappearance of Civil Trial in the United States*, 122 YALE L.J. 522, 563–64. (2012).

[83] *See* Jackson v. Virginia, 443 U.S. 307, 317 (1979) ("Yet a properly instructed jury may occasionally convict even when it can be said that no rational trier of fact could find guilt beyond a reasonable doubt, and the same may be said of a trial judge sitting as a jury. In a federal trial, such an occurrence has traditionally been deemed to require reversal of the conviction.").

[84] Andrew D. Leipold, *Why Grand Juries Do Not (and Cannot) Protect the Accused*, 80 CORNELL L. REV. 260, 294–304 (1995); *cf.* Roger A. Fairfax, Jr., *The Jurisdictional Heritage of the Grand Jury Clause*, 91 MINN. L. REV. 398, 424 (2006) (Rule 7 is constitutionally questionable but the waiver is efficient for government reformers).

Life Insurance Co., the Court struck down as unconstitutional a Pennsylvania statute that permitted a trial judge to find for the losing party after the judge decided that the jury's verdict was not supported by the evidence. The Court cited late eighteenth-century English common law under which a judge could order only a new trial and could not reverse the jury's verdict.[85] The dissenting justices objected to this result, emphasizing efficiency problems. They stated "[t]he serious and far-reaching consequences of this decision are manifest." Because of this decision, Congress could not pass a statute similar to the Pennsylvania statute to reverse a jury's verdict and instead new trials would be required where the judges deemed evidence insufficient. A constitutional amendment would be required to "remedy[] the mischief of repeated trials" and "diminish[] . . . the delays and expense of litigation." They called the Pennsylvania procedure "adopted in the public interest to the end that unnecessary litigation may be avoided."[86] This dissent in *Slocum* signaled the decision two decades later in *Baltimore & Carolina Line, Inc. v. Redman* in which the Court effectively overruled *Slocum* and decided that a judge can review and discard a jury finding based solely on his judgment of the sufficiency of the evidence.[87] In this time period, there was growing criticism by legal elites of the lack of efficiency and the cost of juries including judges championing their own superiority over juries.[88]

Later in the twentieth century, analyses of efficiency and cost continued to affect the jury trial. As mentioned earlier, the Court explicitly characterized its Seventh Amendment analysis on whether a jury should hear a case as based in part on "the practical abilities and limitations of juries" even though these abilities and limitations were not considered at common law. As another example, in the 1980s, the Court held that a judge could dismiss a case before a jury trial if, by viewing the parties' paper record, the judge decided that "a reasonable jury could [not] return a verdict for the nonmoving party,"[89] again a procedure that did not exist at common law. This decision made clear that when judges determined a reasonable jury could not find in a particular way, juries were not necessary. Efficiency continued to become imbedded into the system.

---

[85] *See* 228 U.S. 364 (1913).

[86] *Id.* at 400, 428 (Hughes, J., dissenting).

[87] *See* 295 U.S. 654 (1935).

[88] *See supra* Chapter 3; Stephan Landsman, *The History and Objectives of the Civil Jury System, in* THE VERDICT: ASSESSING THE CIVIL JURY SYSTEM 47–51 (Robert E. Litan ed. 1993).

[89] Anderson v. Liberty Lobby, Inc., 477 U.S. 242, 248 (1986).

In two recent cases, the Court expanded this use of efficiency to the pre-discovery stage of litigation. It decided that before a jury trial and before the parties exchange information, a judge can use her "judicial experience and common sense" to dismiss a case when she finds the claim implausible.[90] In these decisions that changed the standard to dismiss cases before juries heard them, the Court emphasized the costs to parties and courts. It said that

> the threat of discovery expense will push cost-conscious defendants to settle even anemic cases before reaching those proceedings.[91]

> Litigation, though necessary to ensure that officials comply with the law, exacts heavy costs in terms of efficiency and expenditure of valuable time and resources that might otherwise be directed to the proper execution of the work of the Government.[92]

More generally, plaintiffs bringing "frivolous cases" are blamed for increased costs.[93] Citing this justification, legislatures have enacted caps on damages as well as other limitations that affect the jury.[94]

The executive has also justified the transfer of authority from civil juries to administrative law judges due to cost and efficiency concerns. The Securities and Exchange Commission said administrative hearings are "relatively fast, with rulings usually handed down within 300 days of the case being filed, as opposed to years for the typical federal-court case." The head of the Commodities Futures Trading Commission stated the "'overwhelming reason for this change is resources.' . . . The CFTC is 'incredibly stretched' and short of money." Administrative law judges would be "far faster and cheaper."[95]

---

[90] Ashcroft v. Iqbal, 556 U.S. 662, 679 (2009); *see also* Bell Atlantic Corp. v. Twombly, 550 U.S. 544 (2007).

[91] *Twombly*, 550 U.S. at 559.

[92] *Iqbal*, 556 U.S. at 685; Brooke D. Coleman, *The Efficiency Norm*, 56 B.C. L. Rev. 1777 (2015).

[93] *See* Suja A. Thomas, *Frivolous Cases*, 59 DePaul L. Rev. 633 (2010).

[94] *See, e.g.*, Luciano v. Olsten Corp., 110 F.3d 210, 221 (2d Cir. 1997) ("the purpose of the cap [in Title VII] is to deter frivolous lawsuits and protect employers from financial ruin as a result of unusually large awards"); *see also* Lynn Ridgeway Zehrt, *Twenty Years of Compromise: How the Cap on Damages in the Civil Rights Act of 1991 Codified Sex Discrimination*, 25 Yale J.L. & Feminism 249, 263–301 (2014) (describing legislative history of caps on damages in Title VII).

[95] Jean Eaglesham, *CFTC Turns Toward Administrative Judges*, Wall St. J., Nov. 9, 2014; Jean Eaglesham, *SEC Is Steering More Trials to Judges It Appoints*, Wall St. J., Oct. 21, 2014.

The Supreme Court has even declared the Seventh Amendment does not stand in the way of this type of efficiency.

> Congress is not required by the Seventh Amendment to choke the already crowded federal courts with new types of litigation or prevented from committing some new types of litigation to administrative agencies with special competence in the relevant field. This is the case even if the Seventh Amendment would have required a jury where the adjudication of those rights is assigned instead to a federal court of law instead of an administrative agency.[96]

Because of changes in the legal system, including the availability of discovery, which gives parties and the court information about the case before trial, John Langbein has argued that the civil trial is necessarily inefficient and generally unnecessary. Many cases can be settled. Moreover, courts can dismiss unmeritorious cases that litigants otherwise may be forced to settle because of their fear of the cost of discovery.[97]

Although the inefficiency and cost of the jury appears to be assumed by many, the jury may not actually possess these characteristics.[98] Moreover, in some circumstances, the reference to efficiency and cost is simply used to justify taking authority from the jury for reasons related to economics or power. The economic incentives have been evident at times. Support for the jury has waxed and waned between different groups dependent on these incentives. As one example, when Congress enacted civil rights laws in the 1960s, civil rights proponents did not want juries to try their cases because, due to the racial composition of juries at that time, those juries were likely to find against them. This view contrasted with the perspective of defendants. They desired a jury trial, because juries would favor them. Now, with changes to who can serve on a jury, generally plaintiffs alleging discrimination prefer juries. On the other hand, defendants try to avoid them because of their concern that

---

[96] Atlas Roofing Co. v. Occupational Safety & Health Review Comm'n, 430 U.S. 442, 455 (1977).

[97] See Langbein, *supra* note 82, at 551–53; *see also* Lerner, *supra* note 67; Nelson, *supra* note 62. Lerner wrote about changes based on efficiency that began in the nineteenth century. *See* Lerner, *supra* note 67, at 823–24 (in the nineteenth century, some states recognized monetary and other costs of jury trials), 830–31 (shift in states in the mid-nineteenth century to more concerned about inefficiency of jury versus value of jury), 855 (Court upheld summary proceeding of bank against debtors).

[98] Certain groups in the past were under no belief that jury trials were efficient. *See* Wolfram, *supra* note 8, at 671 (discussing anti-federalists).

juries will find against them.[99] So, the demand for efficiency could be simply a screen for a desired result.

Regardless of the reason for the invocation of efficiency and cost, the question remains whether there is constitutional justification for taking them into account to determine whether a jury or another body hears a case. And are there such constitutional grounds for the incentives that the legislature or the executive creates against taking trials? One possible justification for taking into account costs in civil cases that has not been significantly explored is the difference between costs at English common law and costs under the modern system. Under the English system, the losing party would pay the costs of the other party, including attorneys' fees. Although the losing party pays costs under the modern American system, under only certain statutes and rules, does that party pay attorneys' fees. For example, in a Title VII employment discrimination case, if the plaintiff wins, the defendant will be required to pay the plaintiff's attorneys' fees. However, if the defendant wins, only in rare circumstances will the defendant recover its attorneys' fees. Also where the court deems the suit was frivolous, a court may order one party to pay the other party's attorneys' fees. Outside of such special contexts, the losing party does not pay attorneys' fees. Historically, the change from the losing party pays to the current rule came into being across jurisdictions in the United States in the second half of the nineteenth century. Maxeiner has called it the "American practice" as opposed to the "American rule" because jurisdictions can require the losing party to pay attorneys' fees. He argued that the practice against requiring the loser to pay has resulted from the business interests of lawyers who would rather have their own clients pay their own fees. He also emphasized that self-regulation in the system also has caused fees to be high.[100] Add to this that it is difficult to compare the English system to the modern system, because in the eighteenth-century English system lawyers did not play a role in most cases.[101] Moreover, in the American system, legislatures can choose to require parties to pay the attorneys' fees of the other party but they have not done so.

---

[99] See The Right to Jury Trial Under Title VII of the Civil Rights Act of 1964, 37 U. Chi. L. Rev. 167, 167 (1969); cf. Kevin M. Clermont & Stewart J. Schwab, How Employment Discrimination Plaintiffs Fare in Federal Court, 1 J. Emp. Leg. Stud. 429, 442–43 (2004).

[100] James R. Maxeiner, Chapter 26 The American "Rule": Assuring the Lion His Share, 11 IUS Gentium 287, 288–92, 303 (2012).

[101] See Peter King, Decision-Makers and Decision-Making in the English Criminal Law, 1750–1800, 27 Hist. J. 25, 25–27 (1984).

Despite the extensive use of efficiency and costs to justify shifts from the jury to other bodies, the Court has never shown how these considerations are appropriate given the text of the jury provisions. As for the criminal jury, Article III specifically describes the cases in which a jury sits and does not take into account efficiency or cost. None of the words in Article III have meaning associated with efficiency or cost.[102] Also, there is nothing in the Seventh Amendment that permits the consideration of the efficiency or cost to decide whether the jury hears a case. Instead, the Amendment gives certain cases to juries. It in turn permits the judiciary to hear other cases and also to re-examine certain cases heard by juries. Finally, the Fifth Amendment gives certain cases to grand juries without any consideration of efficiency or cost.[103]

Although the Court and many scholars have insisted that efficiency and cost should be examined in determining whether a jury, the judiciary, the executive, or the legislature hears an issue, there is no constitutional basis for this consideration. Instead, the constitutional text gives certain issues to each of these bodies without mentioning efficiency or cost. The Founders may have actually evaluated or alternatively affirmatively decided to disregard efficiency and cost when they decided that certain matters should be placed with juries, the judiciary, the legislature, and the executive.

A curious question in all of this is why the jury is treated any differently than the executive, the legislature, the judiciary, and the states. Authority has never been taken from them on the basis that the Constitution required efficiency or that parties should not bear certain costs that those bodies impose. The Supreme Court has created exceptions for the jury that has suited desires to shift authority to other parts of the government,[104] and the use of efficiency and cost is another such way by which the authority of the jury has been taken.

Conclusion

Currently, the traditional actors exercise significant control over the criminal, civil, and grand juries. This exercise of authority has resulted in a jury with much less authority than in the past. How should the traditional

---

[102] The main words are: Trial, Crimes, Cases of Impeachment, and Jury. U.S. CONST. art. III.
[103] The main words are: answer, capital, infamous, presentment, indictment, Grand Jury, land and naval forces, Militia, actual service, War, and public danger.
[104] See supra Chapters 2 & 3.

actors interpret the authority of the jury? Only the use of originalism can preserve authority in the jury when the traditional actors themselves compete with the jury for power and the jury cannot counter impingements on its authority. Specifically, as described in this chapter, the substance of the English common law in the late eighteenth century should govern the jury's and competing actors' authority when the constitutional text is unclear. Despite the traditional actors' efforts to significantly deviate from this common law, no reasonable constitutional justification exists for such changes, including considerations of efficiency and cost, to shift authority from the jury to another body.

5

Restoring the Jury

Despite the popular image of the American jury and the power possessed by the English jury of our origins, the jury in the United States exercises almost no authority today. It occupies this place even though it was to serve a fundamental role in the checks and balances of the American government established by the Constitution. This chapter addresses how this constitutional role can be restored.

Chapter 4 described how the jury provisions should be interpreted. First, the Seventh Amendment requires the civil jury's authority and the related powers of the traditional actors, including the judiciary, to be governed by the substance of the late eighteenth-century English common law jury trial. Second, because the powers of the criminal and grand juries depend solely upon the traditional actors – who can usurp their authority – the traditional actors' powers in this context must also be restrained in relationship to jury authority. The competing incentives of the traditional actors and their abilities to take criminal and grand jury authority make originalism – primarily, the late eighteenth-century English common law jury trial – the logical reference point limiting the traditional actors' authority. Moreover, due to these relationships, when either actor could arguably possess authority, deference to the jury's competing authority is necessary.

Using the mechanism of originalism, this chapter takes an in-depth look at four major modern procedures that affect jury authority. This analysis shows how they appropriate power from the jury and consequently, how their elimination would help restore the jury. The discussion begins with procedures in criminal cases that shift significant authority to the government. First, a judge's power to free a person whom a jury has found guilty of a crime is considered. Next, the examination turns to a state's authority to prosecute an alleged criminal without a grand jury deciding that the government's case should proceed. This power is particularly potent because the state almost invariably leverages a plea, resulting in a jury never deciding the fate of the accused. After a look at these weighty criminal procedures, the chapter focuses on two civil mechanisms that give the government significant authority where plaintiffs allege defendants committed wrongs. First, Congress's decisions to give judges, instead of juries, certain cases with damages or fines are discussed. Then, a civil procedure analogous to judges freeing criminal defendants is examined. This device permits a judge to dismiss a case before a jury hears it if the judge decides a jury could not find a violation of a law. The chapter then concludes with a discussion of the challenges of restoring the jury, including the difficulties of eliminating these well-entrenched modern mechanisms.

Acquittal of Defendants by Judges

In a criminal case, after the United States government charged two investment portfolio managers with securities fraud, a grand jury indicted them, and a jury unanimously convicted them. The defendants requested that the judge throw out the jury's conviction. Refusing to do so, the judge who presided at their trial sentenced the defendants to several years in prison and also fined them. Later, deciding among other things that there was insufficient evidence for the jury to convict, the federal appeals court that reviewed the case reversed the convictions, setting the defendants free.[1]

Presently, if a jury convicts a person accused of a crime, the judge overseeing the case or the appellate court reviewing the case can acquit or free the person, deciding that there was insufficient evidence to convict. Similarly, prior to the jury deliberating, if the judge concludes that the prosecutor did not present adequate proof of the defendant's guilt, the judge can acquit the defendant. Although this procedure has been accepted for years, the Supreme Court has never analyzed whether it is constitutional.[2] The following examination of the relevant constitutional text as well as its historical meaning shows that the judiciary lacks this authority to usurp the jury's decision.

---

[1] *See* United States v. Newman, 773 F.3d 438 (2d Cir. 2014).

[2] *See Ex parte* United States, 101 F.2d 870 (7th Cir.), aff'd by an equally divided court, United States v. Stone, 308 U.S. 519 (1939); Theodore W. Phillips, *The Motion for Acquittal: A Neglected Safeguard*, 70 YALE L.J. 1151, 1152 & n.8 (1961).

Judgment of Acquittal Under Federal Rule of Criminal Procedure 29

The judge's modern power to acquit is set forth in Federal Rule of Criminal Procedure 29. It provides that before a criminal case goes to a jury or after the jury's verdict, the judge can "enter a judgment of acquittal of any offense for which the evidence is insufficient to sustain a conviction."[3] The motion for judgment of acquittal turns on the judge's assessment of whether there is sufficient evidence that the defendant committed the crime.[4] The judge determines whether "*any* rational trier of fact could have found the essential elements of the crime beyond a reasonable doubt. . . . [with] *all of the evidence* . . . to be considered in the light most favorable to the prosecution."[5] Only in the circumstance where the judge's decision to acquit is rendered after the jury's guilty verdict, can the prosecution appeal the acquittal decision.[6]

Language in Constitution

Whether a judge should be able to acquit a criminal defendant before or after a jury's decision depends on the authority granted to the judiciary and the jury in the Constitution. The language of Article III – "[t]he Trial of all Crimes, except in Cases of Impeachment, shall be by Jury"[7] – gives authority to the jury to try crimes without any concomitant power in the judiciary to affect those jury decisions. This language contrasts with the language of the Seventh Amendment granting the judiciary specific authority over juries trying civil matters.[8] So, under the Constitution, the judiciary lacks any explicit authority to take cases away from the criminal jury.

---

[3] FED. R. CRIM. P. 29; *see also* N.Y. CRIM. PROC. LAW § 290.10(1) (McKinney 2014).

[4] *See* Smith v. Massachusetts, 543 U.S. 462, 469 (2005).

[5] Jackson v. Virginia, 443 U.S. 307, 319 (1979). Instead of freeing the convicted defendant, a judge can grant a new trial under Rule 33(a), if he decides that the evidence is insufficient. *See* FED. R. CRIM. P. 33(a).

[6] Double jeopardy is not violated, because no new trial is required. *See* FED. R. CRIM. P. 29 advisory committee's notes on 1994 amendment.

[7] U.S. CONST. art. III, § 2.

[8] "In Suits at common law, where the value in controversy shall exceed twenty dollars, the right of trial by jury shall be preserved, and no fact tried by a jury, shall be otherwise re-examined in any Court of the United States, than according to the rules of the common law." U.S. CONST. amend. VII.

The Conflict Between the Common Law and Acquittal

As previously discussed, originalism – particularly the English common law of the late eighteenth century – should govern the respective authority of the criminal jury and the judiciary if the constitutional text is unclear and either actor could arguably possess authority.[9] In the absence of any specific constitutional grant of authority to the judiciary over the criminal jury and the lack of any other governing law, such as the equal protection clause, the past authority exercised by the English jury – which was our American model – should be the greatest power the judiciary should exert over the jury in criminal cases today.

Several eighteenth-century English procedures that affected juries' decisions in criminal cases have been compared to modern judicial acquittal. Unlike acquittal, those methods did not permit the jury's decision to be usurped. The following sections describe those mechanisms – the early termination of trials, special verdict, directed verdict of acquittal, reprieve and pardon, and the new trial – and contrasts them with acquittal. Additionally, the differences between acquittal and the core principles or the substance of the common law criminal jury trial are examined.

Early Termination of Trials by Judges v. Acquittal

In eighteenth-century England, the prohibition against double jeopardy – being tried twice for the same offense – did not apply until the jury gave its final verdict. So, if a judge believed the evidence presented at trial was insufficient to convict, he could, and sometimes did, terminate a trial prior to the jury rendering a verdict and he would order the trial to begin again before another jury in the future.[10] This procedure permitted the person prosecuting the case to delay it to obtain more evidence to prove guilt. While English commentator Matthew Hale considered this judicial practice to be "'ordinary,'" John Langbein noted a dearth of these cases in the *Old Bailey Session Papers*. He posited that either the procedure may have been in decline after Hale's era and/or the people who reported the cases chose not to describe trials that were incomplete.[11]

---

[9] *See supra* Chapter 4.

[10] *See* John H. Langbein, *The Criminal Trial Before the Lawyers*, 45 U. Chi. L. Rev. 263, 287 (1978).

[11] *Id.* (quoting 2 Sir Matthew Hale, The History of the Pleas of the Crown 295 (George Wilson ed., 1778)).

There is a similarity between this English procedure and modern judicial acquittal. Under both, a judge can stop a case before the jury's verdict upon a finding of insufficient evidence. However, under the English practice, the judge could only temporarily stop the case, and he did so when he believed the defendant was guilty. In another trial, the prosecutor was given the opportunity to set forth better evidence to prove the defendant's guilt to the jury. In stark contrast to this past English practice under which the jury continued to decide guilt, modern judicial acquittal takes the question of guilt away from the jury, giving the judge the authority to dismiss the case and set the defendant free.

Special Verdict v. Acquittal

The special verdict was another English practice related to the jury. The jury could render a general or a special verdict. Under a general verdict, the jury decided whether the defendant was guilty of the charged crime and did not state the facts that supported its verdict. Under a special verdict, a jury decided the facts and left the determination of whether a crime was committed to the judge. Blackstone described this procedure as "where [the jury] *doubt* the matter of law, and therefore *chuse* [sic] to leave it to the determination of the court." Although the jury could give this matter to the judge, the judge could not require the jury to find a special verdict. The jury possessed "an unquestionable right of determining upon all the circumstances, and finding a general verdict."[12]

There is a similarity between the English special verdict and modern judicial acquittal. Under both, a judge effectively decides whether the defendant is guilty of a crime. However, under the English procedure, the jury plays a decisive role in contrast to its role under the modern procedure. An English jury decided the facts, unlike modern judicial acquittal where the jury plays no such role. Moreover, the English jury exercised the choice to decide the case by either general or special verdict

---

[12] 4 WILLIAM BLACKSTONE, COMMENTARIES ON THE LAWS OF ENGLAND 354 (University of Chicago Press 1979) (1769). Citing another eighteenth-century source from England, James Oldham stated "[e]ven if requested by the judge, the jury could insist on returning a general verdict." James Oldham, *The Seventh Amendment Right to Jury Trial: Late-Eighteenth-Century Practice Reconsidered, in* HUMAN RIGHTS AND LEGAL HISTORY: ESSAYS IN HONOUR OF BRIAN SIMPSON 231 n.33 (Katherine O'Donovan & Gerry R. Rubin eds., 2000). Although Langbein has stated that there were cases in which a judge rejected the jury's general verdict of guilty in favor of a special verdict, he has also acknowledged that in the late eighteenth century, the power to order special verdicts "became controversial." Langbein, *supra* note 10, at 295–96.

and thus, determined whether it or the judge found guilt. In contrast, under modern judicial acquittal, the judge exercises the sole authority to take the case away from the jury when she decides the jury incorrectly convicted the defendant.

Directed Verdict of Acquittal v. Acquittal

A judge's directed instruction or directed verdict to the jury to acquit the defendant is another eighteenth-century English procedure that has been compared to modern judicial acquittal. During a jury trial, after the prosecution presented evidence or after the jury's verdict, a judge could direct the jury to find the defendant not guilty if the judge thought the evidence did not show guilt.[13] While juries "routinely follow[ed] the judge's lead," judges did not frequently tell juries to do this, and juries could reject the recommendation.[14] In the case of Thomas Jones in 1787, after the jury found Jones – who had been accused of stealing sheep – guilty, the judge asked the jury to reconsider its verdict twice. The judge requested a not guilty verdict because he believed that the prosecutor had not proven Jones had stolen the sheep. However, the jury quickly returned from its deliberations responding that all of them believed Jones was guilty. The judge stated that he "was forced at last to receive their verdict."[15] In another case in which the defendant John Barker was accused of highway robbery, when the jury asked to deliberate after the judge summarized the evidence, the judge stated "[a]fter having stated the evidence short, it does not become me to press any thing further to you, it is for your discretion." He further implored them "I never feel any difficulty when in a capital case, where a man's life is concerned, and a Jury pauses so considerably as you do, in such a case I never hesitate to recommend it to them to acquit the prisoner." Despite this direction, the jury found Barker guilty.[16] Peter King, who analyzed many of the cases in

---

[13] See JOHN H. LANGBEIN, THE ORIGINS OF ADVERSARY CRIMINAL TRIAL 321–23 (2003); J.M. BEATTIE, CRIME AND THE COURTS IN ENGLAND, 1660–1800 412–15 (1986).

[14] Langbein, *supra* note 10, at 285, 296; *see* LANGBEIN, *supra* note 13, at 321–23; BEATTIE, *supra* note 13, at 414–15.

[15] P.R.O. H.O. 47/6 Thomas Jones (Brecon). The judge reprieved Jones and recommended that the King pardon him. *See id.* Langbein described a case in which the jury deliberated two additional times upon the judge's direction after the jury originally rendered a not guilty verdict. The jury finally returned with a guilty verdict. *See* Langbein, *supra* note 10, at 291–95. However, such "judicial dominance" was "extremely rare[]." *Id.* at 295.

[16] Old Bailey Proceedings, 15th September 1784, THE PROCEEDINGS OF THE OLD BAILEY: LONDON'S CENTRAL CRIMINAL COURT, 1674–1913, www.oldbaileyonline.org/browse.jsp?

this time period, concluded that "while 'in many cases . . . the jury took its lead from the bench . . . the jury's willingness to do so must be understood in the light of the fact that when the jury wanted to go its own way it had the power to do so.'"[17] As Blackstone had stated, "if the judge's opinion must rule the verdict, the trial by jury would be useless."[18]

There is some similarity between the English practice of a directed verdict of acquittal and modern judicial acquittal. Under both, a judge can exercise influence on whether the defendant goes free. However, different from the English practice under which the jury had final authority to convict or acquit, deciding to follow or not follow the judge's opinion, modern judicial acquittal permits the judge alone to determine the defendant's fate. The judge may acquit the defendant precluding the jury's verdict before deliberations or usurping it after deliberations.

Reprieve and Pardon v. Acquittal

Another English practice that affected the jury's verdict to convict was the judge's power to "reprieve" or stay a sentence. After the jury rendered a guilty verdict and sentence was passed, the reprieve permitted the judge to stay the sentence and ask the King to pardon the prisoner. This procedure delayed the execution of the sentence until the King decided whether to grant the pardon.[19]

The reprieve and royal pardon were considered necessary. While many crimes bestowed the death penalty, ultimately, the government was unwilling to impose this sentence upon a significant number of people.[20]

---

id=t17840915-54-defend684&div=t17840915-54#highlight (last visited Mar. 3, 2015) (reference no. t17840915-54).

[17] PETER KING, CRIME, JUSTICE, DISCRETION IN ENGLAND, 1740–1820, at 251–52 (2000) (quoting THOMAS ANDREW GREEN, VERDICT ACCORDING TO CONSCIENCE: PERSPECTIVES ON THE ENGLISH CRIMINAL TRIAL JURY 1200–1800, at 358 (1985)).

[18] 4 BLACKSTONE, *supra* note 12, at 354–55.

[19] *See* 4 WILLIAM BLACKSTONE, *supra* note 12, at 387. Samuel Johnson defined reprieve as "[r]espite after sentence of death." 1 SAMUEL JOHNSON, A.M., A DICTIONARY OF THE ENGLISH LANGUAGE (5th ed., corrected 1773). Blackstone described a reprieve as "temporary" and "the withdrawing of a sentence for an interval of time" for a variety of reasons including that he "is not satisfied with the verdict, or the evidence is suspicious." 4 BLACKSTONE, *supra* note 12, at 387. The definition of pardon included "[f]orgiveness of an offender," "[f]orgiveness of a crime; indulgence," and "[r]emission of penalty." 1 SAMUEL JOHNSON, A.M., A DICTIONARY OF THE ENGLISH LANGUAGE (5th ed., corrected 1773). Blackstone described a pardon as "permanent." 4 BLACKSTONE, *supra* note 12, at 387.

[20] *See* J.M. Beattie, *The Royal Pardon and Criminal Procedure in Early Modern England*, 22 HISTORICAL PAPERS/COMMUNICATIONS HISTORIQUES 9, 11–12 (1987).

Reprieves were "seen principally as a means of regulating the level of capital punishment so that an acceptable number of offenders would be sent to the gallows."[21]

The power to reprieve was momentous. "Such reprieves were in effect pardons, for the king virtually never refused to spare someone nominated by the judge who had presided at the trial." Judges were not even required to justify their recommendations for pardons partially because of the creation of "transportation" to another place as an alternative acceptable punishment to death.[22]

Because juries and judges generally agreed, cases in which judges reprieved the defendant and sought a pardon were "exceptional." In some of these cases, a judge actually acted in concert with the jury's wish to impose a more lenient punishment; the jury may have been unable to mitigate the death penalty because of the inability to impose a lesser offense or to use the benefit of clergy, another mechanism that could be employed to avoid the death penalty.[23]

In a case in which a judge believed the prosecutor had not proven the defendant's guilt and the jury had disagreed, the judge "often" requested a free pardon.[24] Under this procedure, the prisoner would go free. As an alternative to a free pardon, a judge could request a conditional pardon asking for a reduction in the sentence, for example, to transportation.[25] Several cases, found by Peter King, show the judge recommending a pardon when he doubted the convicted's guilt. At times he asked for a free pardon, and other times, for a lesser sentence such as transportation.[26] In one case, the judge believed that "a Felony not having been proved."[27] In another, the judge "doubted whether the Prisoner ought to have been convicted."[28] In the case of Thomas Jones,

---

[21] BEATTIE, *supra* note 13, at 431.

[22] Beattie, *supra* note 20, at 13.

[23] BEATTIE, *supra* note 13, at 409–10, 435.

[24] BEATTIE, *supra* note 13, at 409–10 & n.13, 431–32; Peter King, *Decision-Makers and Decision-Making in the English Criminal Law*, 27 THE HISTORICAL JOURNAL 25, 46 (1984) (mentioning the case of John Bayne).

[25] *See* BEATTIE, *supra* note 13, at 431; 4 BLACKSTONE, *supra* note 12, at 394.

[26] *See* P.R.O. H.O. 47/11 John Lilly and Robert Heron (transportation recommended).

[27] P.R.O. H.O. 47/6 Thomas Jones (Brecon).

[28] P.R.O. H.O. 47/6 Thomas Jones (Liverpool); *see also* P.R.O. H.O. 47/6 Joseph Wright, John Bayne; *see also* John H. Langbein, *Shaping the Eighteenth-Century Criminal Trial: A View from the Ryder Sources*, 50 U. CHI. L. REV. 1, 30 (1983) (describing a case in which Sir Dudley Ryder of the Old Bailey trial courts reprieved "'because the evidence doubtful'" (quoting Ryder assize diary)).

described earlier, after the judge implored the jury to reconsider their verdict because he believed guilt had not been proven, the jury convicted Jones. The judge's only option to free the defendant was to ask the King.[29] The judge's limited authority to recommend a pardon contrasted with the King's; he "ha[d] an inherent power to pardon all offences against his crown and dignity."[30]

In Peter King's sample study of cases in 1787, at least half of the convicted who claimed innocence received a free pardon. King explained, however, that based on the other statements and behavior of judges, they have not been viewed as "sympathetic" toward prisoners.[31]

In cases in which the judge did not reprieve the sentence, a pardon was still possible. In such cases, the convicted or others could petition the King for a pardon. The judge could continue to have influence here. He was asked for a written report regarding the case, and the King followed the judge's inclinations in most cases.[32]

The English reprieve and pardon share characteristics with modern judicial acquittal. Under both, a case can be dismissed after a jury convicts. However, the English procedure contrasts with the modern procedure because the English judge could not simply dismiss a case. The King acted alone or agreed to the judge's recommendation of freedom, unlike modern judicial acquittal where only a judge decides whether to free the defendant. Although the King almost invariably acquiesced to a judge's recommendation, the judge himself had no authority to set the prisoner free. As Blackstone declared "it would be impolitic for the power of judging and of pardoning to center in one and the same person."[33] Moreover, in England, a judge did not always recommend a free pardon if the evidence was doubted; instead, transportation to another place for a period of years might be requested. The comparison to today's judicial acquittal is also more difficult due to the conditions under which reprieves and pardons were granted, including the prevalence of the death penalty and the ambivalence toward it by the English government.

---

[29] *See* P.R.O. H.O. 47/6 Thomas Jones (Brecon).
[30] [M. Madan], THOUGHTS ON EXECUTIVE JUSTICE, WITH RESPECT TO OUR CRIMINAL LAWS, PARTICULARLY ON THE CIRCUITS 46–47 (London 1785).
[31] KING, *supra* note 17, at 310, 312.
[32] *See* King, *supra* note 24, at 42, 50.
[33] 4 BLACKSTONE, *supra* note 12, at 390.

The New Trial v. Acquittal

The new trial was another English judicial procedure that could affect the jury's verdict. If the jury found the defendant guilty and the Court of King's Bench believed the verdict was "contrary to evidence," the court could grant a new trial.[34] It was used "in many instances."[35] In one case, *Rex v. Simmons*, the King's Bench ordered a new trial after the jurors gave affidavits explaining their misunderstanding of the judge's direction to acquit. Although the justices expressed concern about relying on jurors' affidavits to order a new trial, the court believed there was sufficient support that the jury was mistaken in its verdict. Discussing the importance of the court's authority to order a new trial, the Chief Justice stated that "[t]here is no doubt but a new trial may be granted in a criminal case; and the true reason for granting new trials is for the obtaining of justice."[36] Although Blackstone discussed the general availability of the new trial procedure, a new trial could not be ordered for a felony conviction.[37]

Again, there is a similarity between this English procedure and modern judicial acquittal. Under both, the original jury's verdict is eliminated. However, there is a significant difference between the

---

[34] *Id.* at 355. Bushell's Case recognized the incongruence of a judge rejecting the verdict of a jury. "For if the Judge, from the evidence, shall by his own judgment first resolve upon any trial what the fact is, and so knowing the fact, shall then resolve what the law is, and order the jury penally to find accordingly, what either necessary or convenient use can be fancied of juries, or to continue tryals by them at all?" Bushell's Case, 124 Eng. Rep. 1006, 1010 (C.P. 1670).

[35] 4 BLACKSTONE, *supra* note 12, at 355.

[36] Rex v. Simmons, 95 Eng. Rep. 645, 645 (1752).

The circuit judge would refer a few cases each year to the twelve judges in London who would consider whether a conviction should be overturned or amended upon a legal error or would consider various other issues. *See* James Oldham, *Informal Lawmaking in England by the Twelve Judges in the Late Eighteenth Century and Early Nineteenth Centuries*, 29 LAW & HIST. REV. 181 (2011). "In general, . . . appeal to higher courts played an inconsequential role in English criminal procedure until well into the nineteenth century. Since the jury's verdict gave no reasons, there was little to review." *See* John H. Langbein, *The English Criminal Trial Jury on the Eve of the French Revolution, in* THE TRIAL JURY IN ENGLAND, FRANCE, GERMANY 1700–1900, at 38 (Antonio Padoa Schioppa ed., 1987).

[37] *See* Edith Guild Henderson, *The Background of the Seventh Amendment*, 80 HARV. L. REV. 289, 323, 325 (1966) (describing English procedure where there is no new trial for felony conviction but also describing practice in states in the late eighteenth century or early nineteenth century where a new trial was permitted after felony conviction); *see also* DAVID BENTLEY, ENGLISH CRIMINAL JUSTICE IN THE NINETEENTH CENTURY 281 (1998).

procedures. The English jury continued to exercise final authority to decide guilt, whereas under modern judicial acquittal, a judge decides guilt.

Acquittal by Judges Is Unconstitutional

Each of the English procedures – including the jury's role under the procedures – differs significantly from modern judicial acquittal, evidencing the impropriety of acquittal under the U.S. Constitution. However, whether acquittal is constitutional is best determined by comparing acquittal not only to the English procedures but also to the core principles or substance of the English common law criminal jury trial right. There are two core principles that can be derived from the procedures that governed the criminal jury trial. First, judges had influence over juries but juries chose the effect of the influence that judges had. Second, significant authority to decide the outcome of a case lay outside the jury in the judge's authority to reprieve.

Under the first principle, juries chose the influence judges had over them. Although a judge could temporarily stop a case through early termination of a trial, a jury still decided the case at a later time. Also, while a judge could direct a jury to find a defendant not guilty, the jury – not required to follow the judge's instruction – actually decided the case – finding the defendant not guilty or guilty. Moreover, by deciding by special verdict, a jury could permit the judge to decide guilt or innocence but was not required to do so. In some misdemeanor cases in which juries found guilt, the King's Bench could review the facts, decide they were insufficient, and order a new jury trial. Here, again, a jury still decided the case.

Despite significant authority remaining in the English jury, through the judge's authority to reprieve – the core of the second principle of the English common law criminal jury trial – judges possessed decisive authority in criminal cases. If the jury convicted and the judge, believing the defendant's guilt had not been proven, could not convince the jury to follow him, the judge could recommend a pardon to the King, which was almost inevitably followed by the King. This essentially assured result makes the judicial reprieve an important analogy to modern judicial acquittal.

Nonetheless, this core English principle must be viewed in relationship to the United States Constitution. Article II of the Constitution is the only place in the Constitution to refer to reprieve and pardon authority.

It gives the President the power to "grant Reprieves and Pardons for Offences against the United States, except in Cases of Impeachment."[38] No other provision in the Constitution gives any similar authority to judges.

So, modern judicial acquittal is not equivalent to the English reprieve by judges and pardon by the King. The Constitution gives specific instructions that only the President has reprieve and pardon power. Because the Constitution gives only the President such authority, judges cannot so act.

In summary, the substance of the English common law criminal jury trial authority in conjunction with the text of the Constitution grants juries the authority to choose whether to follow judges' directions to acquit or to permit judges to decide the outcome. Judges also have no constitutional power to reprieve or pardon defendants. It follows that modern judicial acquittal is an unconstitutional usurpation of the authority of the criminal jury.

State Prosecution of Defendants Without Grand Juries

Many states proceed with cases against criminal defendants without requiring grand juries to indict defendants. Instead of a grand jury deciding whether a defendant probably committed an alleged crime, a judge makes this determination. Because a defendant usually takes a plea, the elimination of a grand jury indictment generally results in only the government deciding whether the defendant is guilty and consequently only the government deciding whether the defendant is imprisoned. Say the Connecticut police allege that crack cocaine was found in a car borrowed and driven by Joe Kelly. If the state of Connecticut, which does not require a grand jury to indict a person accused of a crime, charges Kelly with possession of crack cocaine, it is likely that Kelly will go to prison without any community input into whether he should be punished. Connecticut's authority to freely accuse and punish derives in part from the Supreme Court's decision not requiring states to use grand juries.[39] The following section assesses whether the Constitution requires grand juries to check state governments.

---

[38] U.S. Const. art. II, § 2, cl. 1; *see also Recent Case, Criminal Law–Concurrent Jurisdiction,* 8 Harv. L. Rev. 59 (1894) (discussing difference between offenses against the United States and offenses against the states); Hon. Albert Williams Johnson, *Charge to Grand Jury,* 4 F.R.D. 243, 244 (1945) (same).

[39] *See* Hurtado v. California, 110 U.S. 516 (1884).

The Fundamental Right of the Grand Jury

The Supreme Court has decided that states should protect most of the rights set forth in the Bill of Rights. In its most recent decision on this issue, *McDonald v. City of Chicago*, a plurality of the Court decided that individuals in states had rights to possess guns under the Second Amendment.[40] The Second Amendment analysis on whether states should protect the right centered on the Fourteenth Amendment's due process clause, which provides "nor shall any State deprive any person of life, liberty, or property, without due process of law."[41] According to the Court, to decide whether a right is "incorporated" or applies to the states, "we must decide whether the right . . . is fundamental to *our* scheme of ordered liberty, . . . or as we have said in a related context, whether this right is 'deeply rooted in this Nation's history and tradition.'"[42] This examination has consistently involved determining the meaning of due process – specifically, what were fundamental rights at the time of the founding and ultimately at the time of the adoption of the Fourteenth Amendment. In *McDonald*, to decide whether the gun right was fundamental, the Court examined the origin of the right in England, the adoption of the right in the states around the time of the ratification of the Bill of Rights, the meaning of the Fourteenth Amendment, and the protection of the right by the states around the time of the Fourteenth Amendment's ratification. Although an analysis of the privileges and immunities clause, instead of the due process clause, may be the appropriate manner to decide whether rights apply to the states,[43] the limited inquiry here is whether, using the Court's current incorporation jurisprudence, individual states should protect the grand jury right. The following examination of the historical grand jury right shows that states should require them.[44]

The Fifth Amendment Grand Jury Right

In the time period surrounding the founding, indictment by grand juries was a fundamental right, standing in the way of the government

---

[40] *See* 561 U.S. 742 (2010).

[41] U.S. Const. amend. XIV, § 2.

[42] 561 U.S. at 767 (citation omitted) (quoting Washington v. Glucksberg, 521 U.S. 702, 721 (1997)).

[43] *See id.* at 758, 767–78.

[44] For a more extensive examination of the application of the grand jury right to the states, *see* Suja A. Thomas, *Nonincorporation: The Bill of Rights After* McDonald v. Chicago, 88 Notre Dame L. Rev. 159 (2010).

prosecuting a person for a crime in England. In cases where the defendant faced the death penalty, Blackstone stated:

> [T]o find a bill [for a person to be indicted], there must at least twelve of the jury agree: for so tender is the law of England of the lives of the subjects, that no man can be convicted at the suit of the king of any capital offence, unless by the unanimous voice of twenty four of his equals and neighbours: that is, by twelve at least of the grand jury, in the first place, assenting to the accusation.

Grand juries were required in all other cases, except misdemeanors, and they were considered important constraints on government. Discussing this significance, Blackstone proclaimed "[o]ur law has therefore wisely placed this strong and two-fold barrier, of a presentment and a trial by jury, between the liberties of the people, and the prerogative of the crown."[45] Prior to this time, Lord Coke (whom Blackstone later cited) had stated that "[n]o man shall be taken (that is) restrained of liberty, by petition, or suggestion to the king, or to his councell [sic], unless it be by indictment, or presentment of good, and lawfull [sic] men, where such deeds be done."[46]

Blackstone recognized that other procedures may appear better or perhaps more efficient. Discussing these considerations, he emphasized that:

> [H]owever *convenient* [other forms of proceeding] may appear at first, (as doubtless all arbitrary powers, well executed, are the most *convenient*) yet let it be again remembered, that delays, and little inconveniences in the forms of justice, are the price that all free nations must pay for their liberty in more substantial matters. . . .[47]

In America, at the time of the founding, the evidence shows that the grand jury also was a fundamental right. In discussing the inefficiency of civil juries for collecting taxes, Alexander Hamilton contrasted the necessity of the use of the grand jury (and criminal jury) for prosecuting tax avoidance.[48] In the state debates, legislators asserted that the absence of a constitutional provision that required grand juries did not permit judges

---

[45] 4 BLACKSTONE, *supra* note 12, at 301, 305, 343.
[46] EDWARD COKE, THE SECOND PART OF THE INSTITUTES OF THE LAWS OF ENGLAND 46 (London 1809) (footnote omitted).
[47] 4 BLACKSTONE, *supra* note 12, at 344.
[48] *See* THE FEDERALIST NO. 83, at 500 (Alexander Hamilton) (Clinton Rossiter ed., 1961).

to substitute informations – prosecutorial accusations – for grand jury indictments.[49]

Early nineteenth-century commentators also remarked on the fundamental nature of the grand jury right. In his *Commentaries on the Constitution*, including the Bill of Rights, Justice Story stated "it is obvious, that the grand jury perform most important public functions; and are a great security to the citizens against vindictive prosecutions, either by the government, or by political partisans, or by private enemies."[50] When he discussed parts of the Bill of Rights including the grand jury, James Kent stated "[t]he Constitution of the United States, and the constitutions of almost every state in the Union, contain the same declarations in substance, and nearly in the same language" and stated that these provisions were "transcribed into the constitutions in this country" from England to guard the "right of personal security." Kent further stated that where there was no express constitutional provision in the states, these "fundamental" doctrines would have been set forth in the legislative acts, because the "colonies were parties to the national declaration of rights in 1774, in which the trial by jury, and the other rights and liberties of English subjects, were peremptorily claimed as their undoubted inheritance and birthright." Further, Kent specifically discussed the meaning of due process. He stated that "[t]he words, *by the law of the land*, as used in *magna charta*, in reference to this subject, are understood to mean due process of law, that is, by indictment or presentment of good and lawful men. . . ."[51]

In addition to these commentaries, there is other evidence that the grand jury was a fundamental right at the time of the founding in America. Of the fourteen states, four explicitly provided a grand jury for felonies, and four others provided for some form of grand jury.[52]

---

[49] 2 THE DEBATES IN THE SEVERAL STATE CONVENTIONS ON THE ADOPTION OF THE FEDERAL CONSTITUTION AS RECOMMENDED BY THE GENERAL CONVENTION AT PHILADELPHIA IN 1787, at 112–13 (Jonathan Elliot ed., 2d ed. 1836) [hereinafter ELLIOT's DEBATES] (debates of Mr. Gore and Mr. Dawes in the Convention of the Commonwealth of Massachusetts on the adoption of the Federal Constitution on Jan. 30, 1788); 4 ELLIOT's DEBATES 154 (debate of Mr. Spencer in the Convention of the State of North Carolina on the adoption of the Federal Constitution on July 29, 1788).

[50] 3 JOSEPH STORY, COMMENTARIES ON THE CONSTITUTION OF THE UNITED STATES § 1779 (Fred B. Rothman & Co. 1991) (1833).

[51] 2 JAMES KENT, COMMENTARIES ON AMERICAN LAW 12–13 (The Blackstone Publishing Co. 1889) (1827).

[52] *See* Kaitlyn Luther, Table of History of Jury Rights (Feb. 10, 2012) (unpublished table compiled by research assistant) (on file with the author, Suja A. Thomas).

At the time of the Fourteenth Amendment's adoption, there is also significant evidence that the grand jury remained a fundamental right. The Civil Rights Act of 1866 required due conviction by jury, the intention for which could have included a grand jury indictment before a criminal jury conviction.[53] Moreover, the adoption of the Thirteenth Amendment just three years prior to the adoption of the Fourteenth Amendment suggested the importance of the grand jury at the time of the Fourteenth Amendment's adoption. The Thirteenth Amendment specifically stated that slavery and involuntary servitude had been abolished in the absence of a person being "duly convicted."[54] Again, this due conviction could have included a prerequisite indictment by a grand jury. Additionally, evidence existed in the statements of the proponents and opponents of the Fourteenth Amendment that the Fourteenth Amendment incorporated the Bill of Rights, although most of this evidence relates specifically to the Privileges or Immunities Clause.[55]

There is also evidence in the states at the time of the Fourteenth Amendment's adoption that the grand jury right was a fundamental right. Twenty-six out of thirty-seven states guaranteed a right to a grand jury.[56]

Following the Fourteenth Amendment's adoption, the Enforcement Act of 1871, which was enacted to enforce the Fourteenth Amendment, provided for civil and criminal liability and significant penalties for tampering with jurors, showing the general importance of the jury to the liberty of the freed people.[57] Moreover, the Civil Rights Act of 1875 explicitly prevented interference with freed people's right to serve as jurors on grand and petit juries.[58]

Under the Court's current jurisprudence, there is no justifiable reason that the grand jury right has not been applied to the states. Additional support for requiring the grand jury in states comes from the other parts of the Fifth Amendment. In the past, the other rights in the Fifth

---

[53] Civil Rights Act of 1866, ch. 31, § 1, 14 Stat. 27 (1866).

[54] U.S. CONST. amend. XIII, § 1.

[55] For a discussion of these statements, *see* Thomas, *supra* note 44, at 187 n.210.

[56] *See* Luther, *supra* note 52; *cf.* Steven G. Calabresi & Sarah E. Agudo, *Individual Rights Under State Constitutions when the Fourteenth Amendment Was Ratified in 1868: What Rights Are Deeply Rooted in American History and Tradition?*, 87 TEX. L. REV. 7, 78–79 (2008) (stating nineteen states required grand jury indictment for felonies and seven prohibited prosecution solely by information).

[57] *See* Enforcement Act of 1871, ch. 22, § 1–2, 5, 17 Stat. 13, 13–15 (1871).

[58] *See* Civil Rights Act of 1875, ch. 114, § 4, 18 Stat. 335, 336–37 (1875).

Amendment – double jeopardy, self-incrimination, and just compensation – were found fundamental and required in the states under the Fourteenth Amendment.[59] In addition to the rights in the Fifth Amendment, in the past, the Court has opined on whether most of the other rights in the Bill of Rights apply against the states. Of these decisions, the Court has failed to protect only jury rights in the states, including not requiring the grand jury in states.[60]

The evidence from the time of the founding through and around the time of the Fourteenth Amendment's adoption demonstrates that the grand jury was a fundamental right, similar to the other rights that the Supreme Court has applied against the states. To follow its jurisprudence consistently, the Court should require states to convene grand juries to sit in criminal cases.[61]

Administrative Agencies, Bankruptcy Courts, and Other Congressional Actions

Similar to modern judicial authority in criminal cases, in civil cases today, judges exercise significant power. Congress has given authority to judges to decide certain cases that grant money as the remedy, highlighting the question of whether these congressional actions are constitutionally valid.

Congress has created new statutory causes of action under which a plaintiff can recover money damages or the government can recover fines for violations of laws. Juries have been granted authority to decide some of the cases and judges have been given others. For example, juries have authority to hear cases brought by tenants alleging property owners or landlords discriminated against them. On the other hand, in conjunction with the development of new actions, Congress has developed new bodies such as administrative agencies and bankruptcy courts to decide some issues. For example, administrative agencies decide disputes between employers and unions seeking better treatment for their employee members. Recently in conjunction with

[59] Cf. 3 STORY, supra note 50, § 1781 (after discussing the grand jury, Justice Story recognized that the privilege against double jeopardy was "another great privilege secured by the common law").

[60] See Thomas, supra note 44, at 180–83, 203–04.

[61] See id. at 198–203 (discussing stare decisis). For other arguments that the Sixth Amendment unanimity requirement and the Seventh Amendment civil jury requirement should apply against the states, see Thomas, supra note 44.

congressional authority, the executive – seeking monetary recovery for securities fraud – has shifted even more decisions from juries to administrative agencies.[62]

The Supreme Court's assessment of whether a jury trial right exists in these circumstances has been based on some combination of whether an analogous cause of action existed at common law, whether the type of relief sought by the plaintiff was available in the English law courts, the predominance of any claim for equitable relief (such as specific performance of a contract or an injunction of certain action), and a judgment on whether judges might better decide a matter. More specifically, the Court has decided that while juries can decide certain cases involving congressionally created claims with monetary damages, there is no jury trial right where the plaintiff mainly seeks equitable relief even though she also seeks money damages.[63] Additionally, Congress may be able to label relief as equitable or discretionary, giving judges authority over those claims.[64] The Court has also approved Congress's creation of administrative agencies and equity courts to decide rights described as "public."[65] Moreover, the Court believes that the abilities of juries can be assessed. If they are not best able to decide claims with damages, taking cases away from them could be justified.[66] Finally, the possibility that courts themselves can generally determine damages or fines has been left open.[67]

---

[62] Examples include the NLRB, SEC, and the CFTC. See Jean Eaglesham, *SEC Is Steering More Trials to Judges It Appoints*, WALL St. J., Oct. 21, 2014; Jean Eaglesham, *CFTC Turns Toward Administrative Judges*, WALL St. J., Nov. 9, 2014; Jean Eaglesham, *SEC Wins With In-House Judges*, WALL St. J., May 6, 2015.

[63] *See* Katchen v. Landy, 382 U.S. 323, 337 (1966); NLRB v. Jones & Laughlin Steel Corp., 301 U.S. 1, 48 (1937).

[64] *See* Curtis v. Loether, 415 U.S. 189, 197 (1974).

[65] Granfinanciera, S.A. v. Nordberg, 492 U.S. 33, 51–52 (1989); Atlas Roofing Co. v. Occupational Safety & Health Review Comm'n, 430 U.S. 442, 455 (1977). The definition of what qualifies as a public right is unclear. *See Granfinanciera*, 492 U.S. at 66–69 (Scalia, J., concurring); Vikram David Amar, *Implementing an Historical Vision of the Jury in an Age of Administrative Factfinding and Sentencing Guidelines*, 47 S. TEX. L. REV. 291 (2005); Ellen E. Sward, *Legislative Courts, Article III, and the Seventh Amendment*, 77 N.C. L. REV. 1037, 1081–83 (1999); Martin H. Redish, *Seventh Amendment Right to Jury Trial: A Study in the Irrationality of Rational Decision Making*, 70 Nw. U. L. REV. 486 (1975).

[66] *See* Tull v. United States, 481 U.S. 412, 418 n.4 (1987); *see* Ross v. Bernhard, 396 U.S. 531 (1970).

[67] *See Tull*, 481 U.S. at 425–27 (questioning jury right in remedy stage); Feltner v. Columbia Pictures Television, Inc., 523 U.S. 340 (1998) (calling into question the decision in *Tull* that a jury need not determine damages pursuant to the Seventh Amendment).

Using these justifications, the Court has approved several congressional causes of action, permitting judges to decide cases with money damages and fines. An examination of the relevant constitutional text as well as its historical meaning shows, however, that Congress has established procedures to decide cases with money damages and fines that usurp jury authority in contravention of the Constitution.[68]

Language in the Constitution

Under the Court's current jurisprudence, the Seventh Amendment is not viewed as a significant limit or perhaps any limit on Congress. So, what is the extent of the constitutional authority granted to the civil jury in relationship to Congress? The following sections examine the late eighteenth-century English common law and statutory law regarding civil jury trial authority, which the Court itself has never thoroughly analyzed. First, the power divide between juries and judges that existed in the English courts is investigated. Second, the authority of the English parliament is examined. Lastly, the constraints of the U.S. Constitution are considered.

Cases Heard by Juries in England

Blackstone described the courts of "public and general jurisdiction" as of "four sorts . . . [including] the universally established courts of common law and equity."[69] Commentators often referred to the jurisdiction or authority of the courts of law when referring to the authority of the courts of equity and vice versa. In conjunction with his description of the authority of juries in the courts of law to order monetary damages, Henry Ballow described the need for courts of equity, which could order specific performance or an injunction. He stated that

---

[68] For a more extensive examination of the unconstitutional nature of Congress's shift of cases to judges, see Suja A. Thomas, *A Limitation on Congress: "In Suits at Common Law,"* 71 OHIO ST. L.J. 1073 (2010); *cf.* Martin H. Redish & Daniel J. La Fave, *Seventh Amendment Right to Jury Trial in Non-Article III Proceedings: A Study in Dysfunctional Constitutional Theory,* 4 WM. & MARY BILL RTS. J. 407, 408–09 (1995) (Court has treated the Seventh Amendment differently from other constitutional provisions when the Court interprets the power of Congress).

[69] 3 WILLIAM BLACKSTONE, COMMENTARIES ON THE LAWS OF ENGLAND 30 (The University of Chicago Press 1979) (1768). The other courts were ecclesiastical courts, military courts, and maritime courts. *See id.*

[b]ut the law of England was very defective in this particular, and fell short of natural justice, . . . for executory agreements were there looked upon but as a personal security, and damages only to be recovered for the breach of them; most commonly either by an action of covenant, if there was a deed, or by an assumpsit, if without deed. But it proving a great hardship, in particular cases, to be left only to the uncertain reparation by damages, which the personal estate perhaps may not be able to satisfy, courts of equity, therefore, where there was a sufficient consideration, did, in aid of the municipal law, compel a specific performance. And there are many other cases wherein equity will give relief, although there be a remedy at law, if that be insufficient; as for a nuisance by injunction, or the like. . . .[70]

The authority of the courts of law and equity was based on whether the courts of law could provide adequate protection for the plaintiff.[71] Only when the courts of law could not do so, did the courts of equity act. Indeed, the bill or complaint in the court of equity usually stated "and for that your orator is wholly without remedy at the common law."[72]

Cud v. Rutter demonstrates the limited jurisdiction of the courts of equity. Under the alleged facts, the defendant had agreed to sell stock to the plaintiff. Lord Parker decided that the plaintiff could buy the stock with the damages that the courts of law could award. He stated "that a court of equity ought not to execute any of these contracts, but to leave them to . . . law, where the party is to recover damages, and with the money may if he pleases buy the quantity of stock agreed to be transferred to him."[73]

On infrequent occasions, courts of equity determined damages. After discovery – which only equity courts conducted – an equity court might keep the case and decide damages. The eighteenth-century authority John Fonblanque stated that while he could not reconcile when, upon discovery, equity could retain jurisdiction to order relief, he concluded that it was "now settled" that equity courts could not render damages when the plaintiff was there for discovery.[74]

---

[70] 1 HENRY BALLOW, A TREATISE OF EQUITY 27–29 (John Fonblanque ed., 1793).
[71] *See* 12 W.S. HOLDSWORTH, A HISTORY OF ENGLISH LAW 584 (1938) ("equity scrupulously following the law").
[72] 3 BLACKSTONE, *supra* note 69, at 442.
[73] 24 Eng. Rep. 521, 521–22 (Ch. 1719).
[74] 1 HENRY BALLOW, A TREATISE OF EQUITY 663 (John Fonblanque ed., 2d ed. 1835); *see also* 2 HENRY BALLOW, A TREATISE OF EQUITY 494 (John Fonblanque ed., 1795) (in Fonblanque's additions); 1 BALLOW, *supra* note 70, at 38 (in Fonblanque's additions) ("Chancery cannot assess damages.").

There is other limited case law in which an equity court ordered damages when a plaintiff was properly before the court for equitable relief and he desired damages. *Denton v. Stewart* is at the center of much of the discussion of whether the equity courts had power to order these damages. There the plaintiff had possession of a house after the defendant sold it to the plaintiff. However, the defendant subsequently obtained possession after a judgment of ejectment. The plaintiff then brought a bill for specific performance of defendant's agreement to sell plaintiff the house. Lord Kenyon decided that because the plaintiff had done such things as furnishing and repairing the house that specific performance should be ordered. But, the defendant answered that he had sold the house. Lord Kenyon then ordered the master in chancery to determine the damages that the plaintiff had suffered.[75] While *Denton* suggests that courts of equity could order damages when specific performance or an injunction became impossible during the suit, other cases, including *Gwillim v. Stone*,[76] *Todd v. Gee*,[77] and *Sainsbury v. Jones*,[78] suggest that *Denton* was not the rule at the time.

In *Sainsbury*, for example, Lord Cottenham stated that the authority for equity courts to award damages is based on *Denton* but "at the time, very little weight was attached to it."[79] He explained that even in *Greenaway v. Adams*, which "added something to the authority of *Denton*," the master "threw out strong doubts as to the principle" of *Denton*. This supposed principle from *Denton* "lasted but a short time," with Lord Eldon expressly overruling *Denton* in *Todd*.[80]

In addition to these unusual circumstances where equity courts decided damages after discovery or instead of equitable relief, some matters that involve damages were said to be exclusively for equity courts to hear – most notably, trusts.[81] Trusts were carved out for equity jurisdiction because of the special relationship between the parties. One example was a trust created for a wife before marriage.[82] There was some opinion – though at best mixed – that the

---

[75] 29 Eng. Rep. 1156 (Ch. 1786). There were several masters in chancery and the number fluctuated over time.

[76] 33 Eng. Rep. 469 (Ch. 1807).

[77] 34 Eng. Rep. 106 (Ch. 1810).

[78] 41 Eng. Rep. 272 (Ch. 1839).

[79] 41 Eng. Rep. at 273.

[80] *See id.* (mentioning *Greenaway*, 33 Eng. Rep. 149 (1806)).

[81] *See* 1 BALLOW, *supra* note 70, at 10–11 (in Fonblanque's additions); 3 BLACKSTONE, *supra* note 69, at 431–32, 439.

[82] *See* Allen v. Imlett, 171 Eng. Rep. 370 (Assizes 1817).

courts of law and thus juries had jurisdiction over some of the matters of trust.[83]

In summary, while the priority was for a remedy in a court of law, the courts of law and equity operated in conjunction with one another. Parties generally received damages from juries in courts of law. On the other hand, parties received discovery, specific performance, and injunctions from judges in courts of equity. Judges in equity courts also granted monetary relief in at least certain trust cases.

Although there is additional case law in which equity courts decided damages, as explained earlier, this is not authoritative. The courts of law were to decide damages, even when discovery occurred in equity courts. Similarly, even though equity courts decided damages in some circumstances when it considered equitable relief, subsequent courts did not recognize this authority. It also appeared that the plaintiffs themselves preferred that the courts of equity order damages in these unusual circumstances than for the plaintiffs to be required to file again in a court of law.[84] Most importantly, the respective basic division of powers between the courts of law and equity was clear. Juries in the courts of law ordered monetary damages, and the courts of equity ordered equitable relief such as specific performance and injunctions.[85]

Parliament's Authority to Direct Damages to Courts

To answer whether congressional action to direct monetary damages decisions to judges is constitutionally valid, the late eighteenth-century authority of Parliament to send cases with damages to judges must be examined. In the eighteenth century, pursuant to statutes – including usury statutes, labor statutes, bankruptcy statutes, and intellectual property statutes – Parliament gave plaintiffs rights, for example, against oppressive interest rates, wrongful dismissal, creditors, and infringement. Statutory actions like these were heard in common law courts before juries when the remedy was damages. In cases brought under statutes, plaintiffs could seek discovery or equitable relief from equity courts, but

---

[83] 3 BLACKSTONE, *supra* note 69, at 432.

[84] *See also* Peter M. McDermott, *Jurisdiction of the Court of Chancery to Award Damages*, 109 L. Q. REV. 652, 657–72 (1992).

[85] Also, juries decided civil actions for penalties for violating certain laws. *See* Calcraft v. Gibbs, 101 Eng. Rep. 11 (K.B. 1792) (debt for violation of game laws); Atcheson v. Everitt, 98 Eng. Rep. 1142, 1147–48 (K.B. 1775) (characterizing as a civil action with penalties an action of debt for bribery).

not damages.[86] So, in the eighteenth century, Parliament did not change the jurisdiction of the courts of law and equity and thus, the jury.

In the nineteenth century, Parliament acted to change these jurisdictions. It enacted statutes that permitted judges in the courts of law to, among other things, decide cases without juries with the consent of the parties and to grant injunctions and specific performance.[87] In Lord Cairns' Act, Parliament also acted to alter the jurisdiction of the courts of equity to permit those courts to order damages.[88] Eventually, in the late nineteenth century, Parliament merged the courts of law and equity,[89] and also, over time, Parliament made more changes to the jury trial, limiting its availability.[90]

The Unconstitutional Nature of the Shift of Money Damages and Fines Away from Juries

In late eighteenth-century England, the general distinction upon which a jury trial existed was whether the plaintiff sought monetary damages. Courts of law with juries heard claims alleging monetary damages, and courts of equity decided claims seeking specific performance and injunctions. In rare cases, when a court of equity otherwise had jurisdiction, a court of equity might order damages, but this exercise of jurisdiction to order damages was quite controversial. Also, trusts are the notable exception where courts of equity may have had exclusive jurisdiction. Thus, the substance of the difference between the courts of law and equity in England was the remedy, not the type of case, and in the late eighteenth century, through its creation of new causes of action, Parliament did not act contrary to these divisions between the courts of law and equity.

---

[86] See James Oldham, English Common Law in the Age of Mansfield 32–33, 107, 111, 165, 190–99, 346 (2004).

[87] Common Law Procedure Act (1854) 17 & 18 Vict. c. 125 § 1. Clearly, parties sometimes consented to try their cases without a jury prior to this time.

[88] Chancery Amendment Act (1858) 21 & 22 Vict. c. 27.

[89] Supreme Court of Judicature Act (1873) 36 & 37 Vict. c. 66 § 1.

[90] See Joshua Getzler, The Fate of the Civil Jury in Late Victorian England, in "The Dearest Birth Right of the People of England": The Jury in the History of the Common Law 221 (John W. Cairns & Grant McLeod eds., 2002); Michael Lobban, The Strange Life of the English Civil Jury, 1837–1914, in "The Dearest Birth Right," supra note, at 173–209.

In the mid-nineteenth century, Parliament acted to change the authority of the courts. It permitted equity courts to order damages without a jury trial when it otherwise properly had the case and also permitted the parties to agree to try a case in a court of law by a judge without a jury. The jurisdiction of the jury continued to decrease over time in England through statutory developments. Thus, while juries in courts of law had the almost exclusive jurisdiction to determine claims with damages in the late eighteenth century, Parliament later exercised power to change this jurisdiction of the courts, including the jurisdiction of the jury.

Because Parliament exercised power to alter the jury's jurisdiction in the nineteenth century, it appears that Parliament could have exercised such power in the late eighteenth century. So, if Parliament could exercise this power in England in the late eighteenth century at the time when the Seventh Amendment was adopted, the question is whether Congress can similarly chose to give certain matters with monetary remedies to courts.

A comparison of the English system and the United States' Constitution answers this question. Despite the famous early seventeenth-century Bonham's Case, which asserted the authority of English courts over Parliamentary acts,[91] it was generally believed that Parliament could take any actions, including the alteration of the common law.[92] Blackstone stated that Parliament was "always of absolute authority."[93] Moreover, statutes could be "declaratory" or "remedial" of the common law, and it was stated that "the common law gives place to the statute."[94]

---

[91] See Dr. Bonham's Case, 77 Eng. Rep. 646 (K.B. 1610); see also Theodore F.T. PLUCKNETT, A CONCISE HISTORY OF THE COMMON LAW 51, 336–37 (5th ed. 1956) (discussing irrelevance of Bonham's Case).

[92] See 1 WILLIAM BLACKSTONE, COMMENTARIES ON THE LAWS OF ENGLAND 90–91 (University of Chicago Press 1979) (1765); 1 BALLOW, supra note 70, at 17–18 ("But if the law has determined a matter with all its circumstances, equity cannot intermeddle . . . and for the Chancery to relieve against the express provision of an act of Parliament, would be the same as to repeal it. . . . Equity, therefore, will not interpose in such cases, notwithstanding accident and unavoidable necessity."); PLUCKNETT, supra note 91, at 337 ("Parliament could do anything but make a man a woman."). Blackstone also stated that acts contrary to reason would not be enforced, 1 BLACKSTONE, supra note 92, at 90–91, but Fonblanque says his statements of parliamentary supremacy are contradictory to this, see 1 BALLOW, supra note 70, at 23 (in Fonblanque's additions).

[93] 1 BLACKSTONE, supra note 92, at 90, 143 ("the supreme and absolute authority of the state"); A.V. DICEY, INTRODUCTION TO THE STUDY OF THE LAW OF THE CONSTITUTION 37–176 (8th ed. 1915) (parliamentary sovereignty).

[94] 1 BLACKSTONE, supra note 92, at 86–87, 89.

Different from this constitutional structure, the United States Constitution grants Congress certain specified authority in Article I, which does not include giving Congress any authority over the jury. Further, the Seventh Amendment itself grants only the judiciary power over the jury to "re-examine[] [facts tried by a jury] . . . according to the rules of the common law."[95] The separation of powers recognized between the judiciary and the legislature in the Constitution also suggests that Congress should not be able to exercise additional authority over the jury right. The general Seventh Amendment language that "preserved" the jury trial lends more support that Congress does not have authority over the jury.[96] Any implicit grant of power to Congress to eliminate the jury would render the "preserved" language meaningless. Finally, in the late eighteenth century in England, there was no experience with a legislature-dictated jury trial right despite the power of Parliament to alter it. The experience in the late eighteenth century was that juries heard claims alleging damages in the law courts, and Parliament did not interfere. Thus, if it had been the intention to give Congress power contrary to this, Congress's power would have been explicit. Absent this provision in the Constitution, because juries heard claims alleging damages in the common law courts in the late eighteenth century in England, and Congress has no special authority to change this division, juries possess authority to hear claims requesting monetary remedies.[97]

Other authority supports this interpretation. Even though Parliament could change the jurisdiction of the English courts and the jury, Congress operates under a different Constitution than Parliament – one that does not grant it the same authority. Walter Bagehot generally discussed the English Constitution. It did not set forth a division of authority into legislative, executive, and judicial powers that were separate and equally balanced. Instead "[t]he efficient secret of the English Constitution may

---

[95] U.S. CONST. amend. VII.

[96] U.S. CONST. amend. VII.

[97] As a corollary, even the text of the Amendment that references "exceed twenty dollars" suggests a jury trial right in any case where there are claims with damages exceeding twenty dollars. Note, *The Twenty Dollars Clause*, 118 HARV. L. REV. 1665 (2005). Moreover, the somewhat inflexible nature of the Amendment with the $20 clause that must be changed by amendment of the Constitution suggests the overall inflexible nature of the Seventh Amendment. *Id.* at 1672. Also, this specific change to the English common law suggests that the only change to the common law right was a requirement of twenty dollars. Moreover, the Seventh Amendment was not necessary if Congress could decide the jurisdiction of the jury because Congress had already acted to establish a jury trial in civil cases in 1789 prior to the constitutional amendment.

be described as the close union, the nearly complete fusion, of the executive and legislative powers." He explained the basic difference between the English and American systems as fused powers contrasting with the separation of powers.

> Just as the American is the type of *composite* governments, in which the supreme power is divided between many bodies and functionaries, so the English is the type of *simple* constitutions, in which the ultimate power upon all questions is in the hands of the same persons. The ultimate authority in the English Constitution is a newly-elected House of Commons.[98]

A constitutional amendment would be required in the United States to achieve the result reached by the Lord Cairns' Act by which Parliament gave equity courts the power to decide monetary damages.[99]

The constitutional text and English history thus support that the Constitution gave Congress no special authority – to remove or enhance for that matter – the constitutional jury trial authority. Accordingly, if Congress creates a statutory scheme that grants monetary remedies, a jury should determine those claims, as they did in England in the late eighteenth century.

Following the merger of law and equity in the federal rules in the 1930s, the appropriate role of the jury became even more apparent. Because a jury was readily available in all cases after the merger, a jury could decide claims with damages like juries heard them in the common law courts. So, where Congress creates new causes of action with money damages, because juries decided claims with such damages at English common law, juries presently have the authority to decide these cases, including ones currently before administrative agencies and bankruptcy courts.

---

[98] WALTER BAGEHOT, THE ENGLISH CONSTITUTION 2, 10–11, 227 (1872).

[99] A commentator has noted "American judges and legislators are limited throughout this matter by constitutional requirements of jury trials in all cases except those where equity had power to assess damages at the time the constitutions were adopted. Since equity at such times had only a parasitic jurisdiction to award damages for the sake of completeness where some injunctive relief was given, these jury requirements bar any jurisdiction in equity to give damages in entire substitution for equitable relief unless the defendant waives his jury claim. Until constitutional amendments alter this situation, the results of Lord Cairns' Act probably cannot be attained in this country." Note, *Lord Cairns' Act: Statutory Jurisdiction of Modern Equity Courts to Award Prospective Damages*, 38 HARV. L. REV. 667, 671–72 (1925).

Summary Judgment

Even in the civil cases in which jury trial authority is recognized, courts can use procedures to take away that authority. Under one mechanism called summary judgment, a judge can dismiss a case before a jury hears it if the judge decides there is insufficient evidence to support one side. In one recent case, an employee alleged his employer – the federal government – discriminated and retaliated against him by denying him a promotion. The government argued that the plaintiff did not demonstrate the skills necessary for the promotion. In ordering summary judgment in favor of the government and dismissing the case, the judge analyzed the evidence presented by the plaintiff and the government, including the plaintiff's evaluations, and decided that a reasonable jury could not find for the plaintiff.[100]

The use of summary judgments like this has significantly decreased the number of jury trials in civil cases in federal court. Judges use the procedure to clear the federal docket of cases they deem meritless even though many of the dismissed cases are factually intensive. For example, over 70% of employment discrimination cases are dismissed on summary judgment.[101] In these cases, judges use a paper record of what witnesses have said – which does not show demeanor – as well as documents – such as evaluations. The question is whether, under the Constitution, judges should be able to make this assessment. The Supreme Court has not directly analyzed whether summary judgment is constitutional.[102] An examination of the relevant constitutional text as well as the text's historical meaning shows that the judiciary does not possess such authority to preclude the jury's decision and consequently demonstrates that the procedure is unconstitutional.[103]

---

[100] *See* St. John v. Napolitano, 20 F. Supp.3d 74 (D.D.C. 2013). A judge can order summary judgment for the plaintiff, but this rarely occurs.

[101] *See* Memorandum from Joe Cecil and George Cort to Hon. Michael Baylson 2, 6 tbl.3 (June 15, 2007), www.fjc.gov/public/pdf.nsf/lookup/sujufy06.pdf/$file/sujufy06.pdf.

[102] *See* Suja A. Thomas, *Why Summary Judgment Is Unconstitutional*, 93 VA. L. REV. 139, 163–77 (2007).

[103] For a more extensive examination of the unconstitutional nature of summary judgment, *see* Thomas, *supra* note 102. For a more extensive description of common law procedures, *see* Suja A. Thomas, *The Seventh Amendment, Modern Procedure, and the English Common Law*, 82 WASH. U. L.Q. 687 (2004). For the argument that the motion to dismiss under *Twombly* (and now *Iqbal*) is unconstitutional, *see* Suja A. Thomas, *Why the Motion to Dismiss Is Now Unconstitutional*, 92 MINN. L. REV. 1851 (2008).

Summary Judgment Under Federal Rule of Civil Procedure 56

Federal Rule of Civil Procedure 56 provides that "[t]he court shall grant summary judgment if the movant shows that there is no genuine dispute as to any material fact and the movant is entitled to judgment as a matter of law."[104] The motion for summary judgment turns on an assessment of the sufficiency of the evidence. The judge dismisses the case if "the evidence is such that a reasonable jury could [not] return a verdict for the nonmoving party."[105] In making this determination, the judge is required to consider the entire record in the light most favorable to the nonmoving party and draw "reasonable inferences [from the evidence] in favor of the nonmovant."[106] If a judge grants summary judgment, the losing party can ask the appeals' court to review the decision. However, summary judgment decisions are rarely reversed in some types of cases including employment discrimination matters.[107]

Language in the Constitution

Whether a judge should be able to use summary judgment to dismiss a case before a jury's decision depends on the constitutional authority granted to the judiciary and the jury. As described previously, the Seventh Amendment "preserved" the right to jury trial "[i]n Suits at common law." Furthermore, facts tried by juries may be "re-examined" by a judge only "according to the rules of the common law."[108] No other part of the Constitution grants any explicit authority over the civil jury to the judiciary or any other actor.

The Conflict Between the Common Law and Summary Judgment

In assessing whether modern procedures like summary judgment are constitutional under the Seventh Amendment, the Supreme Court has

---

[104] Fed. R. Civ. P. 56; N.Y.C.P.L.R. § 3212(a) (McKinney 2015).

[105] Anderson v. Liberty Lobby, 477 U.S. 242, 248 (1986).

[106] Reeves v. Sanderson Plumbing Prods., Inc., 530 U.S. 133, 149–50 (2000).

[107] *See, e.g,* Kevin M. Clermont, Theodore Eisenberg, and Stewart J. Schwab, *How Employment-Discrimination Plaintiffs Fare in the Federal Courts of Appeals,* 7 Employee Rts. & Emp. Pol'y J. 547, 548, 555 (2003).

[108] U.S. Const. amend. VII. "In Suits at common law, where the value in controversy shall exceed twenty dollars, the right of trial by jury shall be preserved, and no fact tried by a jury, shall be otherwise re-examined in any Court of the United States, than according to the rules of the common law." *Id.*

compared them to procedures existing in late eighteenth-century England and almost invariably has concluded that the modern procedures do not improperly grant authority to the judiciary.[109] In the following sections, the English common law procedures of the demurrer to the pleadings, the demurrer to the evidence, the nonsuit, the special case, and the new trial are examined. How each of the common law procedures is fundamentally different from summary judgment is described. Moreover, how summary judgment conflicts with the core principles or the "substance" of the common law procedures is explained.

Demurrer to the Pleadings v. Summary Judgment

Demurrer to the pleadings is arguably the procedure that is most relevant to whether judges can use summary judgment, because the demurrer was the only English common law device dismissing a case before trial.[110] As James Oldham has stated "[there was no] procedure (other than the demurrer) that would allow a judge to determine before trial that a case presented no issue to be decided by a jury or that an issue in a case should be withheld from the jury."[111] Under the procedure, the demurring party admitted the truth of the opposing party's declaration (complaint) or plea (answer) and asked the court to use the admitted facts to find that he was entitled to judgment under the law. If, as the party contended, no claim or plea existed under the law, the court would find for that party. If there was such a claim or plea, the court found for the other party because the facts had been admitted.[112]

While judges dismiss cases prior to trial under both summary judgment and the common law demurrer to the pleadings, the procedures do not otherwise share any significant characteristics. On a motion for summary judgment by the defendant, a judge uses the facts alleged by both parties to assess whether the case should be dismissed, deciding whether there is insufficient evidence or whether a reasonable jury could not find for the plaintiff. The English courts could not make this determination. A court could use only the facts admitted by the demurring

---

[109] See Fidelity & Deposit Co. v. United States, 187 U.S. 315 (1902); Baltimore & Carolina Line, Inc. v. Redman, 295 U.S. 654 (1935); Galloway v. United States, 319 U.S. 372 (1943). But see Slocum v. New York Life Ins. Co., 228 U.S. 364 (1913) (finding judgment notwithstanding the verdict unconstitutional).

[110] See JAMES OLDHAM, TRIAL BY JURY: THE SEVENTH AMENDMENT AND ANGLO-AMERICAN SPECIAL JURIES 10 (2006); Oldham, supra note 12, at 231.

[111] Oldham, supra note 12, at 231.

[112] See 3 BLACKSTONE, supra note 69, at 314–15.

party to decide whether to grant judgment for one side. So, under summary judgment, unlike the demurrer to the pleadings, the judge does not use admitted facts to decide who wins. Instead he assesses the facts that have been asserted by each side. He then grants judgment for one side if he decides a reasonable jury could not find for the other party.

Demurrer to the Evidence v. Summary Judgment

Demurrer to the evidence, an objection raised during an English jury trial, has similarities to demurrer to the pleadings. Under this procedure, the demurring party admitted the truth and conclusions of the evidence that the opposing party presented during the trial and asked the court to find for him.[113] The court accepted as true any fact or conclusion to be drawn from the opposing party's evidence, whether such fact or conclusion was "probable or not."[114] Because "[w]hether probable or not, [was] for a jury to decide," facts and conclusions must be admitted.[115] In describing this standard for the demurrer to the evidence in *Gibson v. Hunter*, the House of Lords, the supreme judicial body of England, stated that where a "matter of fact be uncertainly alleged, or that it be doubtful whether it be true or no, because offered to be proved by presumptions or probabilities" the demurring party cannot receive judgment "unless he will confess the matter of fact to be true."[116] The court determined whether a claim or defense existed under the law based on the admitted facts and conclusions.[117] If no claim or defense existed, the demurring party received judgment.[118] If, on the other hand, a claim or defense existed, the court found for the opposing party. This procedure was rarely used because only in an unusual case would a party agree to the facts and conclusions of the opposing party's evidence.[119]

---

[113] *See* Francis Buller, An Introduction to the Law Relative to Trials at Nisi Prius 307 (London, W. Strahan & M. Woodfall 1772).

[114] Cocksedge v. Fanshaw, 99 Eng. Rep. 80, 88 (1779); *see also* Gibson v. Hunter, 126 Eng. Rep. 499, 510 (1793) (stating that the defendant must admit "every fact, and every conclusion, which the evidence given for the Plaintiff conduced to prove").

[115] *Cocksedge*, 99 Eng. Rep. at 88.

[116] *Gibson*, 126 Eng. Rep. at 510.

[117] *See Cocksedge*, 99 Eng. Rep. at 88.

[118] *See* Buller, *supra* note 113, at 307.

[119] *Gibson*, 126 Eng. Rep. at 508, 510. Lord Chief Justice Eyre, writing for the Lords, concluded that "after this explanation of the doctrine of demurrers to evidence, I have very confident expectations that a demurrer like the present will never hereafter find its way into this House." *Id.* The House of Lords stated that the procedure was "not familiar in practice" and surmised that following its clarification of the standard for the demurrer requiring the demurring party to admit all facts and conclusions to win, the procedure would rarely be used. *See id.*

The demurrer to the evidence and summary judgment are fundamentally different beginning with timing. The demurrer to the evidence occurred during the trial, and summary judgment occurs before trial. More significantly, on a motion for summary judgment, a judge assesses the facts alleged by both parties to decide whether to dismiss the case, deciding whether a reasonable jury could not find for one party. Again, the English courts could not make this determination. A court could use only the facts and conclusions of the opposing party's evidence admitted by the demurring party to decide whether to grant judgment. So, under summary judgment, unlike the demurrer to the evidence, the judge does not use admitted facts and conclusions to decide who wins. Instead, she assesses the facts. She grants judgment for one side if she decides a reasonable jury could not find for the other party.

Nonsuit v. Summary Judgment

The nonsuit, another eighteenth-century English procedure, was used in two different ways and occurred during and after trial. The first, and more common, occurred during the trial, when the plaintiff did not appear after his name was called in court either because he believed that his evidence was insufficient or because he believed that he had no claim under the law.[120] The plaintiff would be nonsuited and could commence the same suit against the same defendant at a later date. If, however, the plaintiff appeared or, in other words, did not withdraw from the case, the jury would decide the case, and the plaintiff could not try his case again.[121] Under the nonsuit, the plaintiff could not be compelled to withdraw. Thus, "if he insist[ed] upon the matter being left to the jury, they must give in their verdict."[122]

Summary judgment differs from the nonsuit. Different from summary judgment under which a judge dismisses a case, under the nonsuit, the decision to withdraw belonged only to the plaintiff, not to the court. Additionally, after summary judgment against the plaintiff, he cannot bring the case again, while under the nonsuit, the plaintiff could try his case again.

The second type of nonsuit, referred to as the "compulsory nonsuit," was rare.[123] This occurred without the plaintiff's consent and upon the defendant's motion following a jury verdict for the plaintiff.[124] Under the

---

[120] *See* 2 William Tidd, The Practice of the Court of King's Bench, in Personal Actions 586–87 (London, A. Strahan & W. Woodfall 1794).

[121] *See* 3 Blackstone, *supra* note 69, at 376–77.

[122] 2 Tidd, *supra* note 120, at 588.

[123] *See* Oldham, *supra* note 12, at 231 n.35.

[124] *See* Henderson, *supra* note 37, at 301.

compulsory nonsuit, the court would enter judgment for the defendant only if the jury's verdict was unsupported as to a particular matter of law.[125] For example, the plaintiff may not have presented certain specific, required evidence. In one case, the plaintiff had not produced the person who had signed the bond that was at issue in the case. While this was a "technical rule," the witness was required.[126] On the other hand, a court could not order a compulsory nonsuit upon general assertions regarding the insufficiency of the plaintiff's evidence. As Justice Buller stated in *Company of Carpenters v. Hayward*, "[w]hether there be any evidence, is a question for the Judge. Whether [there be] sufficient evidence, is for the jury."[127]

Summary judgment differs from the compulsory nonsuit. First, the procedures occur at different times. Summary judgment occurs before a jury trial, while the compulsory nonsuit occurred after a jury trial. Second, while both procedures involve judicial determinations without the plaintiff's consent, under summary judgment, the court determines the general sufficiency of the evidence. This differs from the compulsory nonsuit, under which the court could play no such role.

Special Case v. Summary Judgment

The special case, also referred to as the "case stated," is another common law procedure that concerned the jury.[128] If the jury found for the plaintiff upon a general verdict, the court could make a legal decision upon the case stated.[129] Here, after the facts of the case were firmly established and stated by the court, either upon the parties' agreement or the jury's determination, the court would decide the legal issue.[130] The parties would argue this legal issue, strictly constrained to the case stated

---

[125] *See* Co. of Carpenters v. Hayward, 99 Eng. Rep. 241 (1780); Pleasant v. Benson, 104 Eng. Rep. 590, 591 (1811).

[126] Abbot v. Plumbe, 99 Eng. Rep. 141 (1779).

[127] *Co. of Carpenters*, 99 Eng. Rep. at 241–42.

[128] *See* OLDHAM, *supra* note 110, at 13 (discussing the case stated and also arguing that Edith Henderson inaccurately described the role of the jury under the case stated); *see also* OLDHAM, *supra* note 86, at 251–52, 258–59. *But see* Henderson, *supra* note 37, at 305–06 (arguing that the jury "scarcely participated at all" under the case stated).

[129] *See* 3 BLACKSTONE, *supra* note 69, at 378.

[130] *See id.*; 2 TIDD, *supra* note 120, at 598 ("In a special case, as in a special verdict, the facts proved at the trial ought to be stated, and not merely the evidence of the facts. It is usually dictated by the court, and signed by the counsel, before the jury are discharged; and if in settling it, any difference arises about a fact, the opinion of the jury is taken, and the fact stated accordingly.").

at the trial.[131] The court decided only a legal issue, which did not involve a question of the sufficiency of the evidence.[132]

Summary judgment again contrasts with this common law procedure. In deciding summary judgment, a procedure before trial, a court assesses whether the evidence is sufficient, without the parties or the jury determining the facts. In contrast, on a special case, after trial, the court used facts agreed to by the parties, or if the parties had disagreed, the jury determined the facts. The facts were conclusively established – or "stated" – prior to the court deciding the legal issues. So under summary judgment, unlike the special case, the judge does not use party or jury-established facts to decide a legal issue. Instead he assesses the facts. He grants judgment for one side if he decides a reasonable jury could not find for the other party.

New Trial v. Summary Judgment

A new trial is another common law procedure that affected the jury trial. After a jury rendered a verdict against a party, the party could move for a new trial. The party could argue that the evidence did not support the jury verdict, and the Court of King's Bench granted the motion if it decided the verdict was strongly against the weight of the evidence.[133]

While there are similarities between the common law new trial and summary judgment, the methods and the result of the procedures differ greatly. For both the motion for a new trial and the motion for summary judgment, the court decides whether sufficient evidence supports the opposing party's case. But on the new trial motion, live evidence at trial was assessed, while on summary judgment, non-live evidence is reviewed. An additional significant difference is the result. The new trial resulted in a new jury trial. On the other hand, under summary judgment, no jury trial occurs and the judge decides in favor of one party.

Summary Judgment Is Unconstitutional

Although each of the English procedures significantly differs from summary judgment, whether summary judgment is constitutional is best decided by comparing summary judgment to the core principles or substance of the English common law procedures that affected the civil jury trial. There are a few core common law principles. First, only the

---

[131] See 3 BLACKSTONE, *supra* note 69, at 378; 2 TIDD, *supra* note 120, at 598–99.

[132] See 2 TIDD, *supra* note 120, at 598–99.

[133] See 3 BLACKSTONE, *supra* note 69, at 387.

jury or the parties determined the facts. The court itself would never decide a case without such a determination of the facts by the jury or the parties. Second, a court decided whether there was sufficient evidence only after a jury rendered a verdict. Even then, the court would order only a new trial. Finally, a jury, not a court, decided a case that had any evidence, however improbable, unless the moving party admitted all of the facts and conclusions of the nonmoving party, including the improbable facts and conclusions.

Summary judgment violates the first core principle that the jury or the parties determined the facts. On a summary judgment motion, the court decides the case without a jury or the parties deciding the facts. The court assesses the evidence, decides what inferences from the evidence are reasonable, and decides whether a reasonable jury could find for the nonmoving party.

Summary judgment also breaches the second core principle of the common law that a court determined whether the evidence was sufficient only after a jury rendered a verdict and ordered only a new trial if the evidence was insufficient. On summary judgment, prior to trial, a court determines that the nonmoving party's evidence is insufficient and finds for the other party, completely eliminating the jury trial.

Finally, summary judgment violates the third core principle of the common law that a jury, not a court, decided a case that had any evidence, however improbable, unless the moving party admitted all facts and conclusions of the nonmoving party, including the improbable facts and conclusions. On summary judgment, a judge decides the evidence is insufficient, removing the case from the jury, without the requesting party admitting the truth of the opposing party's evidence and instead on an assessment of what a reasonable jury could find. So, examining the substance or core principles of the common law, summary judgment is unconstitutional under the Constitution.

*****

Previously, scholars have responded to this argument that summary judgment is unconstitutional. Brunet and Nelson agreed that the common law in 1791 governs the analysis.[134] Nelson also believed that

---

[134] *See* Edward Brunet, *Summary Judgment Is Constitutional*, 93 Iowa L. Rev. 1625, 1627–30 (2008); William E. Nelson, *Summary Judgment and the Progressive Constitution*, 93 Iowa L. Rev. 1653, 1656 (2008).

"a modern judge who is committed to interpreting the Seventh Amendment as its drafters and ratifiers would have applied it should deem summary judgment . . . unconstitutional." Despite this view, Nelson argued that the common law should not govern whether summary judgment is unconstitutional. Because he believed the purpose of the Seventh Amendment – which he asserted was protecting "local self-rule" – does not exist, he argued that the Seventh Amendment is irrelevant today. At most, the Amendment should evolve to meet modern-day needs, and summary judgment must be constitutional by this necessity.[135] Nelson did not recognize that the reasons for the Seventh Amendment went beyond the protection of local self-rule, including the protection against judges. Moreover, the protection of local self-rule arguably continues to be an important policy.[136] More importantly, regardless of opinions on the irrelevance of a constitutional provision or the harm to corporate interests, as discussed by Nelson,[137] the provision stays in force until amended.

Brunet attempted to debate Nelson's, James Oldham's,[138] and this book's conclusion that there is no common law analogy to summary judgment.[139] He pointed out a procedure called the trial by inspection where there was no jury trial. Under this procedure, "the law depart[ed] from it's [sic] usual resort, the verdict of twelve men" if judges could decide an issue "upon the testimony of their own senses." There was a narrow set of circumstances when judges could decide in this manner, for example, to decide if a person was of sufficient age to enter into a contract. A judge would view the person in court and hear additional testimony if by viewing the person, he could not determine the age of the person.[140] Trial by inspection did not involve judges deciding the sufficiency of the evidence as they do

---

[135] Nelson, *supra* note 134, at 1658–66.

[136] *See* Suja A. Thomas, *Why Summary Judgment Is Still Unconstitutional: A Reply to Professors Brunet and Nelson*, 93 Iowa L. Rev. 1667, 1680 (2008) (discussing Charles W. Wolfram, *The Constitutional History of the Seventh Amendment*, 57 Minn. L. Rev. 639 (1973)).

[137] *See* Nelson, *supra* note 134, at 1660.

[138] *Cf.* Oldham, *supra* note 110, at 10 ("[A]lmost all cases in the common-law courts were tried before juries."); *see id.* at 15 ("The Seventh Amendment historical test has become an American legal fiction in application, since many more things were lodged in juries in England in 1791 than modern American courts, including the Supreme Court, are prepared to acknowledge.").

[139] *See* Brunet, *supra* note 134, at 1627–30.

[140] 3 Blackstone, *supra* note 69, at 331–33.

under summary judgment. Instead, it is analogous to judicial notice.[141]

Brian Fitzpatrick has argued that outside of looking at the jury practices and judicial procedures that affect the jury trial in the late eighteenth century, there should be a separate "external frame of reference." These include the founding meanings of the constitutional provision where the text is clear, statements of the Framers regarding the meaning where the text is vague, or where none of this evidence exists, information about the purpose.[142] Here, all of these types of material were examined to explore civil jury trial authority. The jury text, the roles that the jury and the traditional constitutional actors were to play in the constitutional structure, the constitutional text as a whole, and actual jury and judicial practices were all considered to derive the substance or essentials of the late eighteenth-century English common law civil jury trial.

*****

One final note about the attempted comparisons between modern procedures and the English procedures is worthy of mention. Several of the English procedures could be used only by the full Court of King's Bench and not by a lone judge. As examples, only the full court decided whether to grant a new trial or the demurrer to the evidence.[143] So, a group of judges decided these important issues, as opposed to the practice today where one judge decides.

Re-establishing Balance by Recognizing the Other "Branch"

This chapter has demonstrated the constitutional impropriety of four major modern mechanisms that usurp jury authority. With these procedures in place and gainfully used, in essence, the jury ceases to exist. Take these procedures away and the jury re-emerges, becoming a part of

---

[141] *See* Thomas, *supra* note 136, at 1672–78. In another response to the argument that summary judgment is unconstitutional, Luke Meier attempts to compare summary judgment to the compulsory nonsuit, already addressed here and to presumptions and the law of evidence. *See* Luke Meier, *Probability, Confidence, and the Constitutionality of Summary Judgment*, 42 Hastings Const. L.Q. 1, 19–45 (2014).

[142] *See* Brian T. Fitzpatrick, *Originalism and Summary Judgment*, 71 Ohio St. L.J. 919, 925 (2010).

[143] *See* J.H. Baker, An Introduction to English Legal History 84–85 (4th ed. 2011); Oldham, *supra* note 86, at 43.

the governmental structure – beginning to restore the balancing role it was intended to play in government.

In the past, some attempts to question the propriety of modern procedures that take away jury authority have been met with the objection that these criticisms come too late – that these procedures serve as important controls in our system. However, the sources of this disapproval are the traditional actors who cling to authority that they improperly hold or other parties who benefit from this power structure.[144]

What would an objective examination of how the system should be restructured look like? One might argue that "stare decisis" – adhering to the court's past decisions – is one possible manner to evaluate whether the rebalancing should occur through ridding the system of these procedures. This assessment may not be objective, however, because the judiciary, which has benefited from the diminution of the jury and has absconded with jury authority, administers the stare decisis analysis. Previous stare decisis assessments have not recognized these conflict-ridden power dynamics between traditional actors like the judiciary and the jury. The stare decisis analysis also does not take into account the current precarious status of the jury with its inability to protect its own authority in any manner.

The previous chapter resolved this power dynamic between the traditional actors and the jury by recognizing deference due to the jury similar to the respect given to traditional actors under separation of powers and federalism – acquiescing to the competing authority of the jury when the meaning of the text is not clear and either actor could arguably possess authority. Using this test, there is no question about the particular authority of the jury and the traditional actors; the jury held the authority in the past and this power has shifted to the other bodies through modern procedures.

The daunting task remains, however, of reconfiguring a workable system to include the jury to share in authority and serve as a check on the other bodies. Could the balance of authority be re-established without eliminating the existing procedures? It is difficult to conceive of a system where the jury plays an essential role in government where the procedures discussed here continue to exist. They render the jury's authority essentially meaningless. For example, acquittal replaces the jury's decision with the judge's. And summary judgment substitutes a judge's

---

[144] Efficiency issues have already been addressed. *See supra* Chapter 4.

judgment for a jury's. So, the rebalancing must include addressing these procedures that take away significant jury authority.

Because the federal and state governments have adjusted to significant change made by the Court in the past, restructuring has some precedent that can be followed here. And in these circumstances, the Court has often ignored or given short shrift to stare decisis. For example, in *Plessy v. Ferguson*, in 1896, the Court found constitutional under the Fourteenth Amendment a Louisiana law that required "equal but separate" passenger railway cars for whites and people of color.[145] Relying on this decision, states and localities continued to create separate facilities, including schools. However, many years later, in 1954, in *Brown v. Board of Education*, considering schools separated by race, the Court overruled *Plessy*, deciding that such separate facilities could not be equal despite reliance by states and localities.[146] There, the Court ignored stare decisis. Another example is found in sodomy cases. In *Bowers v. Hardwick*, in 1986, the plaintiff had been arrested on charges of sodomy with another male under a Georgia law. The Court decided that the due process clause of the Fourteenth Amendment did not protect gays' engagement in sodomy.[147] Decades later, in 2003, in *Lawrence v. Texas*, the Court overruled *Bowers*, deciding a Texas law forbidding gays from engaging in sodomy, under which the plaintiffs had been convicted, was unconstitutional under the due process clause. Despite some reliance by states and localities, stare decisis was not applied, the Court stating "*stare decisis . . . is not . . . an inexorable command.*"[148] In the final example, in *Ohio v. Roberts*, the Court found constitutional under the Sixth Amendment confrontation clause the admission of certain prior testimony against the accused in a criminal trial. This evidence of a now unavailable witness was deemed reliable by a judge.[149] More than two decades later, in *Crawford v. Washington*, with the concurrence recognizing the same stare decisis language used in *Lawrence v. Texas*,[150] the Court rejected the decision in *Ohio v. Roberts*, deciding actual confrontation was required.[151] While one might argue that these rights are more important than jury authority, the Constitution does not give them such priority.

---

[145] 163 U.S. 537 (1896).
[146] *See* 347 U.S. 483 (1954).
[147] *See* 478 U.S. 186 (1986).
[148] 539 U.S. 558, 577 (2003).
[149] *See* 448 U.S. 56 (1980).
[150] *See* 541 U.S. 36, 75 (2004) (Rehnquist, J., concurring).
[151] *See* 541 U.S. 36 (2004)

Also, this issue of jury authority concerns the significant matter of which entity should have the power to decide crucial questions.

If the procedures at issue here were eliminated, there might be several objections. If acquittal were eliminated, innocent people could go to prison. While new trials were not available for felonies, a new trial does not offend the principles of the common law jury trial. This procedure would be a mechanism to permit the judge to question the jury's verdict but still leave the result to another jury. Other objections to restoring the jury's past role relate to resources. If grand juries were required in all of the states, states may not have the resources to provide these juries. This resource problem is certainly likely. Change would need to occur over time with states being required to shift resources to the creation and sustenance of this body. If other bodies such as administrative agencies and bankruptcy courts did not decide money damages' issues, more resources would be needed in civil trial courts. Finally, another possible resource issue concerns the elimination of summary judgment. More trials would occur without summary judgment, and weaker cases may be brought in the absence of summary judgment. Although these results are possible, parties will continue to settle cases because they can lose at trial before a jury. Also, lawyers have some incentives not to bring weak cases. These include the possibility that they will lose and also that they have limited resources to invest in cases. Moreover, court resources will be saved by courts not reviewing summary judgment motions.

Conclusion

The system proposed here – eliminating the procedures of judicial acquittal, summary judgment, and judges deciding money damages, as well as adding grand juries in states – would require significant changes. On the other hand, it begins to restore the role of the jury under the Constitution. Moreover, other jury-infringing procedures including others discussed in Chapter 2 such as plea bargaining should be reconsidered under originalism.

6

Beyond the Constitution

Affirming a Role for Lay Jurors in America's Government and World-Wide

This book has discussed constitutional necessity thus far. That is, the jury is required under the Constitution, its role has been unconstitutionally usurped, its fall relates to the failure of the traditional actors to view it as an equal – a "branch" – and its revival can occur by restoring it to its former role. Some do not adhere to the past as the constitutional guidepost for the jury and instead view the jury's constitutional role as evolving. For them, for the jury to have a place in the governmental structure, it must have some other value.

Some commentators have rejected any such auxiliary worth for the jury. For example, certain critics consider the criminal jury dispensable for reasons that include the availability of accurate investigative techniques.[1] The grand jury also has been critiqued. The recent failures of grand juries to indict police officers have resulted in calls for their abolition.[2] Even before those events, contrasting politically accountable prosecutors with secretive grand juries, Andrew Leipold argued that prosecutors should be given investigative powers instead of grand juries. He also has asserted that in the absence of grand juries playing any independent function such as working against government corruption, grand juries hold no important role.[3]

Many also argue that the civil jury lacks value. William Nelson and John Langbein both have contended that the civil jury trial has lost its usefulness in light of modern changes. According to Nelson, the reason for juries, which he stated was local self-rule, has disappeared, and the

---

[1] *See* George Fisher, Plea Bargaining's Triumph: A History of Plea Bargaining in America 10 (2003) (discussing Lawrence M. Friedman & Robert V. Percival, Roots of Justice: Crime and Punishment in Alameda County, California, 1870–1910 (1981)).

[2] *See, e.g.*, LaDoris Hazzard Cordell, *Grand Juries Should Be Abolished*, Slate, Dec. 9, 2014.

[3] *See* Andrew D. Leipold, *Why Grand Juries Do Not (and Cannot) Protect the Accused*, 80 Cornell L. Rev. 260, 314–21 (1995).

civil jury appropriately declined in authority as its purpose dissipated.[4] Langbein cited other reasons for the obsolescence of the civil jury. He argued that people do not go to trial in civil cases, because they do not need to do so. In his view, discovery, summary judgment, and settlement effectively substitute for the civil jury trial.[5]

This chapter counters these views, showing value for America's jury through two emerging ideas. First, although the jury is often displayed as a prime example of American exceptionalism, the significant and growing use of lay participation in several other countries – often where a constitution does not require it – displays a generally unrecognized role for lay people in governments throughout the world. In the debate over the importance of juries in America, this place of lay people in other nations' governance largely has been ignored. Although there are differences between lay participation here and abroad, the use of lay jurors elsewhere demonstrates some common value for a role for lay people in judicial decision-making. On the other hand, some other countries' uses of judges to check decisions that involve lay people, similar to judges' reviews of juries' decisions in the United States, display a common distrust of lay decision-making. Finally, because some nations do not engage in this type of judicial review, in certain ways, they actually utilize lay jurors as much or more than the United States despite perceptions of the American jury system leading the world in lay participation.

Because other countries do not provide juries in nearly the set of cases where juries are theoretically available in America – for example, almost never granting a jury in civil cases – arguably, the American jury's formal constitutional role is too extensive. If so, judges in the United States potentially should decide *more* cases. However, the fundamental characteristics of lay jurors, which differ from the judiciary, support instead a more vibrant role for lay participation. These characteristics make the jury an attractive – indeed a more attractive – decision-maker. Specifically, judges and juries have disparate incentives and biases. Among other things, judges have reasons to rule in certain ways for promotion or re-election, while juries do not hold these same monetary or status-related motivations. Moreover, the existing biases of jurors are scrutinized

---

[4] *See* William E. Nelson, *Summary Judgment and the Progressive Constitution*, 93 IOWA L. REV. 1653, 1660, 1662 (2008). Nelson's arguments are addressed in Chapter 4.

[5] *See* John H. Langbein, *The Disappearance of Civil Trial in the United States*, 122 YALE L.J. 522, 542–72 (2012). Langbein's arguments are addressed in Chapter 4.

through deliberations as well as the requirement of consensus at the same time that equivalent checks do not exist for judges.

Possessing some characteristics similar to the judiciary, the executive and the legislature also are vulnerable to prejudices to which the jury is not subject. These differences between the jury and the traditional actors support the jury's restoration in America and the further growth of lay participation in other countries.

A Role for Lay Participation in Governments World-Wide

Despite a declining role of juries in the United States, the participation of lay people in judicial decision-making has a significant world-wide presence and is enjoying a resurgence, posing an interesting counternarrative for the importance of juries. While some countries have used lay jurors for years, others used them in the past and have recently resurrected this form of participation. Still other nations have recently created a form of lay involvement. Tribunals are varied, including panels consisting of all lay people and mixed panels of judges and lay people.

Here, examples of lay participation in other countries – chosen on the bases of significant populations (all rank in the top thirty most populated nations with one exception (Ghana)), geographic diversity, and varied lay systems – are explored.[6] This survey describes the value that several other major countries give lay participation. Additionally, it emphasizes certain similarities between the judicial review of lay decisions in the United States and such controls in some countries abroad. The absence of certain judicial reviews in other nations also shows that in certain respects, these countries actually have more vibrant lay participation than the United States.[7]

United States

Many characteristics of the jury in the United States have already been described. Juries are dictated in some form in both federal courts and state courts. The U.S. Constitution requires criminal, civil, and grand

---

[6] In addition to the citations set forth here, the Acknowledgments list several people who provided information about lay participation in other countries.

[7] Some reviews of decision-making are governed by international covenants and conventions. *See* Peter D. Marshall, *A Comparative Analysis of the Right to Appeal*, 22 DUKE J. COMP. & INT'L LAW 1, 17–22, 24–27 (2011).

juries in federal courts and criminal juries in state courts. Additionally, state constitutions and statutes require criminal, civil, and grand juries in certain cases in state courts.

Selection of jurors generally begins with public databases. In federal court, jurors are chosen from registered voters' lists or other lists such as licensed drivers' lists. U.S. citizens are eligible to serve if they are at least eighteen years old, reside primarily in the relevant federal district for a year, and have never been convicted of a felony. Police and fire department members, active duty armed services' members, as well as "public officers" in federal, state, and local governments are among those who cannot be jurors.[8] Different requirements, though analogous to the federal selection procedures, are in place for state juries.

In federal cases, twelve jurors decide criminal cases, and six to twelve sit in civil cases. Sixteen to twenty-three jurors serve on a federal grand jury panel for about a year. The grand jury determines whether probable cause exists for the charges brought by the government. Once generally selected for service, jurors for criminal, civil, or grand juries may be precluded from serving for cause, including for biases, and before criminal and civil trials, the parties may make a limited number of demands to exclude jurors ("peremptory challenges") for any reasons not related to gender and race. Juries can convict only upon a unanimous vote, and except upon party agreement, to win in a civil case, a jury must find unanimously for the plaintiff.

States have similar but varying decision-making requirements. Six to twelve jurors sit in criminal cases in state court. All states but Louisiana and Oregon require unanimity to convict. (If only six jurors sit, the jury must be unanimous to convict.[9]) In some states, grand juries must decide whether probable cause exists before a case can proceed to trial. In civil cases, the number of jurors varies, and many states do not require a unanimous decision for a plaintiff to win.

In both federal and state courts, jurors and judges have additional influence in cases. Jurors can ask questions; at times, they are permitted to pose them directly to witnesses. Moreover, judges exercise significant power. They may pre-judge cases and second-guess the decisions of juries by dismissing cases before, during, and after the trial, concluding that insufficient evidence exists to support convictions or claims. On appeal,

---

[8] J. George, D. Golash & R. Wheeler, Handbook on Jury Use in the Federal District Courts (Fed. Jud. Ctr. 1989).

[9] *See* Burch v. Louisiana, 441 U.S. 130 (1979).

a panel of judges also has authority. It may dismiss criminal or civil cases for insufficient evidence.

England

The English jury is interesting to discuss for three reasons. First, the American jury was based on it. Second, over time, it has significantly declined in use. Third, despite changes, it continues to be used.

England robustly employed a jury in various forms for many centuries. Because it was never constitutionalized, the power of the jury could be changed by the legislature. The jury began to transform in the mid-nineteenth century when Parliament transferred authority from juries to judges. Judges could decide certain civil cases awarding monetary damages when parties consented.[10] Beginning in this same time period, the legislature began to decrease the jurisdiction of the criminal jury by permitting judges to try certain crimes.[11] In the early twentieth century, the English system continued to undergo transition when the grand jury was eliminated.[12] Although juries continue to hear cases in England, they do not sit for the range of cases that they heard in the past.

Presently, under the English jury system, consisting of only lay people, most are qualified to serve. A person must be registered to vote, be eighteen to sixty-five years old, and be a resident for a period of time.[13] People may be excluded, however, if particular criminal sentences were imposed upon them in the past.[14]

To convene a jury, jurors are selected randomly from a list of qualified people. One of the main reasons a juror may be excluded is for possible bias. Justifications must be provided to exclude jurors because parties cannot exercise peremptory challenges.

---

[10] *See* Conor Hanly, *The Decline of Civil Jury Trial in Nineteenth-Century England*, 26 J. Legal Hist. 253 (2006) (discussing Common Law Procedure Act 1854).

[11] *See* Pendleton Howard, *The Rise of Summary Jurisdiction in English Criminal Law Administration*, 19 Cal. L. Rev. 486, 491–97 (1931).

[12] *See* Albert Lieck, *Abolition of the Grand Jury in England*, 25 J. Crim. L. & Criminology 623 (1934).

[13] Juries Act, 1974, c. 23, § 1; Lorraine Hope & Amina Memon, *Cross-Border Diversity: Trial by Jury in England and Scotland*, in Understanding World Jury Systems Through Social Psychological Research 32 (Martin F. Kaplan & Ana M. Martín eds., 2013).

[14] *See* Alisdair Gillespie, The English Legal System 395–96 (4th ed. 2013) (discussing Criminal Justice Act 2003).

For a criminal trial to take place, twelve jurors are initially required but the trial can continue with less as long as the number does not fall below nine. At the conclusion of a criminal case, although the judge will ask the jury to deliver a unanimous verdict, the vote may be ten to two or nine to one in cases with ten jurors.[15]

Juries can hear only certain types of criminal cases. Juries generally can try crimes where the sentence could be greater than six months' imprisonment.[16] In very limited circumstances where jury tampering may occur, a judge can take these cases away from juries and try them herself.[17]

When a jury sits in a case, with assistance from the judge, jurors can play an active role by asking questions.[18] The judge also has certain duties to influence the jury such as summing up the evidence. Moreover, he is responsible for dismissing cases with insufficient evidence.[19]

If a case goes forward, the judge will instruct the jury on the law, which will be followed by the jury's decision on the question of guilt, and the judge's sentencing. On appeal, the court can review the jury's verdict of guilt and order a new trial or acquittal if it decides the prosecutor presented insufficient evidence of the defendant's guilt such that a reasonable jury could not convict.[20] The prosecution can also assert certain challenges after a defendant is acquitted, including in the circumstance when a judge has dismissed the case for insufficient evidence.[21]

A negotiation process serves as an alternative to trial. While plea bargaining is not statutorily recognized, defense lawyers and prosecutors bargain regularly, and defendants can request a so-called "Goodyear Direction" under which they learn the possible sentence if they plead guilty. The significance of pleas continues to grow, with 70% of defendants in the Crown Court where jury trials occur pleading guilty in 2011, up from 56% in 2001.[22] The English disclaim American-style plea

---

[15] Juries Act, 1974, c. 23, §§ 12, 17(1), 17(4); Gillespie, *supra* note 14, at 425, 445–46.

[16] *See* Gillespie, *supra* note 14, at 403.

[17] Criminal Justice Act, 2003, c. 44, § 44.

[18] *See* Sally Lloyd-Bostock & Cheryl Thomas, *The Continuing Decline of the English Jury*, in World Jury Systems 83 (Neil Vidmar ed., 2000).

[19] *See* Gillespie, *supra* note 14, at 437–40; Lloyd-Bostock & Thomas, *supra* note 18, at 84–89; Regina v. Galbraith, 1 W.L.R. 1039, 1042 (1981).

[20] Criminal Appeal Act, 1968, c. 19, § 2(1) (as amended by the Criminal Appeal Act, 1995, ch. 35); Gillespie, *supra* note 14, at 470; Bron McKillop, *Review of Convictions after Jury Trials: The New French Jury Court of Appeals*, 28 Sydney L. Rev. 343, 343 (2006).

[21] *See* Gillespie, *supra* note 14, at 473–77.

[22] Ministry of Justice, Judicial and Court Statistics 2011, at 9 (June 2012), www.gov.uk/government/uploads/system/uploads/attachment_data/file/217494/judicial-court-stats-2011.pdf.

bargaining, however, stating their procedure does not give the prosecutor authority to direct the process, describing the alleged American practice to attempt to extract a guilty plea by threatening to take away significant benefits as "distaste[ful]."[23]

Civil and criminal cases share some characteristics including most of the same selection procedures. Civil cases usually also consist of a trial by twelve jurors though certain rules such as unanimity requirements may vary from criminal cases.[24] Different from the criminal jury trial in England, the civil jury has almost no presence in England. The civil jury trial is available in only a very small class of cases and even then, jury trials are rare. In the subset of cases where a jury trial may be available – malicious prosecution, false imprisonment, or fraud – a judge may try the case instead of a jury, if she deems the evidence complicated.[25] While juries formerly tried libel and slander, a recent legislature act presumes that judges will try those cases.[26] Outside of cases designated for jury trial, the judge has discretion to order a jury trial in a civil case but this authority is not exercised.[27]

Prior to jury trial, a court can dismiss a civil case upon summary judgment if the "claimant has no real prospect of succeeding on the claim."[28] During or after a trial, a judge can also dismiss a case on this basis, but usually a case thrown out on this ground will be dispensed with prior to this time. After a jury decides liability and damages, on appeal, review of the verdict is possible. After a verdict for the plaintiff, the appellate court can dismiss the case if insufficient evidence for the claim existed such that a reasonable jury could not find for the plaintiff. Also, in a case, if the appellate court deems the damages awarded by the jury "so excessive or so inadequate that no twelve reasonable jurors could reasonably have awarded" them,[29] the court may order a new trial. Alternatively, the court can grant the sum that "appears to the court to be proper."[30]

---

[23] R v. Goodyear, [2005] EWCA Crim. 888, paras. 30, 69 (Supreme Court of Judicature Court of Appeal); McKinnon v. USA and Sec of State, [2007] EWHC 762, para. 54 (High Court of Justice, Queen's Bench Division).

[24] Juries Act 1974, ch. 23, §17(5).

[25] Supreme Court Act, 1981, c. 54, § 69(1).

[26] Defamation Act, 2013, c. 26, § 11.

[27] Supreme Court Act, 1981, c. 54, § 69(3).

[28] Civil Procedure Rule Pt. 24.2.

[29] Scott v. Musial, 2 Q.B. 429, 438 (Eng. C.A. 1959).

[30] Courts and Legal Services Act, 1990, c. 41, § 8 (1) & (2); Kiam v. MGN, Ltd., [2003] Q.B. 281, paras. 16, 17, 48 (Eng. C.A. 2002) (deciding "whether a reasonable jury could have thought the award necessary").

Although juries exist for both criminal and civil cases in England, they do not try many cases, deciding around 1% of criminal cases and less than 1% of civil trials. Cost is one of the reasons cited for the decline of English jury trials and as a reason to have even fewer of them in the future.[31]

*****

The characteristics of jury trials in the United States are significantly different from those in England, including the much larger scope of the jury trial in civil cases in the United States and the unanimity requirement in most American criminal cases. In some ways, though, English practices may provide more protection to the criminal defendant than U.S. procedures. Distinctions in English plea bargaining – imposing stricter rules against coercive practices by prosecutors to obtain pleas – arguably provide English criminal defendants with more protection from wrongful conviction than in the United States – giving English defendants the opportunity to more freely choose a jury trial or a plea. The systems also share similarities to protect the criminal defendant. Like judicial practices in the United States, English judges may preempt the criminal jury's decision as well as overrule its decision to convict when they believe there is insufficient evidence of guilt. Additionally, in civil cases, the American and English systems have commonalities, granting authority to judges over juries. In both, judges can dismiss a claim before a jury hears it and may dismiss it after a jury finds for the plaintiff if they believe insufficient evidence exists. American and English judges also similarly may order a new trial for excessive damages or an alternative reduction in the verdict.

Brazil

The origins of the Brazilian jury date to the early nineteenth century during Portuguese colonization.[32] The English jury is touted as serving as the model for the Brazilian jury that was established after independence.[33] In

---

[31] See Lloyd-Bostock & Thomas, *supra* note 18, at 53, 59, 61.

[32] See Christopher P. Banks & David M. O'Brien, The Judicial Process: Law, Courts, and Judicial Politics 214 (2016); Thomas Flory, Judge and Jury in Imperial Brazil, 1808–1871: Social Control and Political Stability in the New State 116 (1981); Luiz Flavio Gomes & Ana Paula Zomer, *The Brazilian Jury System*, 2001–2002 St. Louis-Warsaw Transatlantic L.J. 75, 75.

[33] See Flory, *supra* note 32, at 142; Tribunal de Justica, Summary: "Institution of Jury in Brazilian Law," www.tjro.jus.br/admweb/faces/jsp/view.jsp?id=a2e835c6-8446-4808-8a9c-d36b050bbedf.

this new system, a grand jury determined if sufficient evidence existed for a trial, and if so, another jury decided whether the accused was guilty.[34] The grand jury was abolished but juries continue to hear certain criminal cases.[35]

Under the current set-up consisting of all lay people, jurors must be citizens and over eighteen. People who meet these qualifications may be excluded from sitting as a juror for reasons that include membership in the judiciary or the legislature.[36] A judge selects a panel of twenty-five jurors to serve for one, two, or three months from the larger set of approved people.[37] Information on the chosen jurors, including their professions, will be published.[38] Under practices currently in place, some jurors will end up serving for years.

By a random drawing from the panel, seven jurors will be chosen to sit on a jury.[39] Each side also may challenge jurors for cause and may exercise peremptory challenges.[40]

Under Brazil's Constitution, juries decide cases involving "intentional crimes against life."[41] In the first instance, a prosecutor decides whether the case involves an intentional act and thus whether a jury hears it. If the case is sent to a jury and the judge decides the case does not involve an intentional act, the judge can send the case to another judge to decide instead of the jury. If the jury hears the case, the jury may decide that intent was not proven, and then, the judge will decide the case. Also, a judge can dismiss a case if he decides that the prosecution presented insufficient evidence.[42]

The procedure in effect for a Brazilian jury trial is particularly unique. Jurors are forbidden from deliberating with one another about the case. They vote privately after being presented with questions about the case and can convict upon a majority verdict.[43] While verdicts are guaranteed "sovereignty,"[44] there are some circumstances for overturning the

---

[34] See FLORY, *supra* note 32, at 119.

[35] See Gomes & Zomer, *supra* note 32, at 75.

[36] See TRIBUNAL DE JUSTICA, *supra* note 33.

[37] See Posting of Hadar Aviram to California Correctional Crisis, *A Jury Trial in Brazil*, http://californiacorrectionscrisis.blogspot.com/2014/08/a-jury-trial-in-brazil.html (Aug. 30, 2014); Tribunal de Justica, supra note 33.

[38] TRIBUNAL DE JUSTICA, *supra* note 33.

[39] See Gomes & Zomer, *supra* note 32, at 76–77.

[40] See Aviram, *supra* note 37.

[41] Tit. II, ch. I, art. 5 XXXVIII, available at www.servat.unibe.ch/icl/br00000_.html.

[42] See Aviram, *supra* note 37.

[43] Tit. II, ch. I, art. 5 XXXVIII, *supra* note. 41; Aviram, *supra* note 37; Gomes & Zomer, *supra* note 32, at 76–77.

[44] Tit. II, ch. I, art. 5 XXXVIII, *supra* note 41.

verdict. For example, on appeal, a new trial may be ordered for a "'decision clearly against the evidence.'"[45] But the verdict will be accepted if the decision is the same in the second trial. With the exception of cases of quite small stature where a defendant can be offered specific discounts, Brazil does not permit plea bargaining.[46]

*****

Lay jurors play a lesser role in Brazil than in the United States in several ways. In the initial selection process in Brazil, judges perform a more extensive screening function over jurors than in the United States, possibly resulting in a less diverse jury in Brazil. Also, when jurors sit in Brazil, they hear fewer types of cases than in the United States including a much smaller set of crimes and no civil cases. Moreover, only a majority vote is required to convict a defendant in Brazil. However, in other ways, lay people in Brazil have a greater role than in the United States. While in the United States and in Brazil, before trial, judges exercise similar control over the jury with the power to dismiss cases where there is insufficient evidence, after trial, with the ability to order only a new trial and limited to only one new trial, Brazilian judges have less review over jury verdicts than the American judiciary.

Other differences between the Brazilian and American jury systems are found in the areas of deliberations and plea bargaining. The prohibition from deliberating makes the Brazilian jury system very different from the one in the United States and many other countries. Finally, because Brazilian prosecutors cannot engage in plea bargaining regarding serious crimes, Brazilian defendants exercise more freedom to choose a jury trial (albeit in the much smaller set of cases subject to jury trial) than American defendants.

China

Efforts to include a jury system in China started in the early twentieth century when a jury with all lay people was proposed. Around 1927, lay jurors began to be employed at some times in some form in Chinese courts.[47] Although a mixed tribunal of judges and lay jurors was formally

---

[45] Gomes & Zomer, *supra* note 32, at 76.

[46] *See* Aviram, *supra* note 37.

[47] *See* Stephan Landsman & Jing Zhang, *A Tale of Two Juries: Lay Participation Comes to Japanese and Chinese Courts*, U.C.L.A. Pac. Basin L.J. 179, 198 (2008); Zhuoyu Wang &

established in 1949 for criminal and civil cases, problems abounded including limited use of lay jurors, insufficient funding, inactive lay people, and use of permanent lay people.[48] A law in the 1980s permitting lay jurors not to be used also contributed to the decline of the use of lay jurors. A new modern system using lay assessors emerged in China as the result of reform efforts in 2004,[49] and recently, China's central authorities, led by the Chinese President, have proposed more significant changes "to promote judicial democracy and fairness" by "enhancing independence in jurors' selection and expanding their participation in trials."[50]

Under the system established in 2004, collegial panels of judges and lay jurors decide cases.[51] The lay jurors must hold a college degree and are chosen after self-nomination, nomination by an employer, or nomination by a local group. The local court and governmental bodies evaluate the potential jurors, and once this selection process is complete, jurors, who serve for five years, undergo training and are randomly selected for cases.[52]

The new proposed rules provide for more people from the general population with less education in comparison to the current more elite composition where personal applications or other nominations have been required.[53] Jurors will be randomly selected from citizens who are at least twenty-eight and who have completed senior high school. People with certain occupations will be excluded including legislators, judges, prosecutors, police officers, and lawyers.[54]

Currently, lay participation occurs in a certain set of cases: "(1) first-instance criminal, civil, and administrative cases with far-reaching social

---

Hiroshi Fukurai, *China's Lay Participation in the Justice System: Surveys and Interviews of Contemporary Lay Judges in Chinese Courts*, in EAST ASIA'S RENEWED RESPECT FOR THE RULE OF LAW IN THE 21ST CENTURY: THE FUTURE OF LEGAL AND JUDICIAL LANDSCAPES IN EAST ASIA 114 (Setsuo Miyazawa et al. eds., 2015).

[48] *See* Wang & Fukurai, *supra* note 47, at 114.

[49] *See* Wang & Fukurai, *supra* note 47, at 115; *Verdict still out on jury system in China*, REUTERS, Sept. 3, 2007, available at www.reuters.com/article/2007/09/04/us-china-jury-idUSPEK6621120070904;

[50] *China pledges education, hospital, juror system reforms*, Judicial News, The Supreme People's Court of the People's Republic of China (Apr. 10, 2015), http://en.chinacourt.org/public/detail.php?id=4972.

[51] *See* Landsman & Zhang, *supra* note 47, at 199, 206.

[52] *See* Wang & Fukurai, *supra* note 47, at 116–18, 130; Landsman & Zhang, *supra* note 47, at 208.

[53] *See* Landsman & Zhang, *supra* note 47, at 207, 210–11.

[54] *See New rules for China's jury system*, XINHUA NEWS AGENCY, May 21, 2015, available at www.globalpost.com/article/6556161/2015/05/21/new-rules-chinas-jury-system.

implications; and (2) any case in which the litigant(s) request the application of a mixed tribunal."[55] The new rules expand the scope of cases subject to lay participation to cases "draw[ing] wide public attention" and cases involving crimes punishable for longer than ten years.[56]

Under the 2004 system currently in place, when jurors sit, they must constitute at least one third of a panel.[57] With two judges and one lay juror in criminal cases as well as a required majority vote, it may be difficult for the lay juror to express himself. As a result, thus far, the effectiveness of lay jurors in these cases is questionable.[58] Jurors can participate in certain ways. They can ask questions.[59] They also may engage in deliberations on the sentence.[60] In civil cases with one judge and two lay assessors, lay people are having an effect in some cases due to bringing perspectives valuable to young judges. They may even constitute a majority and outvote the judge.[61] Panel decisions can be overridden, however. An "'adjudicative committee'" with senior judges can overturn a panel's decision, and the Communist Party has political control of these judges.[62]

A form of plea bargaining exists in China. The "summary procedure" takes place after the defendant confesses and agrees to an abbreviated trial.[63]

Before the new proposed changes, use of jurors had already been increasing. In 2014, 210,000 jurors participated in 2.19 million trials in comparison to 87,000 jurors in the previous year.[64] However, research has found that men, certain occupations, and members of the Communist Party, among other groups, are overrepresented as lay participants on mixed panels. Moreover, jurors are not randomly selected.[65]

The future power of jurors is unclear for reasons related to the review procedures and the varied past reports of former jurors. Some past jurors

---

[55] Wang & Fukurai, *supra* note 47, at 116.

[56] *New rules, supra* note 54; Landsman & Zhang, *supra* note 47, at 206.

[57] *See New rules, supra* note 54; Wang & Fukurai, *supra* note 47, at 129.

[58] *See* Wang & Fukurai, *supra* note 47, at 128–29, 132.

[59] *See* Landsman & Zhang, *supra* note 47, at 207.

[60] *See* Wang & Fukurai, *supra* note 47, at 128, 132–34; Landsman & Zhang, *supra* note 47, at 218.

[61] *See* Landsman & Zhang, *supra* note 47, at 206; Wang & Fukurai, *supra* note 47, at 131–36.

[62] Landsman & Zhang, *supra* note 47, at 199–200, 208, 211, 218.

[63] Elizabeth M. Lynch, *Why Was There a Trial When Gu Kailai Confessed – China's "Plea Bargaining,"* http://chinalawandpolicy.com/2012/08/29/why-was-there-a-trial-when-gu-kailai-confessed-chinas-plea-bargaining/.

[64] *New rules,* supra note 54.

[65] *See* Wang & Fukurai, *supra* note 47, at 122–25.

have described having influence on the outcome and others have stated their presence was ignored. Other problems have included the lack of education of judges and corruption. China also shares some similarities to other countries as expense and efficiency are concerns.[66]

In addition to a form of a criminal jury and a civil jury, a body with some similarities to a grand jury exists in China. "People's Supervisors" are used differently, however, than grand juries in the United States; they review decisions of the prosecutor not to bring charges. The very high conviction rate in China gives prosecutors incentives to bring cases that they can win to keep their conviction rate high. Among other current requirements, supervisors must be twenty-three or older, have the right to vote, and have the right to be elected. Similar to the other juries, they are also selected through nominations, resulting in a lack of diversity.[67]

*****

Chinese jurors exercise less authority than American jurors in several ways. Judges sit with lay jurors with judges outnumbering jurors in criminal cases. The Chinese government closely controls who serves as lay jurors. And Chinese lay people hear fewer types of cases. Moreover, only a majority vote is required to convict or find for a party in China. However, there are some similar limitations on the authority of Chinese lay participants and American jurors. Because Chinese senior judges are permitted to decide against the verdicts of the mixed panels, the Chinese judiciary exercises a control analogous to powers that American judges employ over juries. Finally, Chinese jurors have some additional authority – albeit limited – compared to American jurors. Although a Chinese lay person's vote is not necessary for a conviction, Chinese jurors participate in the deliberations on sentencing unlike American jurors.

France

Emerging during the French Revolution, the criminal jury in France was initially derived from the English system, composed similarly of lay people who were eligible to vote. With different regimes, the criminal

---

[66] *See* Landsman & Zhang, *supra* note 47, at 200–02, 207–09, 212–13.
[67] *See* Hiroshi Fukurai & Zhuoyu Wang, *People's Grand Jury Panels and the State's Inquisitorial Institutions: Prosecution Review Commissions in Japan and People's Supervisors in China*, 37 FORDHAM INT'L L.J. 929, 959–62, 966–68 (2014).

jury changed, becoming more and less restricted over time with, for example, the government sometimes choosing jurors or permitting jurors of only certain professions.[68] In addition to the criminal jury, the grand jury had a historical presence in France. But it, like the traditional criminal jury, was eventually abolished.[69]

The current French jury is very different from the English jury. It includes judges and lay people deliberating together and on appellate review, a second trial before a similar mixed tribunal.[70]

With certain exceptions such as being convicted of a particular crime, lay people are eligible to serve and are randomly chosen from French citizens who are twenty-three to seventy years old. Jurors can be removed for bias, and the prosecution and the defense can preclude the participation of some jurors without giving any reasons.[71]

French panels consisting of three professional judges and six lay people hear serious crimes punishable by a sentence of ten years or more.[72] Before the trial, a panel of judges may dismiss the case for insufficient evidence. After all of the evidence has been presented at trial, French prosecutors themselves may actually argue for acquittal on the basis that they presented insufficient evidence of the crime.

During the trial, lay jurors may pose questions with the permission of the President who leads the panel.[73] Proceeding to deliberations, the judges and lay people – who generally possess the same information – determine both guilt and any sentence.[74] Six votes out of nine votes are required to establish guilt, and only a simple majority is required for the sentencing decision unless the maximum sentence is imposed.[75] Under a new French statute based on a European Court of Human Rights decision, the panel must provide reasoning for their verdict but not their sentence.[76]

---

[68] See McKillop, *supra* note 20, at 343–44; Simeon E. Baldwin, *The French Jury System*, 2 MICH. L. REV. 597 (1904).

[69] See Francois Gorphe, *Reforms of the Jury-System in Europe: France and Other Continental Countries*, 27 AM. INST. CRIM. L. & CRIMINOLOGY 155, 155 (1936).

[70] See McKillop, *supra* note 20, at 343–44.

[71] See Valerie P. Hans, *The French Jury at a Crossroads*, 86 CHI.-KENT L. REV. 737, 747, 750 & n.125 (2011).

[72] See Mathilde Cohen, *The French Case for Requiring Juries to Give Reasons – Safeguarding Defendants or Guarding the Judges?*, in HANDBOOK ON COMPARATIVE CRIMINAL PROCEDURE n.61 (Jacqueline Ross & Stephen Thaman eds., forthcoming).

[73] See Hans, *supra* note 71, at 751.

[74] See Cohen, *supra* note 72 (the president, who is one of the judges, has access to the case file that has the information related to the investigation).

[75] See Cohen, *supra* note 72; Hans, *supra* note 71, at 747, 757.

[76] See Cohen, *supra* note 72.

Both the government and the defendant have the right to appeal the original panel's decision. On appeal, three professional judges sitting with a larger number of lay people – now nine – try the case again.[77] Eight votes are required to convict.[78] Though operating de novo under no deferential standards, almost invariably, the appeals court has decided the same way as the original court.[79] A criminal defendant has one more opportunity for appeal after the second trial, and on this appeal, this new court can order a new trial.[80]

Plea bargaining is not available in cases eligible for jury trial. Existing since 2004, it can be used for only minor crimes and is not used often.[81]

The actual legitimacy of the French jury system has been called into question because of the possibility that judges exercise overwhelming influence over lay jurors due to judges' judicial and legal expertise.[82] Even if judges project such authority, lay jurors constitute the majority on panels and can outvote the judges. Moreover, the rules requiring reasons for the panel's decision arguably place an additional check on judges in these mixed systems.[83] Also, the use of lay people to review the original panel's decision contrasts with other systems where judges alone second-guess juries, demonstrating that the French in fact may trust lay people more than other governments.[84]

Calls for change in the French system have been made, including decreasing the number of jurors to less than the number of judges. Efficiency, including the delay in the time for trials, has been cited to support such shifts in the constitution of these judge/lay people tribunals.[85]

*****

In some ways, the United States has more expansive lay participation than France, with American jurors trying more crimes and hearing civil cases and with unanimity required in most places in the United States.

---

[77] See Cohen, *supra* note 72.
[78] Code de procédure pénale, art. 359.
[79] See Hans, *supra* note 71, at 759–60.
[80] See Cohen, *supra* note 72.
[81] See Cohen, *supra* note 72, at n.52.
[82] See Cohen, *supra* note 72. Aziz Jellab has concluded that the president of the French panel controls the proceedings, resulting in a "'sham democracy.'" DIMITRI VANOVERBEKE, JURIES IN THE JAPANESE LEGAL SYSTEM: THE CONTINUING STRUGGLE FOR CITIZEN PARTICIPATION AND DEMOCRACY 172 (2015).
[83] See Cohen, *supra* note 72.
[84] See McKillop, *supra* note 20.
[85] See Hans, *supra* note 71, at 746, 764–65.

Moreover, American jurors deliberate and decide without the participation of judges. Also, through their power to acquit a defendant without subsequent judicial review, American juries possess authority to nullify that juries in France – which must give reasons for their decisions and whose acquittals can be reviewed – do not hold. Lay jurors there, however, exercise more authority than American jurors in certain ways. They participate in deciding the sentence. Moreover, French lay jurors participate on appeal, whereas in the United States, appellate judges acting alone can question and reverse jury verdicts to convict based on their finding of insufficient evidence. Finally, because plea bargaining does not exist for crimes subject to jury trial, the same sort of potential coercion to forgo a trial that occurs in America does not take place in France, resulting in more opportunity for a French defendant to have lay jurors participate in his trial (albeit in the smaller set of cases subject to jury trial).

Germany

Juries, consisting of all lay jurors, arrived in Germany in the late eighteenth century with French occupation of much of Germany. After independence from the French, in the mid-nineteenth century, jury trials were expanded extensively to most German states. Despite some reform efforts to distance Germany from the French, however, the model remained the French jury. The concept of Volk or German communitarianism was discussed in the debate about the jury in Germany, including the view that the jury served as a protector against biased judges and prosecutors. By the late nineteenth century, juries with three professionals and twelve jurors decided cases involving the most serious crimes.[86] In these cases, the jurors decided guilt and judges sentenced.[87] After changes in the early twentieth century reducing the number of lay jurors and eliminating independent lay courts, lay participation was abolished completely during World War II. Lay participation in a collaborative tribunal was re-established after the war. But by 1974, lay participation

[86] *See* Markus Dirk Dubber, *The German Jury and the Metaphysical Volk: From Romantic Idealism to Nazi Ideology*, 43 Am. J. Comp. L. 227, 229, 232–35, 243 (1995).

[87] *See* Thomas Bliesener, *Lay Judges in the German Criminal Court: Social-Psychological Aspects of the German Criminal Justice System*, *in* Understanding World Jury Systems Through Social Psychological Research, *supra* note 13, at 179.

had been significantly reduced. Three judges sat with only two lay jurors.[88] Mixed tribunals continue to exist today.

Under the current system, lay participants must be twenty-five to seventy years old and may not occupy positions in the judiciary, as prosecutors, as lawyers, or as police.[89] Political parties and other groups nominate lay jurors, and the municipal authorities approve the list, which must include "all sections of the population."[90] This list will be displayed publicly and objections may be made.[91] From this compilation, a group, consisting of a judge and other government-appointed or related people, decides who will be lay jurors, and those jurors will serve for a four-year period.[92]

Lay assessors are then randomly selected for the cases. One additional challenge for bias may be made against lay people, as well as against the judges who sit with the lay jurors on mixed tribunals.[93]

Mixed tribunals will hear cases in which defendants are subject to imprisonments that last longer than two years. One judge and two lay jurors will deliberate over cases with imprisonments of four years or less, and two or three judges (usually two judges) and two lay jurors will hear cases with longer potential imprisonments.[94]

Before the trial, the judges dismiss the case if there is insufficient evidence for going to trial. If the case goes to trial, during the trial, the lay jurors may participate by asking questions.[95] Although the presiding judge runs the deliberation, all participants have equal voting authority.[96] For serious cases, because only a two-thirds' majority is required to convict and sentence, only one lay participant must agree with the judges to convict and sentence.[97]

Although the deliberations are secret, the judge will give reasons for the panel's decision orally in public as well as written reasons. For serious cases, the decision, whether to convict or acquit, can be challenged on

---

[88] *See* Dubber, *supra* note 86, at 237–39.
[89] Walter Perron, *Lay Participation in Germany*, 72 INT'L REV. OF PEN. LAW 181, 190–91 (2001).
[90] Perron, *supra* note 89, at 190–91; Bliesener, *supra* note 87, at 182.
[91] *See* Bliesener, *supra* note 87, at 182.
[92] *See* Bliesener, *supra* note 87, at 182; Perron, *supra* note 89, at 191.
[93] *See* Perron, *supra* note 89, at 191.
[94] *See* Dubber, *supra* note 86, at 239; Sanja Kutnjak Ivkovic, *Exploring Lay Participation in Legal Decision-Making: Lessons from Mixed Tribunals*, CORNELL INT'L L.J. 429, 432 (2007); Perron, *supra* note 89, at 181–82.
[95] *See* Bliesener, *supra* note 87, at 185.
[96] *See* Perron, *supra* note 89, at 186.
[97] *See* Dubber, *supra* note 86, at 239–40.

appeal before judges,[98] and a new trial may be ordered.[99] In some circumstances, though not often, the immediate result on appeal is the opposite of the panel's decision. Appellate judges may reverse the panel's decision, resulting in an acquittal or a conviction, if they believe the fact-finding of the panel and law require that result.

The trial may be supplemented with a form of plea bargaining.[100] According to a decision of the Federal Constitutional Court in 2013, an agreement may occur only after evidence presented at the main trial demonstrates the defendant is guilty, including proof regarding the reliability of the confession. Importantly, it is not possible to buy a better sentence by agreeing to decrease the truth inquiry.[101] However, the truth inquiry will be shortened significantly by a confession. Also, a judge can offer a lower sentence in exchange for a confession.

Prior to the Constitutional Court decision, in the plea-bargaining process as well as at trial, some have questioned the influence of the prosecutor on the judge despite the judge's independent access to the case file.[102] On other hand, others have emphasized the prosecutor's duty to be objective including the requirement to argue the facts for and against conviction in closing arguments. The prosecutor may even argue for acquittal after all of the evidence has been presented.[103]

Because few cases involve the greater sentences that provide for lay participation, lay jurors do not hear many cases in comparison to the total number of criminal cases.[104] The ultimate effect of this participation, when it occurs, is unclear because secrecy in deliberation makes empirical study difficult.[105]

Lay participation in civil cases also occurs in Germany in some limited circumstances. For example, in labor cases, lay jurors may participate as part of a mixed panel of one judge and two lay people with specific

---

[98] *See* Perron, *supra* note 89, at 186–87.

[99] *See* Marshall, *supra* note 7, at 23–24; Perron, *supra* note 89, at 187.

[100] *See* Regina E. Rauxloh, *Formalization of Plea Bargaining in Germany: Will the New Legislation Be Able to Square the Circle?*, 34 FORDHAM INT'L L.J. 296, 298–301, 329 (2011).

[101] *See* Andreas Mosbacher, *The Decision of the Federal Constitutional Court of 19 March 2013 on Plea Agreements*, 15 GERMAN L.J. 5, 7–9 (2014).

[102] *See* Dubber, *supra* note 86, at 270–71.

[103] *See* SHAWN MARIE BOYNE, THE GERMAN PROSECUTION SERVICE: GUARDIANS OF THE LAW? (2014).

[104] *See* Bliesener, *supra* note 87, at 179; Dubber, *supra* note 86, at 240–41.

[105] *See* Bliesener, *supra* note 87, at 185–86.

expertise.[106] For a verdict, in these civil cases, only a majority is required.[107] On appeal, the court can decide differently without ordering a new trial. Also, in some administrative cases in which the government is a party, three judges and two lay people may sit together, and a majority is required for a decision. At times, only one judge may sit in these cases. On appeal, these decisions can be reviewed and new fact-finding may occur.

*****

The German system differs significantly from the American system. In some ways, German lay jurors exercise less authority. Judges and lay jurors deliberate and decide together in Germany; lay jurors hear fewer types of cases than American jurors; the German government chooses the lay jurors who sit; and unanimity is not required in Germany. Also, on appeal, in Germany, judges can even question mixed tribunals' verdicts to acquit. However, German jurors exercise more authority than American jurors by participating in sentencing in addition to voting on guilt. Also, arguably, the decisions of German mixed panels to convict, backed by reasons, may have more authority on appeal than their American counterparts. One additional difference between the American and German criminal systems is the German requirement to hold a trial and not severely compromise the evidence inquiry even when a plea bargain is sought.

Ghana

In Ghana, by 1960, jury trials were available throughout the country.[108] Under the current Constitution enacted in 1992, juries can try certain crimes.[109]

To serve on a jury, a person must be at least twenty-five years old.[110] In consultation with various departments and institutions, the judiciary

---

[106] See Dubber, *supra* note 86, at n.8; Stefan Machura, *Silent Lay Judges–Why Their Influence in the Community Falls Short of Expectations*, 86 CHI.-KENT L. REV. 769, 773–74 (2011).

[107] See Machura, *supra* note 106, at 773.

[108] See Roger Gocking, *The Adjudication of Homicide in Colonial Ghana: The Impact of the Knowles Murder Case*, 52 J. AFR. HIST. 85, 104 (2011).

[109] CONST. OF THE REPUBLIC OF GHANA, ch. 005, § 19(2)(a).

[110] See Gocking, *supra* note 108, at 104.

submits the names of potential jurors, and from this limited list, jurors are randomly chosen to sit on the required jury of seven.[111] Challenges for cause are available to both sides, and peremptory challenges are available to the accused.

Juries sit for crimes punishable by death or life imprisonment, with the exception of high treason and treason. They also hear first-degree felony cases, including murder, rape, and armed robbery. Crimes punishable by death require unanimous verdicts to convict, and a verdict of five to two is required to convict on other crimes.[112]

Prior to trial, the judge can dismiss the case against the accused if there is insufficient evidence. However, the trial judge is bound by the jury's verdict. Moreover, on appeal, the jury's verdict can be overturned only if the judge misdirected the jury on the evidence and the law.[113]

*****

In Ghana, the jury trial is more limited than in the United States in certain ways. There is a more rigorous culling of potential jurors and jurors can hear fewer types of cases than American jurors, including no civil cases. However, where juries try cases, in Ghana, judges cannot overturn convictions based on their determinations that insufficient evidence of guilt existed, unlike judges' power to do so in the United States.

Iran

Iran's relationship with the jury began with the Islamic Lafif. This body originated between the eighth and eleventh centuries, and consisted of twelve members of the community who were required to give a unanimous verdict regarding a matter.[114]

---

[111] See Neil Vidmar, *The Jury Elsewhere in the World*, in WORLD JURY SYSTEMS, *supra* note 18, at 433; Ernest Dela Aglanu, *KKD up for jury trial; case adjourned to April 22*, My Joy Online, Mar. 18, 2015, www.myjoyonline.com/entertainment/2015/march-18th/kkd-up-for-jury-trial-case-adjourned-to-april-22.php.

[112] See Vidmar, *supra* note 111, at 433; Andrew Novak, *The Mandatory Death Penalty in Ghana: A Comparative Constitutional Perspective on* Dexter Johnson v. Republic, 12 CARDOZO PUB. L. POL'Y & ETHICS J. 669, 687, 701 (2014).

[113] See Novak, *supra* note 112, at 691–92.

[114] See Moosa Akefi Ghaziani, *Jury or Judge in the Process of Resolution Disputes: 'Iranian issue,'* www.uaf.edu/files/justice/adr-symposium/symposium-papers/Jury-and-its-obstacles-in-the-process-of-resolution-disputes-Ghaziani.pdf.

Currently, the Head of the Judiciary, who is chosen by the Leader of Iran, directs the juror selection process.[115] To serve on a jury in Iran, a person must be Iranian, at least thirty years old, and have completed secondary education. People apply and are selected from groups that include teachers, lawyers, medical doctors, students, clerics, and farmers.[116] Five people from different organizations such as the judiciary choose the jurors from a larger body of 150–500 people. No more than two people from each group are selected, and jurors may be excluded for the same reasons as judges including a relationship to a party or personal interest in the case.[117] Because of the connections of jury selection to the Iranian leadership, membership on the jury may be limited to those favorable to the government and may lack religious and gender diversity. While fourteen or twenty-one members may serve on a jury, the trial may begin when fewer are present.

The Iranian Constitution provides for a very limited trial by jury – for "political and press offences."[118] In practice, juries do not try political offenses, and there is no other provision for juries in criminal or civil cases. In the limited cases tried by juries, during the trial, juries can present their questions to the judge. A majority vote of the jurors is required for a verdict.[119] In one recent case, a jury convicted a Reuters' journalist of a media-related crime.[120]

Although the articulated purpose of having a jury is to "prevent the judge from committing mistakes and also assist him in the detection of crime," a judge can circumvent the jury. After the jury renders the verdict, the judge decides the case, considering the jury's verdict but not bound by it. If the judge finds the defendant guilty, the judge passes sentence.[121] Finally, while there is some statutory mechanism for

---

[115] See M.A. Ansari-Pour, *Iran*, in 11 YEARBOOK OF ISLAMIC AND MIDDLE EASTERN LAW 324 (Eugene Cotran & Martin Lau eds., 2004–2005); Article 157 of Iranian Constitution.

[116] See M.A. Ansari-Pour, *Iran*, in 10 YEARBOOK OF ISLAMIC AND MIDDLE EASTERN LAW 268 (Eugene Cotran & Martin Lau eds., 2003–2004).

[117] See Ansari-Pour, *supra* note 115, at 324; Ansari-Pour, *supra* note 116, at 268–69 & n.8.

[118] Moosa Afeki Ghazi, *Iranian Judiciary Facing Human Rights Norms or Islamic Criteria*, 5 J. MIDD. E. & ISLAMIC STUDS. (in Asia) 37, 53 (2011); M.A. Ansari-Pour, *Iran*, in 12 YEARBOOK OF ISLAMIC AND MIDDLE EASTERN LAW 415 (Eugene Cotran & Martin Lau eds., 2005–2006).

[119] See Ansari-Pour, *supra* note 116, at 269.

[120] See *Iran jury finds Reuters guilty over video script, pending judge's ruling*, REUTERS, Sept. 30, 2012, available at www.reuters.com/article/2012/09/30/reuters-iran-idUSL6E8 KU1HJ20120930.

[121] See Ansari-Pour, *supra* note 116, at 267–69.

reducing punishment, negotiations through plea bargaining with a defendant is not recognized in Iran.

*****

Iran's jury system is much more limited than the jury in the United States. There, the government controls who sits on the jury, jurors hear only one type of case, and only a majority vote is required. Moreover, the Iranian jury only advises the judge who sits as the final decision-maker. Despite these differences, the countries have some similarity in their judicial controls over juries' decisions to convict. With an American judge able to overrule the jury's guilty verdict, the Iranian judge performs a comparable function when he decides whether to reject a jury's guilty verdict.

Japan

Japan employed a jury for fifteen years until 1943.[122] This all-lay juror system was criticized for its infrequent use. A recurrent argument centered around lay participation being against the "'national identity'" of Japan. Japanese society was homogeneous, the legal system was separated from citizens, and people would prefer to have their fates determined by judges than fellow citizens.[123] In 2009, Japan re-established lay participation in the form of mixed panels, influenced by its status as the only developed country that did not include lay people in its criminal justice system. Lay participation was to result in "better criminal justice by ensuring that verdicts and sentences reflect[ed] citizens' experiences and common sense."[124] Moreover, it was to bolster democracy by "'the promotion of the public's understanding of the judicial system and thereby raise their confidence in it.'"[125]

The current jury consists of three judges and six lay people, or possibly, though currently not in use, one judge and four lay people.[126] Lay jurors are selected from eligible voters who are at least twenty years old.[127] They must have completed compulsory education, and certain people including ex-criminals and lawyers may not serve.[128] Judges may

---

[122] *See* David T. Johnson, *Japan's Lay Judge System, in* HANDBOOK ON COMPARATIVE CRIMINAL PROCEDURE, *supra* note 72; VANOVERBEKE, *supra* note 82, at 91.

[123] VANOVERBEKE, *supra* note 82, at 15–17, 70, 79–80, 91, 162.

[124] Johnson, *supra* note 122.

[125] VANOVERBEKE, *supra* note 82, at 137 (quoting Act).

[126] *See* Johnson, *supra* note 122; VANOVERBEKE, *supra* note 82, at 137.

[127] *See* Johnson, *supra* note 122.

[128] *See* Johnson, *supra* note 122; VANOVERBEKE, *supra* note 82, at 141.

also exclude people who may be biased and who have obligations that prevent them from serving.[129]

Juries hear cases involving serious crimes, including crimes punishable by death and imprisonment for an indefinite period. Most of the cases have involved robbery with an injury, murder, burglary with arson, trafficking drugs, or assault with accompanying injury or death. While the defendant cannot waive the jury trial, judges alone can hear the case if they deem it in the public interest, for example, when lay jurors' lives may be in jeopardy.[130]

Before the trial, the court can acquit, deciding insufficient evidence exists for conviction.[131] During the trial, jurors can actively participate by asking questions of witnesses and discussing the case with one another.[132] Following the presentation of all of the evidence, the judges and jurors deliberate together.[133] A verdict and sentence require a majority vote that includes the votes of at least one judge and at least one lay person.[134] Appeals, including for acquittals, are possible, but changes may occur due to a recent Supreme Court decision holding that mixed panels should be given significant deference regarding verdicts of acquittals.[135]

Instead of a trial, plea bargaining may occur. Although it is illegal, it may take place especially to attempt to obtain a confession.[136]

Similar to many other countries, juries do not hear many cases in Japan. They sat in only about 3% of the criminal trials that took place from May 2009 to May 2012.[137] In the cases that juries hear, the conviction rate is extremely high, although using data available through February 2014, it has gone down slightly from 99% to 97.3%.[138] The conviction rate is somewhat misleading due to prosecutors charging cautiously and defendants not being permitted to plead guilty.[139]

Even though juries do not hear many cases, in the cases in which they participate, juror satisfaction appears high. In a survey, 72% of jurors responded that they sufficiently participated in deliberations

---

[129] See Johnson, *supra* note 122.
[130] See Johnson, *supra* note 122.
[131] See Vanoverbeke, *supra* note 82, at 201.
[132] See Johnson, *supra* note 122.
[133] See Vanoverbeke, *supra* note 82, at 141–42.
[134] See Johnson, *supra* note 122.
[135] See Johnson, *supra* note 122; Vanoverbeke, *supra* note 82, at 210–11.
[136] See Johnson, *supra* note 122.
[137] Johnson, *supra* note 122.
[138] Vanoverbeke, *supra* note 82, at 157.
[139] Johnson, *supra* note 122.

versus about 8% who responded that they were dissatisfied with their ability to do so.[140]

Lay jurors' participation has perhaps most changed judges. They are reported to have begun to question prosecutors because of lay people's influence on them.[141]

A form of grand jury also exists in Japan. This jury, used differently than in the United States, reviews decisions of the prosecutor not to bring charges. Jurors must be Japanese citizens and over twenty years old. The selection procedures, including the requirement to serve for six months, have resulted in criticisms of the representativeness of this jury.[142]

*****

Unlike in the United States, Japanese juries include judges, hear far fewer types of cases including no civil cases, and do not require unanimity. At the same time, lay people in Japan actually participate in sentencing unlike U.S. jurors. While both systems permit some review over verdicts, it appears that Japan exercises less control with no review at the trial level and increasing deference to the mixed tribunal on appeal.

Russia

Russia first established a jury in 1864, with a traditional twelve-juror format. Surviving until the revolution of 1917, a jury trial was available for a wide range of criminal offenses.[143] In the early twentieth century, the Soviet Union established a mixed form of jury trial, with two lay people sitting with a judge. This form of lay participation was not perceived as checking judges. While the judge and lay jurors would hear and decide the case together, "telephone justice" could occur with the case's result being decided by a phone call from a superior court or Communist party officials to the presiding judge.[144] After the fall of the Soviet Union in the 1990s, as a part of reform efforts to include more

---

[140] VANOVERBEKE, *supra* note 82, at 171.

[141] *See* Johnson, *supra* note 122.

[142] *See* Fukurai & Wang, *supra* note 67, at 960, 964–65.

[143] *See* Gennady Esakov, *The Russian Criminal Jury: Recent Developments, Practice, and Current Problems*, 60 AM. J. COMP. L. 665, 667 (2012); Anna Gurinskaya, *Trial by Jury in Russia: From the Cornerstone of the Judicial Reform to the Constitutional History Artifact*, J. CRIM. JUST. & SECURITY 62, 65–66.

[144] *See* Esakov, *supra* note 143, at 669–70; Gurinskaya, *supra* note 143, at 65.

direct citizen involvement, a trial with only lay people – in place in the pre-revolutionary period – was renewed and became "a cornerstone of ... judicial reform."[145]

In the current system, jurors must be twenty-five years old and are randomly selected from a list of registered voters. People with certain characteristics may be excluded including those with criminal records. Jurors also can be excluded for cause and at times, by parties, using peremptory challenges. Twelve jurors will sit to deliberate and will be asked to find a unanimous verdict although a majority vote is permitted.[146]

Russia constitutionalized jury trials for cases punishable by death and in other cases according to federal law.[147] Jury trials currently exist in a limited set of criminal cases, including aggravated murder, aggravated kidnapping, several crimes against state security, and crimes of an inter-national nature.[148]

During the trial, lay jurors may ask questions through the judge who presides in the case. The jury will answer three general questions regarding proof, identity, and guilt.[149]

If the jury acquits, the trial judge must accept the verdict, and on appeal, it may be reversed on only very limited grounds.[150] If the jury finds guilt, the trial judge may accept the verdict, may reject the verdict if the facts found by the jury do not constitute a crime, or may reject the verdict, sending the case to a new trial. On appeal, a conviction can be rejected only for a new trial or sent for new sentencing.[151]

Instead of trial, many cases are subject to a form of plea bargaining known as "special procedure for court hearing." Under this process, which, in 2010, was employed in around 64% of the cases, the defendant accepts the charges without a trial. If so, the defendant cannot be sentenced to the upper third of the sentencing range. However, judges

---

[145] Esakov, *supra* note 143, at 670–71; Gurinskaya, *supra* note 143, at 65.

[146] *See* Esakov, *supra* note 143, at 671–72, 674–75, 678.

[147] *See* Gurinskaya, *supra* note 143, at 66; Nikolai Kovalev & Alexander Smirnov, *The Nature of the Russian Trial by Jury*, Eur. J. Crime, Crim. L. & Crim. Just. 115, 119 (2014).

[148] *See* Sergei Tokmakov, *Jury trials in modern Russia*, XVI The ISCIP Analyst, Jan. 28, 2010, www.bu.edu/phpbin/news-cms/news/?dept=732&id=55374.

[149] *See* Stephen C. Thaman, *Europe's New Jury Systems: The Cases of Spain and Russia*, 62 L. & Contemp. Probs. 233, 250 (1999).

[150] *See* Esakov, *supra* note 143, at 682–87; Peter H. Solomon, Jr., *Courts, law and policing under Medvedev*, in Russia after 2012, at 23 (J.L. Black & Michael Johns eds., 2013) (Supreme Court reviews almost half of acquittals and majority sent for new trial).

[151] *See* Esakov, *supra* note 143, 682–84.

generally do not sentence in this range anyway, so defendants may receive little or no benefit from forgoing a trial through this procedure.[152]

Juries ultimately try few cases – in 2011, trying only about 0.05% of criminal cases.[153] However, they can have a significant impact in those cases.[154] In 2013, juries acquitted 20% of the time, in comparison to judges acquitting around 4.2% of the time.[155] Although many waive their jury trial rights, the government or others involved in the process may coerce defendants into forgoing these jury trials.[156] Also, when jury trials actually occur, to obtain the results that it wants, using informal methods, the state may interfere with trials, for example, requesting jurors whom it thinks are going to acquit the defendant to step off the jury or postponing the trial to a time when jurors whom the state does not desire cannot attend.[157]

Reductions in the Russian jury's authority have been publicly protested with proponents extolling the importance of the jury including to "protect an independent judiciary in Russia and deal with police abuses of power."[158] Judges have been criticized as not independent – as simply "a last link in the chain of agencies." So, the jury trial specifically "serves as a guarantee from any attempts to infringe upon [a] judge's impartiality."[159] While some groups have urged the extension of the jury trial, similar to many other countries, efficiency is cited as a reason to abolish or not extend the jury trial, and judges have also advocated its elimination to garner more convictions.[160]

*****

---

[152] Solomon, *supra* note 150, at 23–24.

[153] Esakov, *supra* note 143, at 692.

[154] In 2011, juries acquitted in around 15% of the cases. Esakov, *supra* note 143, at 688 tbl.1; Solomon, *supra* note 150, at 23 (juries acquit in one out of six cases).

[155] Gurinskaya, *supra* note 143, at 67. In 2011, the Supreme Court reversed 18.2% of acquittals and reversed 7% of convictions. Esakov, *supra* note 143, at 690 tbl.2. These figures are dropping and apparently are attributable to judges' increase in knowledge of the new rules. *Id.* at 692–93.

[156] *See* Thaman, *supra* note 149, at 239 & n.27.

[157] *See* Ellen Barry, *In Russia, Jury Is Something to Work Around*, N.Y. TIMES, Nov. 15, 2010.

[158] Ekaterina Mishina, *Trial by Jury in Russia: Revival and Survival*, Institute of Modern Russia, Jan. 25, 2012, available at http://imrussia.org/en/rule-of-law/186-trial-by-jury-in-russia-revival-and-survival.

[159] Gurinskaya, *supra* note 143, at 68, 76.

[160] *See* Kyra Latukhina, *Chartered will be more: Vladimir Putin instructed to prepare proposals on the justice system*, RG.RU RUSSIAN NEWSPAPER, Jan. 22, 2015, available at www.rg.ru/2015/01/22/prisyajnie-site.html; Kovalev & Smirnov, *supra* note 147, at 123.

Again, similar to the countries already described, Russia has a much less extensive jury trial than the United States, including no civil jury trial. Also, the Russian government will interfere with the composition of the sitting jury to influence the result, and unanimity is not required for a conviction. Following the jury's verdict to convict, however, American judges exercise more control over the jury than Russian judges by possessing the power to acquit based on their opinions that the evidence is insufficient.

Spain

In Spain, beginning in the early nineteenth century, the jury trial was constitutionalized during periods of liberty while not recognized during periods of oppression.[161] Although a civil law country, Spain currently employs a pure jury with only lay jurors.[162]

To sit on a jury, jurors must be eighteen or older, literate, and registered to vote. After the publication of a list of possible jurors and any exclusions, challenges, and petitions, the court randomly chooses potential jurors to sit on a case. At that time, other challenges, including peremptory ones, will occur. People will be excluded for reasons that include having committed certain crimes and possessing particular biases. After this procedure, nine jurors will hear the case.[163]

Certain crimes are subject to jury trial including "crimes against persons," "crimes committed by public officials in the exercise of their duties," "crimes against honor," "crimes against liberty and security," "arson," and "crimes against the environment."[164] Jurors can participate in a limited manner during the trial by posing any questions that they may have to the judge.[165] The judge can preempt the jury's decision by acquitting the defendant, if the judge decides the prosecution presented insufficient evidence of the crime.[166]

---

[161] See Stephen C. Thaman, *Spain Returns to Trial by Jury*, 21 HASTINGS INT'L & COMP. L. REV. 241, 246 (1998).

[162] See Valerie P. Hans, *Jury Systems Around the World*, 4 ANN. REV. L. & SOC. SCI. 275, 278 (2008); Thaman, *supra* note 161, at 252–53.

[163] See Thaman, *supra* note 161, at 263–69, 286–88.

[164] Thaman, *supra* note 161, at 259–60; Elisabetta Grande, *Rumba Justice and the Spanish Jury Trial, in* HANDBOOK ON COMPARATIVE CRIMINAL PROCEDURE, *supra* note 72.

[165] See Thaman, *supra* note 161, at 304.

[166] See Thaman, *supra* note 161, at 316; Grande, *supra* note 164; Mar Jimeno-Bulnes, *Jury Selection and Jury Trial in Spain: Between Theory and Practice*, 86 CHI.-KENT. L. REV. 585, 599–600 (2011).

If the case goes to the jury, jurors fill out a form given to them deciding whether certain facts were proven or not, and they can make changes to the form if necessary. Jury decisions on factual propositions, labeled as "unfavorable" and "favorable" to the defendant, ultimately determine whether the defendant is found guilty. For each factual proposition, seven of nine jurors' votes result in a fact proved unfavorable to the defendant, and five of nine jurors' votes result in a fact proved favorable to the defendant. These decisions are backed by reasons based in evidence.[167]

After the verdict is given, the judge has power over the jury's verdict. He can decide to acquit if he deems there was insufficient evidence to convict.[168] The trial judge can also ask the jury to correct errors in the verdict such as problems with the reasoning. If the jury fails to do so after three times, the case will be retried before a new jury, and the judge can acquit if the new jury has similar problems. On appeal, a conviction or an acquittal can be challenged, and a three-judge panel can acquit or convict for reasons that include, respectively, that there was insufficient evidence to convict or there was sufficient evidence to convict.[169]

The Spanish Constitution gives citizens the explicit right to participate in jury trials and does not give defendants the right to a jury. Thus, it does not justify the jury based on some notion of a biased judge and prosecutor. In connection to this lay people's right, defendants cannot waive the jury trial. However, prosecutors can engage in behavior analogous to plea bargaining.[170]

*****

Spanish jurors exercise less authority than American jurors. They try far fewer types of cases, for example, hearing no civil cases, and unanimity is not required. Also, judicial control over the jury verdict is more expansive in Spain, with judges being permitted to question both convictions and acquittals.

****

This survey of lay participation systems in several other countries in some of the most populous areas of the world shows that people's regular

---

[167] Thaman, *supra* note 161, at 321–22, 336–37, 356, 359, 364–66; Grande, *supra* note 164.

[168] See Grande, *supra* note 164, at n.60.

[169] See Grande, *supra* note 164; Thaman, *supra* note 149, at 256; Thaman, *supra* note 161, at 390–91.

[170] See Thaman, *supra* note 161, at 250–53, 256–58, 309–16.

influence on governmental matters has a historical presence and value. Moreover, it demonstrates the current world-wide importance of lay participation, showing that many of the largest countries (with varied commitments to democracy) presently employ lay people in their judicial decision-making.[171]

There are many recognizable differences between lay systems established throughout the world. Most prominent are the availability of lay participants for criminal and/or civil cases and the form of lay participation, collaborating with or without judges. These distinctions may have an effect on decision-making, including the possible dominance of judges on lay people in mixed tribunals.[172]

However, there are important commonalities between the systems. Although the prevailing view is that the United States has much more extensive lay participation than other countries, as summarized in Table 2, the controls in the American system actually share many similarities to the mechanisms in place elsewhere. In the United States, judges can take cases away from juries based on their view that insufficient evidence to convict exists or they can second-guess juries after they convict. In many other countries, judges may also take these actions in criminal cases. Also, in the United States, although juries have authority to decide many civil cases, judges take cases away from juries before they decide or reject their findings. Even though juries hear few civil cases in other countries, the fact that judges ultimately can decide and do decide many civil cases in the United States makes some of the differences between the U.S. system and other countries more formal than real.

Also despite the view that the American system is more expansive, in many ways, lay jurors in the United States play a less active role than in other countries. In many nations with mixed tribunals, as summarized in Table 1, lay jurors participate in sentencing unlike their role in the United States. Moreover, as denoted in Table 2, the authority of American judges to reject jury decisions to convict before and after jury

---

[171] *See* Cohen, *supra* note 72, at n.26 and n.27 (listing ten traditional common law jury systems and twenty-four mixed jury systems in member states in the Council of Europe). For summary descriptions of criminal jury systems in twenty-eight countries, *see* Ethan J. Leib, *A Comparison of Criminal Jury Decision Rules in Democratic Countries*, 5 Ohio St. J. Crim. L. 629 (2008).

[172] *See* Stefan Machura, *Interaction Between Lay Assessors and Professional Judges in German Mixed Courts*, 72 Int'l Rev. Penal L. 451, 454 (2001).

Table 1 *Lay Participation in Select Countries*

	Crim. Cases	Civ. Cases	All Lay or Mixed	Random Selection	Questions by Lay Jurors	Lay Partic. in Sentencing	Lay Majority on Mixed
United States	Yes	Yes	All Lay	Yes	Yes	No	N/A
England	Yes	Yes	All Lay	Yes	Yes	No	N/A
Brazil	Yes	No	All Lay	No	Yes	No	N/A
China	Yes	Yes	Mixed	No	Yes	Yes	Some cases
France	Yes	No	Mixed	Yes	Yes	Yes	Yes
Germany	Yes	Yes	Mixed	No	Yes	Yes	Some cases
Ghana	Yes	No	All Lay	No	Yes	No	N/A
Iran	Press	No	Advisory Lay	No	Yes	No	N/A
Japan	Yes	No	Mixed	Yes	Yes	Yes	Yes
Russia	Yes	No	All Lay	Yes	Yes	No	N/A
Spain	Yes	No	All Lay	Yes	Yes	No	N/A

verdicts contrasts with judges in some other countries who do not hold such power. So, lay jurors have more power in those countries when they hear a case. The extensive use of plea bargaining in the United States in comparison to the lesser employment by other democratic countries, which is briefly depicted in Table 3, also may result in a less democratic, participatory system in the United States. While America has a more extensive criminal jury system with juries available for many more crimes, it incarcerates people at a much greater rate than other western democracies.[173] Much of this has been attributed to the criminalization of many crimes in reaction to occurrences in society. In many ways, the American jury provides a vehicle to question the legislature's action on a more regular basis particularly because American judges do not interfere with juries' decisions to acquit. However, with extensive plea bargaining in the United States, lay people do not actually participate regularly in decision-making. On the other hand, many other countries with lay

---

[173] *See* Michael Tonry, *Why Are U.S. Incarceration Rates So High?*, 45 Crime & Delinquency 419 (1999).

Table 2 *Review of Lay Participation in Select Countries*

	Acquit. for Insuff. Ev. Before Tr.[a]	Acquit. for Insuff. Ev. After Convict.[b]	App. Acquit. for Insuff. Ev. After Convict.[c]	Convict. for Suff. Ev. After Acquit.[d]	App. Convict. for Suff. Ev. After Acquit.[e]	Civ. Tr. Dismiss. for Insuff. Ev.[f]	Civ. App. Dismiss. for Insuff Ev.[g]	App. Rev. of Mixed: Judge or Mixed[h]
United States	Yes	Yes	Yes	No	No	Yes	Yes	N/A
England	Yes	No	Yes	No	No	Yes	Yes	N/A
Brazil	Yes	No	No	No	No	N/A	N/A	N/A
China	Unavail.	No	Yes	No	Yes	Unavail.	Yes	Judge
France	Yes	No	De Novo Trial	No	De Novo Trial	N/A	N/A	Mixed
Germany	Yes	No	Yes	No	Yes	No	Yes	Both
Ghana	Yes	No	No	No	No	N/A	N/A	N/A
Iran	No	N/A	N/A	N/A	N/A	N/A	N/A	N/A
Japan	Yes	No	Yes	No	Yes	N/A	N/A	Judge
Russia	No	No	No	No	No	N/A	N/A	N/A
Spain	Yes	Yes	Yes	No	Yes	N/A	N/A	N/A

[a] Trial court can acquit for insufficient evidence before trial.
[b] Trial court can acquit for insufficient evidence after conviction by jury.
[c] Appellate court can acquit for insufficient evidence after conviction by jury.
[d] Trial court can convict for sufficient evidence after acquittal by jury.
[e] Appellate court can convict for sufficient evidence after acquittal by jury.
[f] Trial court can dismiss civil case for insufficient evidence.
[g] Appellate court can dismiss civil case for insufficient evidence.
[h] Appellate review of mixed panel decision by judge or mixed panel.

Table 3 *Other Information About Lay Participation in Select Countries*

	Plea Bargaining	Lay Participation in Constitution	Grand Jury
United States	Yes	Yes	Yes
England	Yes	No	No
Brazil	No	Yes	No
China	Yes	No	Yes
France	No	No	No
Germany	Yes	No	No
Ghana	No	Yes	No
Iran	No	Yes	No
Japan	No	No	Yes
Russia	Yes	Yes	No
Spain	Yes	Yes	No

participation limit pressure on defendants through plea bargaining including by limiting the difference between plea and trial.[174]

A Greater Role for Juries in America and World-Wide

Given the existing criticisms of juries that were discussed in other chapters, one might expect that – setting aside the Constitution – there would be no reason for juries to exist. Yet, as just described, in many countries throughout the world, lay jurors participate in adjudication – regardless of the country's location, regardless of the organization of the country's political system, and regardless of constitutional requirements. The following section explores why lay participation should continue, specifically focusing on the jury's value in comparison to other decision-makers.

As described at length in earlier chapters, in the United States, some cases do not go to juries or jury verdicts are overturned against the wishes of some of the interested parties. In some of these circumstances, judges dismiss cases because they decide that a "reasonable jury" could not convict in a criminal case or could not find for one party in a civil case. Juries also may not hear cases when the legislature gives matters to agencies' administrative judges to hear or the executive otherwise exerts authority over cases, referring them to military tribunals. In addition to the judiciary and the executive, the legislature itself exercises decision-making authority over certain types of cases that juries try. When the legislature enacts a damages cap, the legislature will have the final say over the monetary damages that are awarded in a case if the amount that the jury awarded is higher than the cap. Additionally, the legislature, the executive, and the judiciary all work together in the plea-bargaining process, another mechanism precluding jury participation.

So, judges, through executive, legislative, and judicial apparatuses, decide a large number of matters that juries could otherwise determine. Similarly, in other countries, judges, not juries, decide most cases – there especially because the original scope of the jury's authority is usually extremely limited. Recognizing the large role of judges in America and other governments, the following section shows how judges and juries can disagree and argues that judges are less independent than juries, making juries more desirable than judges to decide matters. Because the executive and the legislature share characteristics similar to the judiciary, the jury is also

---

[174] See Darryl K. Brown, *The Perverse Effects of Efficiency in Criminal Process*, 100 Va. L. Rev. 183, 187–88 (2014).

a more attractive decision-maker than them. Moreover, these differences between judges, other governmental decision-makers, and juries support a greater role for lay participation outside the United States.

Can Judges and Juries Decide Cases Differently?

The Reasonable Jury Standard

By concluding that a reasonable jury could not find for one side, judges do not permit juries to decide cases or overrule the jury's verdict in many cases in the United States. This standard has also been used elsewhere in the world, for example, in England.[175] If judges can accurately predict what a reasonable jury could find, this method could save resources and create more just verdicts. On the other hand, if judges cannot perform this analysis, then judges are deciding many cases that juries could determine and could resolve differently.

An important decision that helps show the possible differences between decision-making by judges and juries is the Supreme Court case of *Scott v. Harris*. In that civil case, the plaintiff Victor Harris alleged that the police used excessive force against him after he did not respond to police efforts to stop his car. The plaintiff had been traveling at 73 miles per hour in a 55 miles per hour speed zone when the police pursued him. The chase that followed involved numerous police officers, including the defendant police deputy Timothy Scott. During the chase, the plaintiff left the road and entered a shopping center parking lot, where he continued to evade the police and hit the defendant's car. Back on a road, in an attempt to stop the plaintiff, the defendant rammed the plaintiff's car from behind, which resulted in the plaintiff becoming a quadriplegic after his car tumbled down an embankment.[176]

During the chase, the police videotaped the plaintiff, and after the defendant moved for summary judgment to dismiss the case against him, the courts used the video to evaluate the evidence.[177] The trial court denied the defendant's attempt to avoid liability,[178] and the Eleventh Circuit Court of Appeals affirmed. The appeals' court decided that the

---

[175] *See* Scott v. Musial, 2 Q.B. 429, 437 (1959).
[176] *See* Scott v. Harris, 550 U.S. 372, 374–76 (2007).
[177] *See id.* at 375–76, 378 n.5.
[178] *See* Harris v. Coweta County, No. CIVA 3:01CV148 WBH, 2003 WL 25419527, at *4–6 (N.D. Ga. Sept. 23, 2003), *aff'd in part, rev'd in part*, 433 F.3d 807 (11th Cir. 2005), *rev'd in part sub nom. Scott*, 550 U.S. 372 (2007).

defendant's actions against the plaintiff could constitute deadly force, that the use of such force would violate the plaintiff's Fourth Amendment right to be free from excessive force during a seizure, and as a result, a reasonable jury could find that the defendant violated the plaintiff's Fourth Amendment rights. The Eleventh Circuit emphasized

> taking the facts from [Harris's] viewpoint, Harris remained in control of his vehicle, slowed for turns and intersections, and typically used his indicators for turns. He did not run any motorists off the road.... Nor was he a threat to pedestrians in the shopping center parking lot, which was free from pedestrian and vehicular traffic as the center was closed. Significantly, by the time the parties were back on the highway and Scott rammed Harris, the motorway had been cleared of motorists and pedestrians allegedly because of police blockades of the nearby intersections.[179]

Writing for the majority of justices on the Supreme Court, Justice Scalia disagreed with the Eleventh Circuit, deciding that no reasonable jury could find for the plaintiff. Reversing the appeals' court decision, the Supreme Court ordered summary judgment, dismissing the case against the police deputy. In his decision, Justice Scalia described what he and his colleagues saw when they viewed the videotape. He stated

> we see respondent's vehicle racing down narrow, two-lane roads.... We see it swerve around more than a dozen other cars.... We see it run multiple red lights.... Far from being the cautious and controlled driver the lower court depicts, what we see on the video more closely resembles a Hollywood-style car chase of the most frightening sort.

The police videotape demonstrated that no reasonable jury could believe the plaintiff's version of the facts and established that the defendant's decision to ram the plaintiff's car was "objectively reasonable."[180]

The sole dissenter on the Supreme Court, Justice Stevens, sided with the lower court judges, stating that a reasonable jury could find for the plaintiff. He chided the Court for attempting to act as a jury and discussed other facts including that the plaintiff had not run any red lights and that the roads had been cleared.

> My colleagues on the jury saw [Harris] 'swerve around more than a dozen other cars,' and 'force cars traveling in both directions to their respective shoulders,' ... but they apparently discounted the possibility that those cars were already out of the pursuit's path as a result of hearing the sirens.

---

[179] See *Harris*, 433 F.3d at 813–21, *rev'd in part sub nom. Scott*, 550 U.S. 372 (2007).
[180] *Scott*, 550 U.S. at 374–86.

Even if that were not so, passing a slower vehicle on a two-lane road always involves some degree of swerving and is not especially dangerous if there are no cars coming from the opposite direction. At no point during the chase did [Harris] pull into the opposite lane other than to pass a car in front of him; he did the latter no more than five times and, on most of those occasions, used his turn signal. On none of these occasions was there a car traveling in the opposite direction. In fact, at one point, when [Harris] found himself behind a car in his own lane and there were cars traveling in the other direction, he slowed and waited for the cars traveling in the other direction to pass before overtaking the car in front of him while using his turn signal to do so. This is hardly the stuff of Hollywood. To the contrary, the video does not reveal any incidents that could even be remotely characterized as 'close calls.'

Justice Stevens stated that "eight of the jurors on this Court reach a verdict that differs from the views of the judges on both the District Court and the Court of Appeals who are surely more familiar with the hazards of driving on Georgia roads than we are."[181]

The case demonstrates that judges can disagree on what a reasonable jury could find. Although the law assumes that the highest court correctly decides what a reasonable jury could find, there is no reason to believe that the majority in a case (with possibly five judges in the majority deciding one way and four judges the other way[182]) can decide the verdict of a reasonable jury any better than the other judges on the Supreme Court or the lower court judges. In fact, *Scott v. Harris* itself strongly suggests that instead of deciding what a reasonable jury could find, the judges in the case used their own opinions of the evidence to decide whether to dismiss the case. Although the judges in *Scott v. Harris* stated that they determined what a reasonable jury could find, there is no indication in their opinions that they actually factored in the possible viewpoints of jury members and their possible deliberations.[183] The judges' disagreement with each other as well as the descriptions in the opinions of what each judge saw – not what a jury could see – indicate that judges substituted their opinions for the jury's, whether they realized it or not. In other cases, disagreements among judges, descriptions of what judges themselves think about the evidence, as well

---

[181] *See id.* at 389–97 (Stevens, J., dissenting).
[182] *See* Suja A. Thomas, *The Fallacy of Dispositive Procedure*, 50 B.C. L. Rev. 759, 772–73 (2009) (discussing Matsushita Elec. Indus. Co. v. Zenith Radio Corp., 475 U.S. 574 (1986)).
[183] *See* Thomas, *supra* note 182, at 775–77.

as judges' interchangeable use of terms such as reasonable jury and reasonable juror in the standard to dismiss a case – terms that can have very different meanings – show judges are substituting their own opinions for juries' decisions and are not determining what reasonable juries could find.

In *Scott v. Harris*, the judges disagreed about facts – even though they were displayed in an easily viewable, seemingly objective video. Various studies show that judges may disagree about facts, and they may have different opinions for a variety of reasons including ones related to their backgrounds such as prior work experiences.[184]

If judges can disagree, can lay people also disagree with judges, which could mean juries can have different opinions than judges? Using the video in *Scott v. Harris* and studying the responses of a diverse group, Dan Kahan, David Hoffman, and Donald Braman examined the issue of whether lay people can have different opinions than judges. Although a large majority of the people who viewed the videotape reacted similarly to the Supreme Court in *Scott*, 75% agreeing that deadly force was warranted, certain subgroups had significantly different reactions. African-American, Democratic, liberal, egalitarian, communitarian, lower income, more educated, single, and older subjects generally appeared more pro-plaintiff than their respective counter-groups. Thus, the study's authors showed that people's views of the facts could be based on many characteristics and experiences, including their race, political affiliation, education, and age. They argued that their results conflicted with the Supreme Court's conclusion that reasonable people would agree regarding the risk involved in the chase or the role of the police in increasing or decreasing the risk. Because the study demonstrated that people, including those with different characteristics, could disagree, the authors argued that the Supreme Court incorrectly referred to such group members as unreasonable.[185]

Disagreement does not necessarily demonstrate that one side is unreasonable. After all, such a conclusion would require a finding that the lower court judges and Justice Stevens were unreasonable in *Scott*. The

---

[184] *See, e.g.,* Gregory C. Sisk, Michael Heise & Andrew P. Morriss, *Charting the Influences on the Judicial Mind: An Empirical Study of Judicial Reasoning,* 73 N.Y.U. L. Rev. 1377 (1998).

[185] *See* Dan M. Kahan, David A. Hoffman, and Donald Braman, *Whose Eyes Are You Going to Believe?* Scott v. Harris *and the Perils of Cognitive Illiberalism,* 122 Harv. L. Rev. 837, 848–902 (2009).

different reactions of the lower court judges and the Supreme Court justices in *Scott v. Harris* show that reasonable people can disagree.

The Supreme Court decided not to send the *Scott* case to a jury because of its view that a reasonable jury could decide only in favor of the defendant. The psychology literature provides a possible explanation for this decision. It shows that people tend to think others should think similarly to themselves. The false consensus effect is a well-established cognitive bias that leads a person to assume that others share their own opinions. In their study, Lee Ross, David Greene, and Pamela House found that people tend to "see their own behavioral choices and judgments as relatively common and appropriate to existing circumstances while viewing alternative responses as uncommon, deviant, or inappropriate."[186] Several other studies have confirmed the existence of people's false beliefs that their views are shared. Different reasons are proffered for the false consensus effect including that people spend time with other people similar to themselves and then evidence of such similarity is more easily available from memory.[187] The authors of the video study labeled the bias that the Court showed for privileging its own views in *Scott* as "cognitive illiberalism,"[188] a bias that shares characteristics with the false consensus effect.

The disparate decisions by the judges in *Scott*, the Kahan study, and psychology literature at least suggest that a jury composed of lay people might reasonably find differently from at least some judges. This question of whether juries can make reasonable decisions that are different from those of judges is difficult for several reasons though, including that judges themselves can disagree. A jury could agree with one or more judges but disagree with other judges. The agreement and disagreement of juries and judges is exhibited in a study on summary judgment. The author sought to determine whether trial judges correctly decided the question of what a reasonable jury could find on their orders of summary judgment. He examined 263 cases decided from 2000 to 2006 in which the trial judge ordered summary judgment, the appellate court reversed

---

[186] Lee Ross, David Greene, & Pamela House, *The "False Consensus Effect": An Egocentric Bias in Social Perception and Attribution Processes*, 13 J. EXPERIMENTAL SOC. PSYCHOL. 279, 280 (1977).

[187] *See* Gary Marks & Norman Miller, *Ten Years of Research on the False-Consensus Effect: An Empirical and Theoretical Review*, 102 PSYCHOL. BULL. 72, 72–75 (1987).

[188] *See* Kahan, *supra* note 185, at 896.

the trial court decision, and the jury decided for one party. The study found that in 25% of the cases, the jury found for the party against whom the judge had granted summary judgment. Assuming these juries were "reasonable," the trial judges incorrectly decided these cases. In 38% of the cases, the jury decided for the same party for which the trial judge had found. The rest of the cases were irrelevant to the study. In all of the relevant cases, the jury both *agreed and disagreed* with various judges at the trial or appellate level.[189]

*****

In summary, judges can disagree about what a reasonable jury could find. In their decisions, they may actually decide what they think, not what a jury could find. Moreover, jurors may agree and disagree with different sets of judges. So, judges are dismissing cases that jurors and perhaps juries, and perhaps reasonable juries, could decide differently.

Comparing Decision-Making by Judges and Juries

Deciding a reasonable jury could not find for a party is one of the ways judges take cases from juries. Administrative, military, and other "non-Article III" judges also decide cases that juries could decide. Comparing decision-making between judges and juries can inform whether it matters that judges decide so many cases. To understand possible differences between judicial and jury decision-making, a comparison of the demographics of the judiciary and general population, from which the jury is derived, is useful. Although studies are not consistent, some research shows that if the composition of the judiciary is diverse, the outcomes of decision-making may change.[190] Diversity can be particularly relevant in certain types of cases, including discrimination cases.[191] Other indications of the influence of diversity are found elsewhere

---

[189] *See* Michael W. Pfautz, *What Would a Reasonable Jury Do? Jury Verdicts Following Summary Judgment Reversals*, 115 COLUM. L. REV. 1001 (2015).

[190] *See* Sisk, *supra* note 184 (finding some statistically significant difference between African-Americans and whites but no such difference between the opinions of men and women on issues related to the constitutionality of sentencing guidelines); Sean Farhang & Gregory Wawro, *Institutional Dynamics on the U.S. Court of Appeals: Minority Representation Under Panel Decision Making*, 20 J.L. ECON. & ORG. 299, 302 (surveying different studies with different results), 324–28 (describing effects of women and minorities on appellate panels) (2004).

[191] *See* Farhang & Wawro, *supra* note 190, at 303; Cass R. Sunstein, David Schkade & Lisa Michelle Ellman, *Ideological Voting on Federal Courts of Appeal*, 90 VA. L. REV. 301,

in judges' speeches as well as in judicial opinions. Sherrilyn Ifill has written that most, if not all of us, understand the value of diversity in the judiciary. For example, Supreme Court Justices Ruth Bader Ginsburg and Samuel Alito suggested the importance of diversity in their opening statements at their confirmation hearings when they both emphasized their first-generation and working-class backgrounds. Ifill contended "[a]ll judges ... are the product of all of their experiences," not just women and minorities. In addition to legitimacy, she argued that diversity in "backgrounds and experiences makes for *better* judicial decisionmaking." Specifically, Ifill argued that "the interaction" of people with diverse backgrounds could aid decision-making. While she recognized that outcomes may not be different in all circumstances, the actual process of rigorous decision-making enhanced by diversity is important.[192]

Although diversity may affect outcomes, the bench does not reflect the diversity of the general population. As for race, the federal judiciary was 85% white as of 2009[193] although whites constituted only approximately 75% of the population in the 2010 census.[194] The federal judiciary was only 8% African-American in 2009[195] as compared to African-Americans comprising approximately 13% of the general population in the 2010 census.[196] And the federal judiciary was 5% Hispanic in 2009[197] in contrast to a general Hispanic population of around 16% in the 2010 census.[198]

319–25 (2004); Sherrilyn A. Ifill, *Racial Diversity on the Bench: Beyond Role Models and Public Confidence*, 57 WASH. & LEE L. REV. 405, 449–55 (2000).

[192] *See* Sherrilyn A. Ifill, *Judicial Diversity*, 13 GREEN BAG 2D 45–57 (2009); *see also* Joy Milligan, *Pluralism in America: Why Judicial Diversity Improves Legal Decisions About Political Morality*, 81 N.Y.U. L. REV. 1206 (2006) ("beneficial effect of judicial diversity in the aggregate, developed through judges' interactions with one another and public over time" resulting in "making judicial reasoning more open and rigorous, ... improv[ing] its results").

[193] RUSSELL WHEELER, THE CHANGING FACE OF THE FEDERAL JUDICIARY 1 (Governance Studies at Brookings Aug. 2009), www.brookings.edu/~/media/research/files/papers/2009/8/federal-judiciary-wheeler/08_federal_judiciary_wheeler.pdf.

[194] LINDSAY HIXSON, BRADFORD B. HEPLER & MYOUNG OUK KIM, THE WHITE POPULATION: 2010, 3 (United States Census Bureau Sept. 2011), www.census.gov/prod/cen2010/briefs/c2010br-05.pdf.

[195] WHEELER, *supra* note 193, at 11 tbl.1.

[196] SONYA RASTOGI, TALLESE D. JOHNSON, ELIZABETH M. HOEFFEL & MALCOLM P. DREWERY, JR., THE BLACK POPULATION: 2010, 3 tbl.1 (United States Census Bureau Sept. 2011), www.census.gov/prod/cen2010/briefs/c2010br-06.pdf.

[197] WHEELER, *supra* note 193, at 11.

[198] SHARON R. ENNIS, MERARYS RÍOS-VARGAS & NORA G. ALBERT, THE HISPANIC POPULATION: 2010, 3 (United States Census Bureau May 2011), www.census.gov/prod/cen2010/briefs/c2010br-04.pdf.

Although the numbers of African-Americans and Hispanics have continued to grow with many diverse appointments by President Obama, the federal bench continues not to match the general population.[199]

In state courts, the racial judicial make-up also does not match the general population.[200] A 2010 study of ten states by the Brennan Center for Justice looked at these compositions. Note that the study also concluded that the lawyer populations did not match the general populations. The Brennan Center found that in Arizona, 100% of the Supreme Court, 82% of the appellate court, and 84% of the district court was white as opposed to 60% of the general population. In New Mexico, 60% of the Supreme Court, 85% of the appellate court, and 82% of the district court was white as opposed to 43% of the general population. In Missouri, 86% of the Supreme Court, 84% of the appellate court, and 99.3% of the district court was white as opposed to 84% of the general population.

The gender make-up of the federal judiciary also does not reflect that of the general population. Men comprised 80% of the federal bench in 2009[201] when they were around 49% of the general population in the 2010 census.[202] Women constituted 18% of the federal bench in 2009[203] when they were around 51% of the general population in the 2010 census.[204] The number of women in the federal judiciary has increased since that time with a recent report showing women constitute around 25% of the federal bench.[205]

In state courts, the female judicial population is also proportionately much less than the female general population.[206] For example, in Arizona, the general population is equally 50% men and women, but the state supreme court is 60% men and 40% women, the appeals court is 77% men and 23% women, and the trial court is 73% men and 27% women. In New Mexico, the general population is about 49% men and

---

[199] See Jeffrey Toobin, *The Obama Brief: The President considers his judicial legacy*, THE NEW YORKER, Oct. 27, 2014.

[200] CIARA TORRES-SPELLISCY, MONIQUE CHASE & EMMA GREENMAN, IMPROVING JUDICIAL DIVERSITY 49 app. D, available at www.brennancenter.org/sites/default/files/legacy/Improving_Judicial_Diversity_2010.pdf.

[201] WHEELER, *supra* note 193, at 1.

[202] THE HISPANIC POPULATION: 2010, 3 (United States Census Bureau May 2011).

[203] WHEELER, *supra* note 193, at 1.

[204] LINDSAY M. HOWDEN & JULIE A. MEYER, AGE AND SEX COMPOSITION: 2010, 3 (United States Census Bureau May 2011), www.census.gov/prod/cen2010/briefs/c2010br-03.pdf.

[205] NATIONAL WOMEN'S LAW CENTER, WOMEN IN THE FEDERAL JUDICIARY: STILL A LONG WAY TO GO 2 n.2 (Feb. 2016).

[206] TORRES-SPELLISCY, *supra* note 200.

51% women, while the state supreme court is 60% men and 40% women, the appeals court is 70% men and 30% women, and the trial court is 84.5% men and 15.5% women. In Missouri, the general population is 48.9% men and 51.1% women, at the same time that the state supreme court is 71% men and 29% women, the appeals court is 75% men and 25% women, and the trial court is 94.3% men and 5.67% women.

In addition to insufficient racial and gender diversity, the federal judiciary has been criticized as lacking professional diversity, including representing greater business and governmental interests.[207] For example, looking at recent nominations, 71% of the district court judges and 73% of the court of appeals' judges nominated by President Obama primarily served business clients prior to their appointment. Many of President Obama's nominees also were formerly prosecutors. Over 42% of the district court judge nominees and around 40% of the appellate court choices served as state or federal prosecutors, while only around 15% of the district court and 7% of the courts of appeals selections were public defenders. Also, over 40% of his nominees served as government lawyers in civil cases.[208]

So, the judiciary looks much different from the general population from which juries are derived, including significant race and gender differences. Moreover, judges and the general public likely differ regarding many other characteristics including wealth. Its decision-making may be affected by these differences though the extent to which it may be so affected is unclear.

Various studies have attempted to compare the decision-making of judges and juries by examining how judges would hypothetically decide the same cases that juries decided.[209] The classic jury–judge study of Harry Kalven and Hans Zeisel concluded that juries and judges generally would agree. The authors asked judges who presided over 3576 criminal jury trials how they would decide the same cases. In 78% of the cases, the judges agreed with the jury's verdict. In the cases in which they disagreed, judges were more likely to convict. The researchers also examined civil

---

[207] See Ifill, *supra* note 192, at 49.
[208] ALLIANCE FOR JUSTICE, BROADENING THE BENCH: PROFESSIONAL DIVERSITY AND JUDI-CIAL NOMINATIONS 8–10 (Nov. 4, 2014), www.afj.org/wp-content/uploads/2014/07/Prof-Diversity-Report-11.4.2014-FINAL.pdf.
[209] See Jennifer K. Robbennolt, *Evaluating Juries by Comparison to Judges: A Benchmark for Judging?*, 32 FL. ST. U. L. REV. 469 (2005) (discussing empirical research comparing jury and judicial decision-making).

cases where there was a similar result. In 78% of the approximately 4000 cases, judges reported agreement with the jury's liability determination. But juries exceeded judges' damages awards by around 20%.[210] More recently, others have reported similar findings to the Kalven and Zeisel study. In one study, of seventy-seven criminal jury trials, judges agreed in around 71% of the cases. And of the sixty-seven civil jury trials, judges agreed in around 63% of the cases.[211] In another study, in three hundred criminal trials, judges reported agreement with the jury over 70% of the time.[212] Bornstein concluded that "these studies suggest considerable agreement between judges and juries; yet in the minority of cases where they do differ, judges could be characterized as somewhat 'tougher': They would award less in civil cases, and they *may be* (depending on the strength of the evidence) more likely to convict in criminal cases."[213] The rate of agreement in these studies tracks the agreement of judges and other decision-makers such as employment interviewers and doctors diagnosing certain diseases.[214]

Several important studies are consistent with these results. They show that judges are affected by many of the same influences as lay people. One study showed that cognitive illusions, such as anchoring, affect judges too. Anchoring, for example, can cause an individual to overvalue or undervalue some determination based on a value that is initially provided to them. As a result, a damages cap may cause a judge to believe that the capped amount is the highest award a plaintiff could receive, resulting in the plaintiff receiving less than what the judge might award if the cap did not anchor her thoughts.[215] Other important studies have shown that judges hold the same biases as jurors.[216] And they also

---

[210] HARRY KALVEN, JR. & HANS ZEISEL, THE AMERICAN JURY 55–65 (The Legal Classics Library 1993) (1966).

[211] Larry Heuer & Steven Penrod, *Trial Complexity: A Field Investigation of Its Meaning and Its Effects*, 18 LAW & HUM. BEHAV. 29, 48 tbls.12–13 (1994).

[212] Theodore Eisenberg et al., *Judge-Jury Agreement in Criminal Cases: A Partial Replication of Kalven and Zeisel's "The American Jury,"* 2 EMP. LEG. STUD. 171, 173, 182 tbl.2 (2005).

[213] Brian H. Bornstein, *Judges vs. Juries*, 43 J. AM. JUDGES ASS'N 56, 57 (2006).

[214] *See* Robbennolt, *supra* note 209, at 479–80.

[215] Chris Guthrie, Jeffrey J. Rachlinski & Andrew J. Wistrich, *Inside the Judicial* Mind, 86 CORNELL L. REV. 777, 793 (2001).

[216] Jeffrey J. Rachlinski, Sheri Lynn Johnson, Andrew J. Wistrich & Chris Guthrie, *Does Unconscious Racial Bias Affect Trial Judges?*, 84 NOTRE DAME L. REV. 1195 (2009) (unconscious racial biases affect trial judges but adjustments can be made to avoid their effects).

react to evidence in a manner similar to jurors.[217] Bornstein concluded that "[o]n the whole, judges' decision making adheres to the same psychological principles as jurors' decision making; they are much more similar than they are different, including their susceptibility to errors in reasoning."[218]

Studies, including those discussed earlier, do show some differences between decision-making by judges and juries. And some studies emphasize distinctions, for example, finding differences in the award of punitive damages and in the award of damages in patent cases.[219] In many of the studies that have been mentioned, however, it is difficult to compare jury and judicial decision-making when juries and judges do not hear the same cases, and juries may decide cases that have a tendency to result in greater damages.[220]

Deliberations by Juries

All of this information continues to establish that people including judges can agree and disagree regarding evidence, and diversity may affect decision-making. Not yet discussed is the fact that jury decision-making includes deliberations, not simply individual decision-making.[221] While not studying juries, Sean Farhang and Gregory Wawro's study of appellate decision-making found deliberations influential, with male judges being influenced to vote more liberally when a woman served on a panel with them.[222]

The effects of jury deliberations have been studied, but much more study is necessary.[223] Most research fails to account for deliberations and may discount it, including Kalven and Zeisel's study. In asking judges to state the result that they would have reached in the jury trials they presided over,

---

[217] Andrew J. Wistrich, Chris Guthrie & Jeffrey J. Rachlinski, *Can Judges Ignore Inadmissible Information? The Difficulty of Deliberately Disregarding*, 153 U. Pa. L. Rev. 1251 (2005).

[218] Bornstein, *supra* note 213, at 58.

[219] *See* Chris Barry, Ronen Arad, Landan Ansell & Evan Clark, 2014 Patent Litigation Study: As case volume leaps, damages continue general decline 9 (PricewaterhouseCoopers LLP July 2014), www.pwc.com/en_US/us/forensic-services/publications/assets/2014-patent-litigation-study.pdf; Joni Hersch & W. Kip Viscusi, *Punitive Damages: How Judges and Juries Perform*, 33 J. Legal Stud. 1 (2004).

[220] *See* Barry, *supra* note 219, at 9.

[221] The *Scott* video study describes only individuals' opinions of the video and does not actually include the results of deliberations. *See* Kahan, *supra* note 185, at 849.

[222] *See* Farhang & Wawro, *supra* note 190, at 324–25.

[223] *See* Jessica M. Salerno & Shari Seidman Diamond, *The promise of a cognitive perspective on jury deliberation*, 17 Psychonomic Bull. & Rev. 174 (2010).

and in comparing those outcomes to the jury verdicts, the researchers did not directly consider the role of deliberations and thus the conclusions judges could reach upon deliberating with others. But Kalven and Zeisel concluded the role of deliberations to the juries' decisions was insignificant. To reach this opinion, they used the set of cases where there was information on the first votes of the jury and where a majority ruled one way. 90% of the first votes matched the final verdicts, leading Kalven and Zeisel to conclude that jury deliberations did not significantly affect the result. There are various flaws with this methodology including that the initial votes most often come after deliberations begin.[224]

Some other studies show that jury deliberations may affect results.[225] For example, in one study, 20% of jurors reported that they did not favor one side before deliberations began.[226] Other studies including ones showing significant differences between predeliberation damages' assessments and damages actually awarded also suggest deliberations may matter.[227] Moreover, a study of fifty actual jury trial deliberations revealed "jurors make use of discussion periods available – not only in terms of the frequency of case-relevant discussion, but also in terms of substantive exchange. . . . [and] discussion about what was actually said at trial does assist the jurors in reconstructing the evidence."[228] As Jessica Salerno and Shari Seidman Diamond have concluded "[m]uch jury decision-making research challenges the popular and convenient conclusion that the deliberation process is not important" and shows "there is much room for the deliberation process to have an impact on jury verdicts" though how much is unclear at this time.[229]

Who Should Decide: Judge or a Jury?

So, we know a decision by a judge may be different from a decision by a jury but it may not be different. If a decision by a judge could be different, which body should decide? Currently, judges take some cases from juries on the basis of what a reasonable jury could find which, as discussed

---

[224] See Salerno & Diamond, *supra* note 223, at 175–76 (discussing Kalven's and Zeisel's recognition of this potential flaw).

[225] See Salerno & Diamond, *supra* note 223, at 175–76 (discussing studies).

[226] See PAULA L. HANNAFORD-AGOR, VALERIE P. HANS, NICOLE L. MOTT & G. THOMAS MUNSTERMAN, ARE HUNG JURIES A PROBLEM? 63 (National Center for State Courts 2002).

[227] See Salerno & Diamond, *supra* note 223, at 175–76 (discussing several studies).

[228] Shari Seidman Diamond, Neil Vidmar, Mary Rose, Leslie Ellis & Beth Murphy, *Juror Discussions During Civil Trials: Studying an Arizona Innovation*, 45 ARIZ. L. REV. 1, 47 (2003).

[229] See Salerno & Diamond, *supra* note 223, at 178.

earlier, may be based on only the judge's view of the facts. Moreover, the question of what a reasonable jury could find is a complicated, unresolved question.[230] Other current law permits judges to decide many other cases that juries could decide.

People, including from different groups, have preferences for juries versus judges and juries versus mixed tribunals.[231] Juries have many potential shortcomings[232] and judges share some, but not all, of these problems. While people could value the legal qualifications of judges that most jurors on juries do not have, juries have three characteristics that judges do not possess that favor juries over judges. First, juries represent the general population better than judges; second, juries deliberate; and third, judges have incentives and biases that juries do not have.

If people can disagree for different reasons including their characteristics, having juries, which include more people from the general population, decide permits more viewpoints to be considered. Moreover, if judges themselves can disagree, and judges and juries can disagree, juries, which include deliberation as well as consensus, can improve the possibility of the "correct" decision.

In addition to diversity, the presence of deliberations, and the requirement of consensus, juries and judges differ significantly as to their incentives and some biases. In some ways, juries and judges are treated similarly to remove possible biases. Jurors with possible interests are removed from the jury in advance, and judges must recuse themselves from cases in which they have obvious connections. Judges are not however screened by others for conflicts.[233] Also different from juries, judges have career incentives to act in certain ways. Where judges are appointed or elected, dependent upon their decisions, they may be retained, promoted to other positions, or criticized.[234]

---

[230] See Thomas, *supra* 182 (arguing the standard is impossible and judges use their own opinions of the evidence instead of deciding what a reasonable jury could find).

[231] See John H. Langbein, *Mixed Court and Jury Court: Could the Continental Alternative Fill the American Need?*, 1981 AM. B. FOUND. RES. J. 195.

[232] See *supra* Chapter 3.

[233] See Stephan Landsman, *Appellate Courts and Civil Juries*, 70 U. CIN. L. REV. 873, 883 (2002); *see also* Pennsylvania v. Williams, 105 A. 3d 1234 (Pa. 2014), *cert. granted*, Williams v. Pennsylvania, 136 S. Ct. 28 (2015) (considering question of whether Pennsylvania Supreme Court justice should have recused himself from case in which, as a prosecutor, he sought the death penalty).

[234] See Jean Eaglesham, *SEC Wins With In-House Judges*, WALL ST. J., May 6, 2015 (one SEC judge "came under fire from [the chief administrative law judge] for finding too often in favor of defendants").

There are other relationships that may indirectly affect judges' careers and thus their decision-making. As a part of government, judges may favor the government when the government is a party in a criminal or civil case.[235] Moreover, unlike jurors who serve limited terms on juries, in their courtrooms, judges encounter some of the same people representing parties as well as some of the same parties. Because biases have been found when repeat players appear before decision-makers, judges are subject to these problems.[236] For example, the same prosecutor appears before the judge and the judge may be friendly with this person. A juror with a similar type of relationship with a party may be precluded from participation. Judges also will have seen other cases that may seem similar and cause the judge to prejudge the case. Additionally, a judge's early involvement in a case may cause the judge to form impressions about the parties and the evidence before the case goes to trial. The judge may also be affected by prejudicial information that the judge herself must screen out of consideration.[237]

Although results between judges and juries may be similar, judges and juries can disagree. If a choice must be made between a judge or a jury deciding, the diversity, availability of deliberations, the requirement for consensus, the lack of monetary and promotion incentives, and the jury's fresh examination of evidence all make the jury the most attractive, least biased decision-maker.[238]

The Federal and State Executives and Legislatures versus Juries

Thus far, because judges decide many cases instead of juries, the decision-making of judges and juries has been compared. As first described in Chapter 2, similar to judges, the federal and state executives and legislatures decide matters that juries could otherwise determine. For example, because a federal or state prosecutor can offer a sentence that the defendant cannot otherwise obtain through the jury, the executive

---

[235] See, e.g., Ashcroft v. Iqbal, 556 U.S. 662 (2009).

[236] Cf. Lisa B. Bingham, On Repeat Players, Adhesive Contracts, and the Use of Statistics in Judicial Review of Employment Arbitration Awards, 29 McGeorge L. Rev. 223 (1998).

[237] See Landsman, supra note 233, at 883–84.

[238] Cf. Cheryl Thomas, Are juries fair?, Ministry of Justice Series (Feb. 2010), www.justice.gov.uk/downloads/publications/research-and-analysis/moj-research/are-juries-fair-research.pdf (analyzing decision-making of juries in the United Kingdom and concluding that they are fair generally, showing, for example, similar conviction rates for whites and minorities).

and legislature often decide the fate of a defendant instead of a jury. As another example, the Securities and Exchange Commission has been granted authority to try claims that juries would otherwise decide. And the legislature can limit the amount of damages a plaintiff can receive, precluding a jury from giving a larger amount. Because of these types of shifts in authority, the question is whether the executive and legislature are better decision-makers than the jury.

The executive has incentives similar to the judiciary that cast doubts on its ability to act as well as the jury. The prosecutor may be re-elected or may be appointed to a more prestigious position based on her actions in office. Similarly, a person in an executive agency may act to dismiss claims or act more quickly to dispose of matters in order to advance in their employment. Juries lack these same incentives.

While the legislature is elected and may act in the public interest,[239] in some ways, the incentives of the legislature compare to the biases of the judiciary. Legislators, similar to judges, have career reasons to decide in certain ways. If they do not vote in certain ways, they may not receive funding for their re-election from particular interest groups in the future.[240] They also work with other legislators and in order to garner their vote on particular legislation, they may need to promise their vote for other legislation. Although these descriptions do not describe all of the incentives, jurors simply do not have the same incentives as legislators. With respect to the civil jury, for example, Stephan Landsman has argued that at times it may be "democracy's only effective voice." The legislature may be "in the thrall of special interests or . . . imprisoned by gridlock, . . . [so that] it cannot act in a fashion that reflects the popular will."[241]

Conclusion

For some, the constitutional requirement of the jury or the jury's past role is not enough to support vibrant grand, criminal, and civil juries in America. They think other bodies should decide questions that juries previously decided. The presence and growth of juries world-wide affirms some value for lay participation. While the American jury arguably

---

[239] *See* Daniel Shaviro, *Beyond Public Choice and Public Interest: A Study of the Legislative Process as Illustrated by Tax Legislation in the 1980s*, 139 U. Pa. L. Rev. 1, 31–35 (1990).

[240] *See* Shaviro, *supra* note 239, at 36–50, 64–71.

[241] Landsman, *supra* note 233, at 882–83.

decides too many cases, the difference in biases and incentives of judges and juries, in addition to the presence of diversity, deliberations, and consensus, make the jury a better decision-maker than a judge. Moreover, because the executive and the legislature have similar biases and incentives as the judiciary, the jury also is the better decision-maker than those bodies. At the same time, given these differences, juries should arguably play a larger role in other countries around the world.

A Branch Among Equals in American Democracy

A Conclusion

This book has recognized the jury's fundamental constitutional role alongside the executive, the legislature, the judiciary, and the states. It has also discussed the jury's innate value over these traditional actors for deciding the questions of whether a person is punished and whether a person receives monetary damages. Outside of the jury's constitutional necessity and inherent comparative importance, it can serve another particularly significant role – for civil liberties and civil rights.

Writing about the mass incarceration of African-Americans in this country, Michelle Alexander has written about the New Jim Crow in criminal law. Much of the modern segregation about which Alexander writes is actually connected to the lack of jury trials. As discussed in Chapter 2, the community generally does not determine whether crimes have been committed and whether to punish. It also does not decide whether people should be compensated for wrongs committed against them. Instead, the executive, the legislature, the judiciary, and the states decide. The most vivid display of this authority is the imposition of punishments through plea bargaining. In this system, a person can be forced into prison by the false choice of a plea to a charge with less punishment or a jury trial on the threatened charge with a higher sentence. In other circumstances that involve civil liberties, juries may not decide the issue of whether people should be compensated where the government improperly treated them. So, if the government takes land from a family or imprisons a person unjustly, often a judge, not the community, is given the opportunity to decide whether a remediable harm occurred. As a final example, civil rights laws gave people the ability to challenge discrimination in the workplace. However, a jury may never decide this issue if a judge determines the employee does not have sufficient evidence of discrimination.

The most consistent themes against the jury deciding these cases have been cost and efficiency. As discussed in Chapter 4, the Founders either considered those factors in framing the government or rejected their relevance. Indeed, many major changes for the advancement of civil liberties and civil rights have occurred despite increased costs coming with change. Although its economic impact was far-reaching, slavery was eliminated. Although there would be costs to enforcing civil rights, those laws were enacted.

The missing jury is a new civil liberties and civil rights frontier because its restoration could support the protection of these and other essential rights. At the same time, it is important to recognize that juries have taken different positions over time, for example, against civil rights and for them – both not convicting slave traders and awarding damages in discrimination cases. It may shift positions – positions with which people may disagree, just as people may agree or disagree with other governmental actors. The significance of the jury is not in the particular view that it may take at any point in time but in its role, described in Chapter 3, as one of the branches among equals that individually and together protect American democracy.

As described in Chapter 5, the jury's revival primarily depends on eliminating the modern procedures infringing its authority. However, a few words are warranted about the present system in which these mechanisms continue to operate. Despite their use, there still may be ways to restore a more vibrant role for the jury. As previously mentioned in Chapter 5, eighteenth-century English judges could order new jury trials in non-felony cases when they thought the first jury incorrectly convicted. Now, instead of ordering acquittals in circumstances when they think the jury erred, judges should be encouraged to use their current authority under the rules to order new trials. Another jury can test the reasonableness of the first jury's decision, instead of a sole judge deciding whether the first jury was wrong. Four additional new ideas – "the reasoning requirement," "the plea offer requirement," "the sentence requirement," and "the consensus requirement" – briefly introduced here and about which more will be written in the future, also show the possibility of a tenacious, dynamic jury in the continued presence of the jury-infringing modern procedures.

As described in Chapter 6, in some nations, reasoning is required for final decisions of mixed jury tribunals, and this requirement may reduce the questioning of verdicts. If prescribed in the United States, jury verdicts may face less unwarranted scrutiny. While juries were not required to give reasons in the past, judges also were not permitted to pre- and second-guess juries as they do now. Under "the reasoning requirement," juries would justify their verdicts, and consequently, it would permit judges to actually consider a jury's reasoning instead of speculating on how the jury should have or could have decided a case.

The "plea offer requirement," another mechanism to restore a more vibrant jury, provides a balance to plea bargaining. To counter the potential coercive effect of plea bargaining – forcing defendants not to take jury trials – prosecutors would be required to present any charge that the criminal defendant was offered in plea bargaining also at the jury trial. So, instead of losing the opportunity for a jury to decide whether he is guilty by being compelled to plead guilty to a charge with a lesser punishment, the defendant would have a choice. The defendant could go to trial where the prosecutor would present the jury with the same alternatives that the defendant faced in the plea bargain. In addition to giving the defendant a real choice for the jury to decide his fate, if the case is tried, the community itself through the jury is given the opportunity to determine whether and on what to convict the defendant.

Under the next idea, "the sentence requirement," judges would be required to inform juries of the sentence associated with each crime, giving the jury the opportunity to consider the same type of information that it examined at the time of the founding. Similar to the English procedure, perhaps juries should be able to take into account the seriousness of the offense and the conduct and character of the accused, along with the punishment in deciding on what crime to convict.

Finally, "the consensus requirement" would require agreement of all judges for the Court of Appeals or the Supreme Court to affirm orders for summary judgment or judgment as a matter of law or for the courts to order either motion in the first instance. The consensus requirement lessens the problems with the present summary judgment and judgment as a matter of law standard under which judges appear to use their own opinions of the evidence instead of determining whether a reasonable jury could find for the non moving party. When judges disagree, there is even less justification to permit summary judgment or judgment as a matter of law. Under this rule, when all judges agree that a reasonable jury could not find for the nonmovant, summary judgment or judgment as a matter of law will be granted, making the grant of summary judgment or judgment as a matter of law more defensible.

Although the second best result to eliminating constitutionally impermissible procedures, exploring the use of these types of alternatives could lead the jury to occupy a place more akin to the constitutional role it was intended to serve in the government.

INDEX

Printed in the United States
By Bookmasters

SEP -- 2016
9504791

DISCARD

SEP -- 2016
3509791